To John Taylor –
who recognized a good idea
when he heard it – and kn[ew]
what to do about it.

from Cheryl Dickson
on behalf of the
Minnesota Humanities Commission

5/15/85

THE CURVE OF THE ARCH

THE CURVE OF THE ARCH

THE STORY OF
LOUIS SULLIVAN'S OWATONNA BANK

"It [the arch] is a form so much against Fate, that Fate, as we say, ever most relentlessly seeks its destruction. Yet does it rise in power so graciously, floating through the air from abutment to abutment, that it seems ever, to me, a symbol and epitome of our own ephemeral span."

–Louis Sullivan, in *Kindergarten Chats*

Larry Millett

Minnesota Historical Society Press / St. Paul, 1985

This book was published with the assistance of the
Minnesota Humanities Commission in cooperation
with the National Endowment for the Humanities
and the Northwest Area Foundation.

The views expressed in the book do not necessarily
represent the views of the Minnesota Humanities
Commission, the National Endowment for the
Humanities, or the Northwest Area Foundation.

MINNESOTA HISTORICAL SOCIETY PRESS,
St. Paul 55101
© 1985 by Minnesota Historical Society
All rights reserved
Manufactured in the United States of America
10 9 8 7 6 5 4 3 2 1

International Standard Book Number:
0-87351-181-6 Cloth
0-87351-182-4 Paper

LIBRARY OF CONGRESS CATALOGING IN
PUBLICATION DATA
Millett, Larry, 1947–
  The curve of the arch.
  Bibliography: p.
  Includes index.
  1. National Farmers' Bank (Owatonna, Minn.)
2. Owatonna, (Minn.)–Public buildings. 3.
Sullivan, Louis H., 1856–1924. 4. Elmslie, George
Grant, 1871–1952. 5. Bennett, Carl Kent. I. Title.
NA6243.09N385 1985 725'.24'0924 84-25528

To Dave Bowers, who laid the foundation

CONTENTS

ILLUSTRATIONS

ACKNOWLEDGMENTS

ONE OF THE PLEASURES of writing a book is that when the work is finally done, the author has a chance to acknowledge those who helped make it possible. There are three people in particular who made vital contributions to this book.

In St. Paul, Dave Bowers of the architectural firm of Val Michelson and Associates freely shared with me his deep knowledge of the National Farmers' Bank building and the men who made it. In 1976, while working on plans for a possible expansion of the bank, Dave undertook a study of the building's history. His research resulted in a documentation project prepared for the building's owners, the Northwestern (now Norwest) Bank of Owatonna. Much of my research consisted of going down avenues Dave had already explored in preparing his report, and his trail blazing made my task far easier than it otherwise would have been. Dave also made available to me his copious research notes as well as a large number of documents he had assembled during the course of his studies. Moreover, he helped me find photographs, plans, and drawings of the bank; he read and offered valuable criticisms of my first drafts of the book; and he interrupted his own busy work schedule countless times to answer my questions, which I never seemed to run out of. In short, this book simply could not have been written without his help and encouragement.

In Minneapolis, Alan Lathrop, curator of the Northwest Architectural Archives at the University of Minnesota, provided me with ready access to the wealth of material in the archives relating to Sullivan, Elmslie, and Bennett. Much of this book is based on what I discovered in the archives with Alan's help. He also read my early drafts and offered several suggestions, most of which I had the good sense to accept. In addition, he helped with the chore of finding and selecting illustrations for the book.

In Chicago, Tim Samuelson provided invaluable assistance in my efforts to learn about the life and work of Louis Sullivan. Tim, a historian with the Commission on Chicago Historical and Architectural Landmarks, gave me access to a large number of letters, notes, and other items relating to the bank that were collected by Richard Nickel, perhaps the greatest of Sullivan scholars, before his untimely death in 1972. Tim also read early drafts of the book and saved me from some egregious errors, particularly in my account of how the bank's terra cotta was manufactured. He also helped in finding photographs of Sullivan and his buildings. Finally, Tim provided me with a memorable, if at times surreptitious, tour of the Auditorium Building in Chicago, a tour that brought home to me the genius of Sullivan.

Many other persons shared their knowledge with me as I was researching this book. Among those I wish to thank are Lydia Bennett Freeman and Arabella Bennett Winston, Carl Bennett's two surviving daughters, who kindly consented to interviews and who provided me with a great deal of information about their father that simply could not have been obtained elsewhere. Clifford Sommer, who was president of the bank during the 1957–58 remodeling, provided me with much important information during an interview. I also received valuable information from David Gebhard, Harwell H. Harris, Mark Hammons, Mayo Stuntz, Connie Lorch Osler, and Betty Lorch Bailey.

In Owatonna, I was fortunate to have help from many people. At the bank, President Kenneth Wilcox kindly permitted me to spend several days rummaging through historical documents in the bank's possession, many of which proved invaluable to my research. Members of the bank staff, particularly Jeanne Blanchette, also were unfailingly helpful. Others in Owatonna to whom I owe a debt include: Marjorie Bennett, the widow of Carl Bennett's nephew, Leonard Bennett; Graham Benoit and his staff at the Owatonna Public Library; Gail Lippelt, clerk of court for Steele County; and Carl Kottke, Robert Adair, Benjamin Darby, Jr., Larry Berghs, and Calvin Anderson, all of whom shared their memories of the bank and the Bennett family with me.

I also owe thanks to Chris Johnson and her staff at the School of Architecture Library at the University of Minnesota; the staffs of the St. Paul and Minneapolis Public Libraries; Dallas Lindgren and her staff at the Minnesota State Archives; and Russell W. Fridley, John McGuigan,

Sally Rubinstein, and others at the Minnesota Historical Society who helped this book come about.

There are others to whom I owe a debt as well. John Finnegan and Deborah Howell at the *St. Paul Pioneer Press & Dispatch* kindly granted a leave of absence that enabled me to complete my research. Noel Bredahl carefully read the manuscript and made many valuable suggestions. John Mallander, an old friend who shares my love of architecture, occasionally helped with the research and offered encouragement. My late father, Samuel Millett, and my mother Agnes provided financial assistance during a critical stage of the project. My children, Matt and Molly, were uncommonly understanding during the three years it took to complete this book, and they did not complain (too much) when I disappeared for hours on end almost every night to stare at the screen of my home word processor. Finally, I want to thank Mary for all the good years and for her help during the time this book was in progress.

INTRODUCTION

Every building tells its story, tells it plainly. With what startling clearness it speaks to the attentive ear, how palpable its visage to the open eye, it may take you some little time to perceive. But it is all there, waiting for you.
— *Louis Sullivan*[1]

IT BEGAN, as all great buildings do, with a dream. In the small farming town of Owatonna, Minnesota, just after the turn of the century, a banker named Carl Kent Bennett dreamed of creating "a true and lasting work of art" in his community. Being a banker, Bennett also wanted to make money. A new bank building, he believed, would enable him to do both. He envisioned a building that would stand proud and strong, announcing to the world that here was a safe place to keep valuables. It would be a regal building, commanding its site with power and grace, yet it also had to meet the down-to-earth banking needs of the common man. But Bennett wondered where he would find the right architect to design such a building. Banks, like cars, tended to come in only a few basic models in those days. Mostly, banks were designed to resemble Roman temples, with big Ionic columns and plenty of marble to impress customers. Bennett, however, did not want a building that harkened back to some lost age of imperial splendor. He wanted instead a building that would express his own ideals and those of the culture in which he lived. For many months, Bennett searched for an architect to build his dream. In early 1906, he found the man he was looking for.[2]

The architect chosen for the new bank was Louis Henry Sullivan, a passionate idealist who saw his life's work as nothing less than a holy mission. His greatest dream was to create, singlehandedly, an authentic American architecture free from the tainting influence of European design. He proposed to achieve this lofty goal through the application of his famous motto, "form follows function," by which he meant that the design of a building should always unfold organically from the building's purpose and use. In pursuing his vision, Sullivan took a high and lonely road that left him increasingly alienated from the architectural establishment. Moreover, he had a rigid and often abrasive personality that caused him to lose both friends and clients. For a few glorious years in the 1890s he had been the most famous architect in Chicago, but by 1906 economic slumps, changing tastes, and his own intransigence had brought him low. Out of style, out of work, and desperately short of money, Sullivan turned increasingly to alcohol for solace. Yet despite all of these troubles, his vision and his belief in himself never wavered, and when the call came from Owatonna he responded with a masterpiece.

Working beside him was George Grant Elmslie, a quiet Scotsman who had a gift for drawing ornament of the utmost delicacy and grace. He had been Sullivan's chief draftsman for almost fifteen years and was, in fact if not in title, his working partner. Elmslie was a shy, self-effacing man given to terrible bouts of melancholy. Sensitive by nature, he was an impractical dreamer who often seemed to be overwhelmed by life. At the drawing table, however, he had the easy confidence of a master, and the bank in Owatonna was to be perhaps the summit of his ornamental art.

Together, in a quiet corner of the American heartland, these three men in 1907–08 built what is very probably the most famous small-town bank in the world. Their creation, the National Farmers' (now Norwest) Bank, is only sixty-eight feet square and forty-nine feet high. The entire building could fit easily within the rotunda of the United States Capitol. Yet almost from the day it was finished, the bank has drawn the attention of architects and art lovers the world over. At the request of French admirers, Sullivan sent a duplicate piece of the bank's terra-cotta ornament to the Louvre in what was surely the first, and possibly the last, time that Paris ever looked to rural Minnesota for inspiration. A leading Dutch architect of the time, Hendrik Berlage, believed the bank to be one of the great buildings of its age and even planned a visit to Owatonna to see it while on an American tour. "Owatonna has long been marked on the map of the world because of its possession of this distinguished structure," wrote architectural historian Henry-Russell Hitchcock. "Certainly no other town of its size has a commercial building of equal distinction."[3]

Designed by Sullivan and Elmslie to resemble a giant treasure chest for the safekeeping of depositors' money, the bank was unique in its time and remains so to this day. Its genius lies in the resonant simplicity of its basic form, the wealth and originality of its ornament, the earthy glory of its colors, and the superb craftsmanship of its builders. Constructed from materials of the old order—stone, brick, terra cotta, iron, and stained glass—the bank is little more than a cube punctured by two huge arched windows. Sullivan and Elmslie took this simple volume and filled it with ornament so beautiful and varied, so full of curving energy, that the building has an air of almost Oriental voluptuousness. The bank was also intended to be, in Sullivan's words, "a color symphony." Burgundy and multicolored tapestry brick, green and brown terra cotta, blue and gold glass mosaic, black Belgian marble, pink sandstone—all became part of the carefully orchestrated design. Working with Chicago artist Louis Millet, Sullivan and Elmslie brought their color symphony to its climax in the banking room, where about two hundred shades of color are united and harmonized by the blue-green light that filters through the great stained-glass windows.

Sullivan once wrote that "as you are, so are your buildings." In other words, he believed that architecture, at its best, is a means by which human beings express their aspirations and ideals. He also understood that buildings, in time, become containers of human history, revealing (both literally and figuratively) the shape of the past. Much has been written about the bank in the years since it was built, and the tendency has been to treat it as simply one more beautiful object in the grand procession of art history. But the bank—in many ways an improbable building in an improbable place—cannot be fully appreciated without knowing something of the rich human history that is as much a part of it as its stained-glass windows or terra-cotta ornament. And so this book, which is an attempt to tell the story of the bank within the context of the lives of the three men most responsible for its creation.[4]

The lives of Sullivan, Elmslie, and Bennett at once illuminate and are illuminated by the bank. As a work of art, it reflects their confident creativity, their passion for perfection, their vision of architecture as a means of ennobling everyday life. By the same token, the creation of the bank was a pivotal event in the lives of all three men. For Sullivan, it was the key that opened the door to other bank commissions in small midwestern towns—commissions that provided him with virtually his only work during his later years. For Elmslie, the bank marked the end of his association with Sullivan and the beginning of a long and fruitful friendship with Bennett, who helped secure many commissions for Elmslie and his new partner, William G. Purcell. For Bennett, the bank was the realization of a dream and the start of a fifteen-year period during which he perhaps did as much as any man in America to advance the cause of what he liked to call "the new architecture."[5]

Through the years, the bank building has undergone many changes. Some of its finest ornament was lost forever in a brutal and senseless remodeling in 1940, and much of its original floor plan was altered in an even more extensive, if far more sensitive, remodeling sixteen years later. But the bank has survived, in Sullivan's words, "to tell its story." A monument to the enduring power of human dreams, it also serves as a reminder that dreams can sometimes take a dark turn. For in the years after the bank was built, Sullivan, Elmslie, and Bennett all met tragedy on the downward curve of the arch.

1

A BANKER'S DREAM

This bank began in a very small way, but prospered with the growth of the surrounding country. — *Carl Bennett*[1]

ON MARCH 15, 1907, the most exciting news in the southern Minnesota farming community of Owatonna concerned a local butcher who, dissatisfied with the progress of his two-week-old marriage, had decided to do himself in with one of the utensils of his trade. The man chose to make his final gesture in a meat market on Owatonna's main street, much to the interest of practically everyone in town. But he failed to slash his wrists with sufficient vigor, and the *Owatonna Journal-Chronicle* reported in a breathlessly detailed front-page story that the man was expected to recover in body, if not in spirit. There was also an intriguing story on the adventures of a local harness maker, who claimed to have been attacked and bitten by a "huge pickerel" after falling through the ice on a nearby lake. Aside from these tales of human and piscatorial mayhem, however, there was little out of the ordinary to be found in the paper's news columns. But those readers who bothered to comb through the *Journal-Chronicle* that day might have found a notice of more than passing interest. The notice announced that the National Farmers' Bank of Owatonna had decided to erect a new building:

For several years past the officers and directors of this bank have felt the need of a larger banking room and more facilities for the convenience of customers.

The rapid increase of this bank's business during the past five years has now made a new bank building imperative and the Board of Directors has authorized its construction during the coming season. The plans and details of construction will gladly be made public when they are fully determined.[2]

The bank was then the largest in Owatonna, with assets approaching eight hundred thousand dollars, and its name told its story. Agriculture had built the bank, just as it had built the town of Owatonna itself. The rich, rolling farmland around Owatonna had become an especially productive dairying region by the turn of the century. Steele County, of which Owatonna is the county seat, boasted twenty-one creameries in 1907, many of them co-operatives. The sixteen square miles around Owatonna, it was said, produced more butter than any comparable region in the country. This led Owatonna to advertise itself as the "Butter Capital of the World." It gained that exalted status in part because of a mechanical butter churn that was Owatonna's most famous export. Invented in Owatonna in 1889, the churn revolutionized the dairy industry and helped bring prosperity to Steele County. The importance of dairying to Owatonna's economy is duly recognized in the bank itself, where one wall is covered by a large mural depicting a pasture full of cows.[3]

Located in the valley of the Straight River about sixty-five miles south of Minneapolis-St. Paul, Owatonna in 1907 had a population of fifty-five hundred, making it one of the largest towns in southeastern Minnesota. Served by two railroads, the town was the commercial hub for a large area. It had more than one hundred retail stores, four hotels, three banks, and many fine houses. There were also several manufacturing plants in town that turned out farm equipment and other products. Owatonna even had an automobile plant that managed to produce three cars before it closed in about 1910. Yet the town still had something of the raw look of a pioneer community, and its dirt streets accommodated far more horses than automobiles.[4]

It was not the sort of place where much exciting ever happened – the butcher's adventures notwithstanding. The most pressing social issue of the day was prohibition, and the town went through at least one short-lived dry spell as the electorate tried to sort out its ambivalent feelings toward Demon Rum. Fortunately for Sullivan, who was a practiced drinker, the town's saloons were open for business when he made his first visit in late 1906.

In matters of architecture, which is how a community presents itself to the world, Owatonna offered little out of the ordinary. The town had some impressive Victorian houses, but there were no buildings that aspired to architectural originality. The National Farmers' Bank was typical. It was housed then in an undistinguished three-story brick building overlooking the town's central square. Facing the bank across the square was Owatonna's major piece of architecture, the Steele County Courthouse. A mildly Romanesque structure dating from 1891, the courthouse was a rather standard design for its day – competent but uninspired.[5]

Owatonna did have a varied cultural life that reflected its rich mix of ethnic groups, including large numbers of Germans, Czechs, and Scandinavians in addition to the old Yankee families who had founded the community in 1855. Each of these groups formed cultural organizations, some of them quite impressive for a town of Owatonna's size. As early as 1873, for example, the town had a large choral group, called the Beethoven Society, which performed regularly. By 1875 Owatonna had an opera house seating twelve hundred people, even though the town's population then was less than three thousand. The opera house, which was reputed to be the largest in the state outside of the Twin Cities and

Central Park was the hub of Owatonna business and government activity. The top of the newly completed bank is visible above the trees (right center).

Duluth, often attracted nationally known performers. The town also had a good-sized public library housed in a handsome new building. Owatonna, to be sure, was no Athens of the prairie, but it was a place where the traditional emblems of culture – music, art, literature, drama – were valued and respected.[6]

Still, there was nothing about Owatonna that made it greatly different from any of a thousand other farming towns scattered across America or that would explain why, in 1907–08, a great work of art was created in its midst; nothing, that is, except for the presence of Carl Bennett. The bank was built in Owatonna primarily because Bennett was a man of unusually sophisticated tastes who dared to seek out a truly original design for his new building.

Yet it was Owatonna's agrarian wealth that enabled Bennett to build his dream. The town was booming in 1906 because the first decade of the twentieth century was a time of heady prosperity for the American farmer. Only a few years before, rural America had plunged into a depression as commodity prices hit rock bottom following the panic of 1893. But farm prices, as well as the economy as a whole, rebounded sharply at the turn of the century. Fueled by high demand for foodstuffs at home and abroad, farm prices rose by more than 50 percent between 1900 and 1910. During that same period, the price of farmland doubled from an average of twenty dollars to forty dollars an acre. Bennett's bank shared in this explosive growth of agricultural wealth. As a result, when Bennett and his board of directors decided to build a new bank, they were able to spend about $125,000 for the project.[7]

That amount sounds like a paltry sum today, but at the time it was an enormous expenditure for a small-town bank building. Other buildings of comparable size erected in Owatonna during the same period cost nowhere near as much. In 1907, the year construction began on the bank, a new city hall was completed in Owatonna. A three-story brick structure vaguely Romanesque in style, the building had room for city offices as well as the fire department. Yet it cost only about fifteen thousand dollars, an amount that at least some Owatonnans considered excessive at the time. The public library, completed in 1900 and located a block east of the bank, provides another comparison. An impressive Beaux-Arts composition with a strong Greek feeling to it, the library was built and equipped for about thirty-two thousand dollars.[8]

The high price tag of the bank was not the result of any huge cost overruns on Sullivan's part. Carl Bennett knew from the outset that his new building would be very expensive, but the general prosperity of the region made it possible for him to spend a small fortune to get what he wanted. It is doubtful whether any other businessman in Owatonna would have spent that kind of money for a building, but then Carl Bennett was not like most businessmen. For he not only envisioned a costly work of art but also was able, against long odds, to get it.[9]

Carl Kent Bennett was a man who sought to live like a Renaissance prince in a world of Babbitts. Banker, businessman, public servant, musician, art lover — he was a shrewd idealist who believed that beauty was not only good for people but good for business as well. His beliefs are perfectly expressed in the bank itself, which is one of the happiest marriages of art and commerce in American architecture. Yet he was in many respects a most unlikely client for Sullivan. Typically, clients of progressive architects such as Sullivan or Frank Lloyd Wright were self-made businessmen, rough and ready types who were seldom pillars of the community. Bennett, however, was nothing if not a community pillar. He presided over the biggest bank in town, was a prominent member of the Baptist church, belonged to such civic organizations as the Masons and Commercial Club, and was a firm supporter of the Republican party. Moreover, he represented old money (by Owatonna's standards), for he was a member of one of the town's oldest and wealthiest families.[10]

The patriarch of the Bennett family and the president of the bank in 1907 was Leonard Loomis Bennett, a physician by training who had moved to Owatonna in 1864, just nine years after the founding of the community. Like many of Owatonna's early settlers, L. L. Bennett (as he was usually called) was of Yankee stock, although he had been born in Illinois. He arrived in Owatonna two years after graduating from Rush Medical College in Chicago and a year after his marriage to Arabella Brown, who also traced her ancestry to colonial New England. For nine years, Bennett practiced medicine in Owatonna and the surrounding countryside. Soon, he became a familiar figure to the farm families who were struggling to live under frontier conditions. "He saw the sad side of the farmer's life," his daughter-in-law recalled many years later. When arthritis finally forced Bennett to give up his medical practice, he looked for another way to help the rural families who had once been his patients.[11]

His work as a doctor had enabled him to learn a great deal about the local farm economy, and so he decided to enter the banking business. In 1873 he was among sixteen investors who contributed a total of fifty thousand dollars in capital stock to start what was to be Owatonna's second bank. Called the Farmers' National Bank, it opened for business on July 1, 1873, with Bennett as its president. The bank was reorganized in 1893, when its capital stock was increased to eighty thousand dollars.

For reasons unknown, its name was changed that year to the National Farmers' Bank.[12]

By 1907 L. L. Bennett was well into his sixties. An imposing figure with a great thatch of white hair, he was known to virtually everyone in the Owatonna area. Out of respect, most people still called him "doctor," despite the fact that he had not practiced medicine in more than thirty years. Although he still held the title of bank president, he had recently

Carl Bennett at about age 20

turned the day-to-day operation of the business over to his two sons, Carl and Guy. Carl, born in 1868, was officially vice-president of the bank, but he functioned in effect as the chief executive officer and made most major decisions. Guy, born in 1871, was the bank's cashier. An affable, outgoing man who thrived in the intimate, neighborly atmosphere of small-town life, Guy was on friendly terms with just about everybody in Owatonna and did much of the bank's public relations work.[13]

But Carl was different. He was more reserved than his younger brother and less inclined to become involved in the social side of banking, which is extremely important in a small community. In fact, it appears he was not very well liked in Owatonna because of his rather ostentatious lifestyle and his cultural aspirations. He could often be seen riding through town on one of his fine horses, with his young wife Lydia at his side, both of them dressed in expensive English riding clothes. It was this sort of activity that made some people in town think Carl was a trifle uppity, that his tastes were perhaps a bit rich for a place like Owatonna. Still, Carl was well respected if not always well liked, for as

The old National Farmers' Bank building

de facto president of the town's largest bank he held a position of great power and influence in the community.[14]

Both Carl and Guy had been born in Owatonna, in their parents' big white house on Main Street just a few blocks from the bank. Both went to public schools before entering Pillsbury Academy, a private school located across the street from the Bennett family home. The academy, founded by the Baptist church, attracted children of the well-to-do from Owatonna and elsewhere in Minnesota. One of Carl's instructors at the academy was A. C. Gutterson, who taught music. (Gutterson had for many years directed the Beethoven Society, which drew its singers from some of Owatonna's most distinguished families. Gutterson was also one of the original stockholders of the bank and for many years its head cashier.) Carl's love of music – a passion he shared with Sullivan – was nurtured by Gutterson, who by all accounts had a magnetic personality and was a fine teacher.[15]

As the son of a wealthy small-town businessman with impeccable Yankee credentials, Carl Bennett was a natural candidate for an Ivy League education. After graduating from Pillsbury Academy in 1886, he enrolled at Harvard University to pursue a special course of study in music. (Guy also went to Harvard but followed the regular academic program.) Carl's musical talents were such that by 1889 he was selected to lead the Pierean Sodality, Harvard's symphony orchestra. It was a prestigious position because the sodality was one of the best-known musical organizations in America.[16]

Bennett, who also became interested in drawing while at Harvard, wanted to continue his musical career after leaving college. His exposure at Harvard to the larger realm of people and ideas had not made him anxious to return to the cloistered world of small-town life in Owatonna. He apparently was interested in becoming either a concert pianist or a conductor, but his father would not hear of the idea. L. L. Bennett expected his elder son to return to Owatonna to enter the family business, and that is exactly what Carl did in 1890. "He would have been much happier as an artist than a banker, I'm sure," his wife once said. Many years later, Bennett was deeply to regret his decision to return to Owatonna, even though it had made possible the creation of his beloved bank building.[17]

Once home in Owatonna, Bennett threw himself into the life of the community, devoting himself to private enterprise and public service in equal measure. He began by learning the family business. Starting as a bookkeeper in his father's bank, he soon was named assistant cashier and, in 1893, he replaced the retiring Gutterson as head cashier. In that same year, Bennett – barely twenty-five years old – was elected to the Owatonna city council. He remained an alderman for six years and played an important role in securing a publicly owned power plant for Owatonna. In 1898, Bennett was appointed to the town's first library board. He also served for several years as president of Owatonna's park commission.[18]

Meanwhile, he built a business career that was eventually to make him even wealthier than his father. In addition to his work at the bank, Bennett was president of at least three manufacturing firms in Owatonna, part owner of two creamery supply companies, and a member of the *Journal-Chronicle's* board of directors. Moreover, he served as a trustee of Pillsbury Academy and, later, Carleton College in nearby Northfield. He also raised a family after marrying Lydia H. Norwood of Owatonna in November 1898. At the time of the wedding she was barely eighteen years old, a full twelve years younger than her husband. Like Bennett, she had attended Pillsbury Academy. Later, she studied music at Carleton and graduated from the music conservatory there. The marriage appears to have been a happy one, and the couple eventually had four daughters, the last being born in 1913.[19]

Bennett was a patrician figure in those days, part of the monied class that dominated Owatonna's economic and cultural life. In addition to his horses, he maintained a prize herd of dairy cows at a large farm he owned a mile south of town. His bank also owned a number of other farm properties around Owatonna, and he would sometimes take inspection tours to see how the tenants were faring. He had a summer cottage on Lake Minnetonka just west of Minneapolis and could often be seen boating with his brother, who was an avid yachtsman. In short, Bennett seemed to be a perfect representative of Owatonna's gentry, the very model of a man of sober substance. Yet his artistic impulses set him apart from his peers in Owatonna and elsewhere. Music was an especially important part of his life. He was the organist at the First Baptist Church in Owatonna and directed a choral group that performed cantatas by Bach as well as other formidable works.[20]

A small man with delicate features, Bennett looks much younger than his age in most photographs. He wore wire-rim glasses and, for a time, sported a thick mustache, perhaps in an attempt to make himself appear older. A fastidious dresser, just as Sullivan was, Bennett usually wore dark three-piece suits, and photographs always show him with his thin, sandy hair carefully parted, his tie neatly in place, and his suit immaculately pressed. He was, his daughters remember, a quiet, gentle man never given to displays of temper. Although he loved to garden, music was always his chief passion, and he and his wife would often while away the evenings by playing four-hand arrangements on the grand piano in their living room. Beginning in the fall of 1906, another man would often play at that piano. His name was Louis Sullivan, and he had come to Owatonna to design the "true and lasting work of art" that was Carl Bennett's dream.[21]

Although the National Farmers' Bank was flourishing in 1906, it did have one problem. Its quarters on the first floor of a forty-year-old building in downtown Owatonna were becoming cramped, and there was even some fear that the building might be structurally unsound. The bank, Bennett believed, needed a new facility to provide better service to its customers. Moreover, he felt that a new building, especially an impressive one, would help solidify the bank's position as Owatonna's leading financial institution.[22]

Carl and Lydia Bennett with their daughters Beatrice, Sylvia, and Arabella in about 1912

No one in Owatonna would have raised an eyebrow had Carl Bennett decided to build his new bank in the style of a Roman temple or a Renaissance palace. Banks of this sort – complete with Ionic columns, intricate scrollwork, and imported white marble – were the standard of the day. Full of pomp and pretense but lacking originality, these banks were built across America by small-town businessmen who shared many of Bennett's values and beliefs. But they lacked Bennett's shrewd artistic judgment and his willingness to go beyond conventional architecture to obtain exactly the building he wanted.

In an article written in 1908 for *The Craftsman* magazine, Bennett explained what he and the bank's officers sought in their new building and why Sullivan was chosen to design it:

With increasing business came the natural need for a larger and more convenient banking room, and the officers of the bank not only felt the necessity of adequate and practical housing for its business, but also desired to furnish its patrons with every convenience that was necessary and incident to its environment. But this was not all. They believed that an adequate expression of the character of their business in the form of a simple, dignified and beautiful building was due to themselves and due to their patrons, through whose generous business co-operation had been made possible the financial preparation for a new building. . . .

The layout of the floor space was in mind for many years, but the architectural expression of the business of banking was probably a thing more felt than understood. Anyhow, the desire for such expression persisted, and a pretty thorough study was made of existing bank buildings. The classic style of architecture so much used for bank buildings was at first considered, but was finally rejected as being not necessarily expressive of a bank, and also because it is defective when it comes to any practical use.

Because architects who were consulted preferred to follow precedent or to take their inspiration "from the books," it was determined to make a search for an architect who would not only take into consideration the practical needs of the business but who would heed the desire of the bank officials for adequate expression in the form of the building of the use to which it would be put. This search was made largely through the means of art and architectural magazines, including *The Craftsman,* with the hope of finding some architect whose aim it was to express the thought or use underlying a building, adequately, without fear of precedent, – like a virtuoso shaping his material into new forms of use and beauty. From this search finally emerged the name of one who, though possibly not fully understood or appreciated at first, seemed to handle the earth-old materials in virile and astonishingly beautiful forms of expression. The work and personality of Mr. Louis H. Sullivan, of Chicago, was then carefully investigated, with the result that he was the man sought to solve the problem of an adequate expression of banking in this new bank building.[23]

Bennett's article shows his enlightened approach to both business and architecture, but it does not tell the full story behind his selection of Sullivan as architect of the bank. For one thing, the article suggests that Bennett was simply one of several bank officers involved in the selection process and that they all played roughly equal roles. It seems likely, however, that Bennett was the man in charge of selecting an architect and that the other bank officials relied heavily on his judgment. He was a natural choice for the job because, as will be seen, he knew far more about architecture than anyone else connected with the bank. L. L. Bennett, for example, apparently viewed the new bank as a copy of ancient buildings he had seen elsewhere. "The ideas embodied in its construction were suggested to L. L. Bennett, president of the bank, by a number of buildings which he visited during the course of a recent trip to Europe," he told *Bankers Magazine* in 1908, adding that "the interior will be finished in the Grecian and Mosaic style of architecture." Although the bank does indeed show some resemblance to Byzantine architecture in its use of great semicircular arches set within a cube, it hardly can be classified as an example of the "Grecian" style, whatever the elder Bennett may have meant by that term. By contrast, Carl Bennett's 1908 article for *The Craftsman* is an exceptionally clear statement of the aesthetic and functional considerations that underlay Sullivan's design.[24]

Bennett's article leaves the impression that he first became acquainted with Sullivan's work and ideas by reading about him in various art and architectural journals. This may not, however, have been the case. To be sure, Sullivan wrote frequently for such publications, and early in 1906 one of his typical essays was published in the *American Contractor* and reprinted in *The Craftsman* later that year. Entitled "What Is Architecture: A Study in the American People of Today," the essay was a powerful, if florid, statement of Sullivan's theories about architecture and life, and it is very probable that Bennett read it. As always, Sullivan called for a new architecture to express the democratic spirit of the American people. But much of the essay was a jeremiad against historically inspired styles of architecture and the evils of materialism. "The attempt at imitation, by us of this day, of the by-gone forms of building, is a procedure unworthy of a free people," Sullivan wrote. The derivative architecture of the day, he added, was an outward sign of an inner malaise:

As you are, so are your buildings; and, as your buildings, so are you. You and your Architecture are the same. . . . This Architecture is ashamed to be natural, but is not ashamed to lie; so you, as a people, are ashamed to be natural but are not ashamed to lie. This Architecture is ashamed to be honest, but it is not ashamed to steal; so, then . . . you are ashamed to be honest but are not ashamed to steal. This Architecture is filled with hypocrisy and cant. So, like-wise, are you, but you say you are not. This Architecture is neurasthenic; so have you burned the candle at both ends. Is then this Democracy? This Archi-tecture shows, ah, so plainly, the decline of Democracy, and a rank new growth of Feudalism – sure signs of a people in peril! . . . In these buildings the Dollar is vulgarly exalted – and the Dollar you place above Man. You adore it twenty-four hours each day: it is your God! . . . These buildings show no love of country, no affection for the people. So have you no affection for each other, but secretly will ruin each and any, so much do you love gold, so wantonly will you betray not only your neighbor but yourselves and your own children, for it![25]

All of this must have been pretty heady reading for Bennett, a man who, after all, made his living by taking care of other people's money. In fact, Sullivan's fulminations on the topic of the Almighty Dollar would have caused most bankers to think twice before handing him a lucrative commission. Bennett, however, appears to have had no hesita-tions about hiring Sullivan. The likely reason for this is that Bennett was familiar with Sullivan's writings and designs long before plans were laid for the new bank.

There is no question that Bennett knew far more about architecture than the typical businessman of his day. His interest in art and architec-ture dated from his college days, when he apparently had taken a trip to Europe. His wife later recalled that he had made "some pencil drawings of European cathedrals" and had always had a strong artistic bent. But it appears that Bennett acquired his detailed knowledge of architecture from his activities as a member of Owatonna's first library board. The board was created in 1898 after a local woman left the town fifteen thou-sand dollars to build a library. That year, Bennett and James W. Ford, another member of the board, were sent to the Boston area to study innovations in library design there. Among the libraries Bennett saw was the Boston Public Library, completed just three years earlier and de-signed by the famous New York firm of McKim, Mead and White. Bennett was doubtlessly impressed by the Boston library, a huge build-ing done in the manner of an Italian Renaissance palace. But he also may have learned something of the library's practical deficiencies, for like many buildings of its time it tended to celebrate form over function.[26]

While on the tour, Bennett also visited libraries in the towns of Quincy and Malden, Massachusetts, that were the work of Henry Hobson Richardson. Completed in 1893, the Quincy library is done in the stripped-down Romanesque style that became Richardson's hallmark. The library is distinguished for its simplicity and strength, two qualities

Bennett was later to seek in his bank. Richardson was the one architect of his time whom Sullivan genuinely admired, and it is likely that Bennett, after seeing two examples of Richardson's work firsthand, shared that admiration.[27]

When Bennett and Ford returned to Owatonna, they submitted a summary of their findings. Their report recommended in great detail how the proposed Owatonna Public Library should be built, covering everything from the heating and ventilating system to lighting arrangements to the placement of the librarian's desk. The location of the main desk so as to "allow ease of control by one person" was crucial, the report said. It continued:

To this [ease of control by one person] your committee gave special attention as an essential for our library. This will practically decide the shape of the building. It will also decide the location of the main entrance.

The main body of the building should be a rectangle, say 80 by 40 feet. The librarian's desk should . . . be the division between the stack room and the reading room. There should be no partition between these two rooms, no corners or alcoves in the reading room. In such an interior every part is visible from the librarian's desk.

The main entrance should be at about the middle of one side of the building, so that the visitor appears at once before the librarian's desk at the left for business there or turns to the right to the reading room.[28]

What the report recommended, in other words, was that the new building should be designed from the inside out, that its function (to provide a comfortable and well-equipped library that could be supervised by one person so as not to strain the library board's budget) should determine its form. The library was built in 1900 closely in accord with Bennett's recommendations, and it remained in use eighty years later. In helping to plan the library, Bennett learned firsthand how the design process works, and this experience must have been of great value to him when the time came a few years later to search out an architect for his new bank.

Another recommendation in the library report shows that Bennett, as early as 1898, had very definite ideas about how a building should appear. Specifically, the report suggested that the exterior of Owatonna's new library should be similar to that of a library Bennett and Ford had seen in Westford, Massachusetts:

This building is rich in color, plain, massive, substantial, with hardly any ornament. It looks as if it would be there just the same in a hundred years. . . . The arrangement and quality and color of material, the chaste, neat, substantial style of building we should do well to follow. This building does not conform to any one style of architecture.

Bennett's wish for a building "rich in color" as well as being "massive" and "substantial" was realized ten years later in the bank. Of course, the bank fails to meet one of Bennett's architectural criteria in that it is heavily ornamented. However, there is some evidence that the bank, at Sullivan's insistence, was given more lavish ornamentation than Bennett desired. In any event, Bennett's report to the library board shows that, well before the bank was built, he had strong ideas about architecture that were in tune with Sullivan's own beliefs.

Moreover, it is likely that Bennett was acquainted with some of Sullivan's work before 1906. Beginning in the 1890s, Bennett is known to have made periodic trips to Chicago to attend dairy shows and other events. The Chicago Loop during that time was full of buildings designed by Sullivan and his partner, Dankmar Adler. Bennett, with his interest in drawing and architecture, undoubtedly spent some time on his trips looking at buildings in the Loop, and he could not have failed to see such Adler and Sullivan monuments as the Auditorium Building, the Chicago Stock Exchange, and the Schiller Building.[29]

It also seems probable that Bennett, like just about everyone else in the Midwest who had the time and money to do so, went to the 1893 World's Columbian Exposition in Chicago, better known as the Chicago

The Owatonna Public Library shortly after it was built

World's Fair. One of the fair's great attractions was Sullivan's Transportation Building, which featured a huge arched entryway surrounded by dazzling golden ornamentation within a rectangular frame. This entryway adumbrated the basic form Bennett's bank was to take fifteen years later. Although the evidence suggests that Bennett was aware of Sullivan's work in Chicago as early as the 1890s, there is no way now to know for certain that this was the case. But at the least it seems likely that Bennett had Sullivan's name in the back of his mind when he began his search in 1906 for someone to design a new bank.[30]

There are other reasons, not fully dealt with in Bennett's article for *The Craftsman*, that help to explain why he took the radical step of hiring Sullivan. Bennett was, for all of his idealism, a very pragmatic man who knew that any bank design had to be approved by the bank's board of directors. Although the Bennett family held a controlling interest in the bank, the board's views on the matter of a new building could not be ignored. The board consisted of local businessmen and farmers, men not given to visionary thinking in matters of architecture. Bennett knew that above all else these men would demand a practical building, regardless of what qualities it might have as a work of art. By hiring Sullivan, Bennett was able to address the practical concerns of his board. Sullivan had years of experience in the design of commercial buildings, in which practical demands were paramount. And even though Sullivan had acquired, perhaps unjustly, a reputation as an "expensive" architect, he was adept at providing quick and usually accurate cost estimates for his designs. Sullivan's ability in this regard was undoubtedly a strong selling point when Bennett recommended him to the bank's board of directors.[31]

Historian Alan Lathrop has observed that all of Sullivan's small-town banks are "exquisite amalgams of shrewd business and aesthetic principle." This is particularly true of the Owatonna bank. In his article for *The Craftsman*, Bennett touched on this mixing of business and aesthetics, and his comments shed light on another reason for his choice of Sullivan. Referring to the bank's officers (but probably speaking of himself), Bennett wrote: "They believed that a beautiful business house would be its own reward and that it would pay from the financial point of view in increased business." In other words, Bennett was convinced Sullivan could create a building so impressive that it would attract new customers to the bank.[32]

Bennett, in fact, launched a sophisticated advertising campaign in the Owatonna newspapers as soon as final plans for the bank were completed by Sullivan and Elmslie in March 1907. The advertisements extolled the beauty and convenience of the new bank and also emphasized how secure it would be. Security was a particularly important consideration for the bank's officers and board of directors, who wanted a building that would convey a sense of invulnerable strength so that customers would feel comfortable about depositing their money. Bennett obviously believed that Sullivan could create such a building and, as it turned out, he was right.[33]

Although Bennett had good reasons for hiring Sullivan, it still took considerable courage on his part to do so. Sullivan's practice by 1906 had shriveled almost to nothing, his ideas were anathema to the architectural establishment, and he had a reputation for explosive confrontations with his clients. Moreover, Sullivan had never built a bank before, although he had designed banking rooms for several of his large commercial buildings in Chicago and elsewhere. But Bennett took the risk because he was an uncommon man – uncommon in his desire for a great building in his community, uncommon in his willingness to spend a small fortune to get it, uncommon in his ability to perceive true quality in architecture.[34]

It is not known when or how Bennett first contacted Sullivan (or Elmslie, who dealt with clients when his employer was indisposed, which was often). But it is known that Bennett made arrangements for Sullivan to visit Owatonna in the fall of 1906 to look at the bank site and prepare a preliminary plan. And so, in September or early October of that year, Sullivan headed north out of Chicago by train, across the prairies that for him had always symbolized America's vast power, toward a bustling little farm community, to meet a banker with a dream.[35]

2

THE MAN FROM CHICAGO

Sullivan was a faithful worker, a tireless thinker, an extraordinary talker; wherever he sat was the head of the table. . . . He was the most fascinating, inspiriting and encouraging companion anyone could have. He believed in himself and had reason to do so. He had a true message to deliver and delivered it with eloquence, virility and great power. — *George Elmslie*[1]

AS HE JOURNEYED NORTH from Chicago that autumn of 1906, Louis Sullivan was a man on the edge of personal and professional failure. He was fifty years old, had been a practicing architect for three decades, and had already designed a series of magnificent commercial buildings that would one day make him known throughout the world. But the fame and fortune that had been his in the 1880s and 1890s, when he had helped make Chicago the architectural capital of America if not the world, were long gone. Hard times, along with Sullivan's own reckless arrogance, had taken their toll, and he was fast becoming the forgotten man of American architecture. His last significant commission had been the Schlesinger and Mayer (now Carson Pirie Scott) department store in Chicago, completed in 1903. But much of that building had actually been designed years earlier. With so few commissions, his financial situation had grown precarious. He could no longer afford the rent for his offices atop the seventeen-story tower of the Auditorium Building, which he had designed twenty years earlier as a partner in Chicago's most famous architectural firm, Adler and Sullivan. His staff of draftsmen and engineers, which once numbered fifty, was now almost gone, although

Louis Sullivan at about age 45 at the turn of the century

the loyal George Elmslie stayed on. But even Elmslie, working at half pay, was beginning to wonder how much longer the great man could continue.[2]

Sullivan's finances were not his only problem. He had a fondness for the consolations of the bottle and was very likely an alcoholic. He suffered from periods of deep gloom, and his personal behavior was becoming increasingly erratic. To add to these woes, Sullivan's wife of seven years, the beautiful but extravagant Margaret Hattabough, had finally despaired of straightening out either his drinking habits or his finances and would soon leave him for good. But although Sullivan had lost much, he still had his pride and his genius, and those long, slender fingers that observers were always quick to notice could still transform a pencil into an instrument of magic.[3]

Louis Henry Sullivan was in many respects like the lavishly ornamented skyscrapers that made him famous – romantic and passionate on the outside but with an inner frame of cold steel. Often it seemed there were two different men behind those intense brown eyes that, as Elmslie remembered, "no living man could cause . . . to waver or to flinch." On one hand, Sullivan was a thoroughgoing romantic given to rhapsodic pronouncements on the mystic unity of all things. A lover of nature and of nature's ways, he blossomed amid the rock-hard realities of 1880s Chicago like some exotic flower, bright and beautiful but destined not to last. His romantic credo included faith in the natural goodness of man and in the unlimited potential of American democracy. Above all else, he was a man in a hurry to remake the world, for he saw his architecture as a way to shape and transform the human experience. "The form, American architecture, will mean, if it ever succeeds in meaning anything, American life," he wrote, and he was convinced that one day his work would help usher in a golden age in American civilization.[4]

But there was a cold, hard edge to his passion – the "tiger element," Elmslie called it – and in his day-to-day dealings with people, Sullivan the man was often far different from Sullivan the romantic dreamer. Although his philosophy embraced all mankind, Sullivan was close to no one. To be sure, he could be charming and sociable at times, but he was by nature a loner. Proud, willful, unforgiving, with a kind of savage certitude about himself and his work, he careened through life without much regard for the feelings of others, and in the long run it cost him dearly. "The simple, fundamental trouble that has caused all my unhappiness, bitterness, misery . . . is none other than my persistent lack of kindly feeling toward my fellow men," Sullivan wrote during one of his many crises, yet he never really learned how to deal with other people. He worked his staff of draftsmen like a Prussian drillmaster and would tolerate no deviation from his own ideas. He got into needless arguments with prospective clients and often lost commissions because of it. He coldly rejected his long-time business partner Dankmar Adler when Adler sought to renew the partnership after a breakup. "We did not love him," said one of Sullivan's draftsmen, "but we had a great respect for him."[5]

Yet for all the discipline he brought to his work, he was never quite able to master his own appetites and passions. His drinking and carousing made him something of a notorious figure in Chicago, and his personal finances were almost always in a precarious state, no matter how much money he was earning. "He didn't have a perfect grip on himself, which is very essential," a friend recalled, and as Sullivan grew older that grip seemed to become ever more tenuous.[6]

Sullivan seized upon the idea of creating a new American architecture when he was very young, and he never let go of it. He could not understand why others failed to experience his vision with the same intensity, and so he spent much of his life waging war against the architectural establishment. In 1900 he announced with his usual scorn that "American architecture is composed, in the hundred, of ninety parts aberration, eight parts indifference, one part poverty and one part Little Lord Fauntleroy."[7] This sort of rhetoric did not endear him to his colleagues, but he would never back down. Compromise simply was not Sullivan's way, as more than one client discovered, and he remained fiercely independent to the very end. Yet Sullivan also had the weakness that comes with an inflexible outlook. He could not adjust to shifting tastes, as so many of his fellow architects were able to do, and so he finally was broken.

Like Walt Whitman, his favorite poet, Sullivan was an elemental force, full of raw energy and bristling with contradictions that were evident in his personal life, his thought, and his work. For example, he spent virtually his entire professional career working in Chicago, where he designed scores of buildings and achieved his greatest success, yet he believed the city to be a place of "vacant, sullen materialism." Contending that the city was inimical to the human spirit, he took to the countryside, which he viewed as the only true source of inspiration. Asa Gray's *School and Field Book of Botany* was one of his favorite books, and he often encrusted his large commercial buildings with stylized ornament derived from his study of plants. There was also an inconsistency between his avowed hatred of unbridled capitalism and his willingness to serve its needs. He condemned the venality of American society, complaining that "the growl of a glutton hunt for the Dollar" could be heard everywhere. American business, he said, had become "a war of extermination among cannibals." Yet his finest works of architecture – such as the Wainwright Building in St. Louis, the Carson Pirie Scott store, and the Owatonna bank – sanctify the commercial instinct through their extraordinary beauty. In fact, much of Sullivan's output consisted of office buildings, where money is made; retail stores, where money is spent; and banks, where money is kept.[8]

His philosophy was at odds with his practice in other ways as well. He called for a native, democratic architecture that would be "interwoven with the needs, the thoughts, the aspirations of the people." Yet he showed little interest in designing for the common man (as Wright did, in theory at least), and he had trouble obtaining commissions in his later years because of his reputation as an "expensive" architect. Moreover, his personal tastes – fine books, luxurious furnishings, exquisite art objects – were hardly of the common variety. "He lived in some ways like an intellectual aristocrat, [all] the while preaching democracy," Elmslie once wrote. Sullivan also held contradictory views about writing. He was a compulsive writer who poured out his ideas in a prose style that was as dense and ornate as his buildings. He even produced reams of mawkish poetry, which he delighted in inflicting upon captive listeners such as Elmslie and Frank Lloyd Wright. Yet despite his literary aspirations, Sullivan professed nothing but contempt for book learning. "The bright spirit of art must be free," he said. "It will not live in a cage of words."[9]

His designs also showed contradictory impulses. He popularized the idea that "form follows function," yet he sometimes violated this credo in his own work because he believed that a building's ultimate function is spiritual rather than practical. Some of his houses, in particular, failed to meet the practical requirements of their owners and seem to have been based more on formal than functional considerations.[10]

The tensions and contradictions that marked Sullivan's life were at once expressed and transcended in his art. His best buildings – the Owatonna bank among them – pulsate with ornamental energy yet have a classic sense of symmetry and repose. Sullivan described the effect he was trying to achieve as "mobile serenity," a quality he saw as the ultimate product of living and creating in harmony with nature. He once wrote:

There can be no doubt that the most profound desire that fills the human soul . . . is the wish to be at peace with Nature and the Inscrutable Spirit; nor can there be a doubt that the greatest Art Work is that which most nearly typifies a realization of this ardent, patient longing. All efforts . . . tend, consciously or unconsciously, toward this consummation, tend toward this final peace: the peace of perfect equilibrium, the repose of absolute unity, the serenity of complete identification.[11]

Born in Boston in 1856, Sullivan was the son of an Irish dancing master and a German-Swiss mother who was a fine musician and amateur artist. Sullivan spent much of his youth, however, on his grandfather's farm in rural Massachusetts, where he developed his love of nature. In *The Autobiography of an Idea,* Sullivan's not entirely candid account of his early life and career, he described how at age twelve he decided to become an architect (Sullivan, ever the formalist, always refered to himself in the third person):

One day, on Commonwealth Avenue [in Boston], as Louis was strolling, he saw a large man of dignified bearing, with beard, top hat, frock coat, come out of a nearby building, enter his carriage and signal the coachman to drive on. The dignity was unmistakable, all men of station in Boston were dignified; sometimes insistently so, but Louis wished to know who and what was behind the dignity. So he asked one of the workmen, who said:
"Why he's the archeetec of this building. . . . He lays out the rooms on paper, then makes a picture of the front, and we do the work under our own boss, but the archeetec's the boss of everybody."
Louis was amazed. . . . Then and there Louis made up his mind to become an architect and make beautiful buildings "out of his head."[12]

In 1872, at the age of sixteen, Sullivan enrolled at the Massachusetts Institute of Technology to study architecture. At the institute, he learned drawing techniques and familiarized himself with the classic orders of architectural design. But he clearly chafed under the school's emphasis on teaching the traditional architectural styles. The ancient orders "were fairy tales of the long ago," he decided, "now by the learned made rigid, mechanical and inane in the books he was pursuing."[13]

After barely a year at the institute, Sullivan left to look for work in an architect's office. He went to Philadephia, where his uncle and grandfather were living. He was only seventeen, but he was brash and talented and soon talked his way into a job in the offices of Frank Furness, an original if highly eccentric designer. Furness had already begun to develop his own brand of Victorian Gothic architecture and would eventually go on to design some of the most delightfully insane buildings ever seen in America. His buildings usually were heavily ornamented and extremely colorful – two traits that were to characterize Sullivan's mature work, although Sullivan never produced anything as wildly picturesque as some of Furness's creations. Furness's stylized botanical ornament seems to have had an especially strong influence on Sullivan, as his own drawings from the period show. While working for Furness, Sullivan also undoubtedly saw in Philadelphia a number of Gothic Revival style office buildings that may have influenced his later skyscraper designs.[14]

Sullivan stayed with Furness for only three months. Just down the street from Furness's office was the banking house of Jay Cooke, who had compiled a vast fortune by speculating with other people's money. On September 17, 1873, Cooke's financial empire collapsed, touching off a nationwide financial panic that brought building construction to a halt. Furness soon found it necessary to cut back his staff; Sullivan, with the least seniority, was the first to go. It was Sullivan's initial, but by no means his most costly, experience with the vagaries of the American business cycle. But the panic of 1873 actually proved beneficial to Sullivan by forcing him to look elsewhere for work. His parents were living in Chicago by this time, and Sullivan decided to join them. As it turned out, he could not have picked a better place to pursue his visions of a new American architecture.[15]

The great Chicago fire of 1871 had devastated more than three square miles in the heart of the city, destroying eighteen thousand buildings and leaving three hundred people dead and one hundred thousand homeless, all at a cost of more than $200 million. A great rebuilding was already under way, and Sullivan was excited by the possibilities Chicago presented. He wrote: "Louis thought it all magnificent and wild: A crude extravaganza: An intoxicating rawness: A sense of big things to be done." Despite the panic, he wrote, "there was stir; an energy that made him tingle to be in the game." He soon became part of the game by obtaining a job in the offices of Major William Le Baron Jenney. Jenney was a hard-working, hard-drinking bon vivant who presided over one of Chicago's largest architectural firms. He was also a fine engineer who, in 1884–85, would build the world's first all-metal-frame skyscraper – the Home Insurance Building in the Chicago Loop. Sullivan stayed in Jenney's firm for about a year. He then decided that he needed more formal training, so in July 1874 he set sail for France to enroll in the École des Beaux-Arts, which was then the most famous school of architecture in the world.[16]

He found the bohemian life of a Parisian art student to his liking and soon decked himself out in the student uniform of the day: silk hat, tail coat, dark trousers, carefully polished shoes, gloves, and a cane. It apparently was in Paris that he acquired certain affectations, such as his insistence that his first name be pronounced "Louie" in the French manner. He also Gallicized his middle name to "Henri" instead of the more prosaic "Henry." During his first weeks in Paris, Sullivan put in long hours of study, including a crash course in French, to prepare himself for the École's rigorous entrance examinations. He passed the three-week-long series of tests with ease and then turned to the serious business of being a full-time student of architecture.[17]

Drawing on classical antecedents, the École emphasized a highly disciplined and orderly approach to design. Students selected a project and then were given several months to work out a suitable solution. Initially, Sullivan welcomed this approach, but once his first project was completed, he grew restless. He found that the École's systematic approach to architecture contained "a fatal residuum of artificiality. . . . And there came the hovering conviction that this Great School, in its perfect flower of technique, lacked the profound animus of a primal inspiration."[18]

In February 1875, Sullivan left the École. After a quick tour of Europe, he returned to Chicago, where he was to work for the rest of his life. Yet Sullivan's brief stay at the École influenced all of his later work. The École, for example, taught that an initial sketch, or *esquisse*, should be the first step in designing a building. The entire design, down to the working out of its smallest details, was to flow out of this sketch. Sullivan adopted this method in his own work, relying on a quickly drawn sketch rather than elaborate preliminary studies to arrive at the basic form and ornamentation of his buildings. The École also emphasized that a building's exterior should be an expression of its interior arrangement, a concept Sullivan celebrated in his famous motto: form follows function. Despite his professed unhappiness with the École's rigid curriculum, Sullivan later admitted that "it was at the School that I first grasped the concrete value of logical thinking." Moreover, Sullivan's best buildings, with their classic restraint of form, clearly reflect the lessons he learned at the École.[19]

After returning to Chicago, Sullivan's first job was with a small firm headed by John Edelmann, an architect who had worked with Sullivan in Jenney's office. Most of Sullivan's work at this time was as a decorator, and a number of his frescoes for churches and synagogues received favorable notice in the Chicago newspapers.[20]

Sullivan's designs also attracted the eye of Dankmar Adler, one of Chicago's most respected structural engineers. In 1878 Sullivan was introduced to Adler, who was then a partner with Edward Burling in a large architectural firm. A native of Germany, Adler was only thirty-four years old but already well entrenched in the Chicago building establishment. "He was a heavy-set short-nosed Jew, well bearded, with a magnificent domed forehead which stopped suddenly at a solid mass of black hair," Sullivan later recalled. "He was a picture of sturdy strength, physical and mental."[21]

The first meeting between the two men, who were so different in many ways, did not have immediate results. But in early 1879 Adler dissolved his eight-year partnership with Burling. Adler realized that he needed a "design" man as partner, since his own skills were largely in the area of engineering. A second meeting was arranged with Sullivan, who in 1880 agreed to join Adler's office. Three years later, Sullivan — barely twenty-seven years old — became a full partner in the newly created firm of Adler and Sullivan. What followed were the twelve most productive and successful years of Sullivan's life, when the name of Adler and Sullivan came to stand for the very best in Chicago architecture.[22]

Much of Sullivan's success during these years must be attributed to Adler. Many of the practical innovations found in the firm's commercial buildings were the work of Adler, who was a superb engineer with an encyclopedic knowledge of construction techniques. Moreover, Adler had all of the personal qualities his young partner lacked; he was levelheaded, tolerant, wise in the ways of the world, and deft at handling clients. "A solid block of manhood," Wright called him, "inspiring the confidence of everyone, a terror to any recalcitrant or shifty contractor." In the office, Adler was known fondly as "the big chief," and he was far more popular among the firm's employees than was Sullivan. Yet Adler understood and unfailingly supported his high-strung young partner. He saw Sullivan's genius and provided an atmosphere where it could be nurtured toward its fullest blossoming. "In Dankmar Adler," Wright said, "Louis H. Sullivan had a heavy champion."[23]

Sullivan, in turn, looked on Adler as a surrogate father, since his real father had been a distant and often absent figure. Recalling his first years as Adler's office manager, Sullivan wrote: "He found in Adler a most congenial co-worker . . . opening to Louis every opportunity to go ahead on his own responsibility, posting him on matters of building technique of which he had a complete grasp, and all in all treating Louis as a prize pet — a treasure trove. Thus they became warm friends." Sullivan summed up their relationship succinctly when he described Adler as "the sturdy wheel-horse of a tandem team of which Louis did the prancing." And in the 1890s, in that great city by the lake, Sullivan had plenty of room to prance.[24]

Sullivan's rise to partnership with Adler came at a time when Chicago's building boom was nearing its peak. Rebuilding after the Great

Fire had gone slowly at first because of the recession that began in 1873. But by 1880 the economy had recovered, and Chicago began a period of explosive growth. The city's population grew from 300,000 in 1870 to 1,100,000 in 1890, making it the nation's second largest city. The construction fueled by this phenomenal growth produced some of the most powerful and original architecture ever seen in this country: the so-called Chicago Commercial Style that flourished from 1880 to about 1900. Not everyone agrees that the style originated in Chicago or even that it was a distinct style in the first place. But there is no question that the modern skyscraper was in good measure the creation of architects working in Chicago. And it was Sullivan who gave this new kind of building its most dramatic and appealing expression.[25]

Many of Chicago's early skyscrapers, which were quite small by later standards, have long since given way to the wrecking ball, and those that remain might seem rather ordinary looking to modern eyes. But these buildings were extraordinary in their time because they represented a clean break with the past. For more than two hundred years, American architecture had looked to Europe for inspiration. Sullivan, and a handful of other Chicago architects, managed to turn that gaze inward, if only for a little while.[26]

The rise of a new kind of building in Chicago was especially remarkable in view of the prevailing architectural tastes of the day. A kind of frenzied eclecticism characterized much of American architecture in the 1870s and 1880s as various "revival" styles vied for the public's fancy. In general, architects preferred French Second Empire for public buildings, Victorian Gothic for churches and colleges, and various styles of gingerbread (such as Eastlake and Queen Anne) for houses. Buildings done in one or more of these revival styles tended to be exuberantly picturesque, if not always in the best of taste. Sullivan was among the first to condemn this sort of architecture as decadent and un-American. He was, perhaps, a little overheated on the subject, since some of these revival-style buildings had considerable charm and inventiveness. But there is no question that the lean, straightforward commercial buildings produced in Chicago came as a breath of fresh air amid the stifling excesses of Victorian design.[27]

By 1886 the firm of Adler and Sullivan had designed more than sixty buildings, many of them quite small, in Chicago. The firm's work included office buildings, retail stores, churches, houses, and railroad stations, few of which were still standing in the 1980s. For the most part, these early works showed that Sullivan was still groping for a distinct style. In particular, he experimented with various types of ornament as he sought to find a personal expression of his ideas. But he was less successful in finding clear, simple forms for his buildings. His early commercial loft buildings, for example, tended to be rather fussy and did not always present a unified facade.[28]

Then, in 1885, Sullivan and every other architect in Chicago received a revelation. In that year, construction began on a huge wholesale store for the Marshall Field Company. The store, in the Chicago Loop, was designed by Henry Hobson Richardson, the architect whose libraries Carl Bennett had admired. Like Sullivan, Richardson trained at the École des Beaux-Arts, except that he stayed two years rather than only a few months as Sullivan had. In the 1870s, Richardson developed a highly personal style based on the Romanesque buildings of eleventh-century France and Spain. Richardson's buildings, usually constructed of massive granite blocks, had a kind of dense grandeur that struck a new note in American design. His Trinity Church in Boston, completed in 1877, was the most original American building of its time and inspired a popular revival style that later came to be known as Richardsonian Romanesque. For the Marshall Field wholesale store, Richardson designed a stone building of seven stories with clean, simple lines and virtually no ornamentation. The store's massive simplicity was in sharp contrast to the rather picturesque Victorian structures that still dominated the Chicago Loop, and its effect on Sullivan was strong and immediate.[29]

As Richardson's store neared completion, Sullivan was beginning work on his greatest commission, the Auditorium Building in Chicago. Begun in 1887, the Auditorium Building was a work of daunting size and complexity. As originally built, its block-long, ten-story mass included a forty-two-hundred-seat theater designed primarily for opera, a four-hundred-room hotel, plus 136 business offices. Some of the offices were housed in a seventeen-story tower. The building was so big that it required more than forty miles of plumbing, two thousand lock and door plates, twenty-four hundred sash lifts for windows, and an estimated ten million marble tiles or tesserae for the mosaic floors.[30]

The theater takes up about half of the building and is its most famous feature. At the time, it was the largest theater ever built in the United States, with a stage ninety-eight feet wide and sixty-two feet deep. Above and below the stage was a fantastic assortment of machinery that could create virtually any dramatic effect. All of this apparatus was the work of Adler, who also designed an ingenious system of partitions so that the theater's seating capacity could be adjusted to suit various kinds of performances.[31]

Auditorium Building, Chicago

While Adler wrestled with the engineering problems presented by the Auditorium complex, Sullivan worked on the building's facade and its interior ornamentation. His first sketches, done in 1886, show a nine-story building topped by a steep roof with dormers and small corner turrets. But the influence of Richardson's store less than a mile away became apparent in Sullivan's final design. The dormers and turrets, as well as other picturesque effects, were discarded in favor of a powerful, straightforward exterior with very little ornamentation. But Sullivan, for whom ornament was "a perfume," pulled out all the stops in designing the building's sumptuous interior. Walls, columns, ceilings, stairways, doors – all were energized with Sullivan's uniquely rhythmic ornament. Some of his finest effects were created for the theater, which was restored in the 1960s after years of neglect. Sullivan showed a particularly original touch in his method of ornamenting the four huge elliptical arches that flow across the theater's ceiling. He incorporated electric lights – a recent invention in the 1880s – into the ornament of these arches, which gleam like ethereal rainbows when the theater is lighted. The arches, incidentally, have no structural purpose but were placed across the ceiling for purely acoustical reasons. This was the work of Adler, who in addition to his other skills was one of the outstanding acoustical engineers of his day.[32]

Among the draftsmen Sullivan hired to work on the Auditorium plans in 1887 was a nineteen-year-old Wisconsin farm boy named Frank Lloyd Wright. In those days, Wright recalled, Sullivan was:

a not so tall young man with a stride seeming quite too long for the length of his legs. The net result of the stride was a pompous strut. Carrying a dark pointed beard well in front of a dark-brown head of hair trimmed fairly short, already "losing" at the crown, he came immaculately – as always – dressed in brown. His eyes were large, also brown; burning, "seeing" eyes that had a glint of humor in them to make the arrogance of his bearing – bearable.

Sullivan had a knack for picking gifted assistants (he hired Elmslie in 1889 and had a number of other outstanding draftsmen on his staff), but he was not an easy man to work for, as Wright discovered during his first day on the job:

About 10:30 the door opened. Mr. Sullivan walked slowly in with a haughty air, handkerchief to his nose. Paid no attention to anyone. No good mornings? No. No words of greeting as he went from desk to desk. Saw me waiting for him. Came forward at once with a pleasant "Ah! Wright, there you are," and the office had my name. . . .

"Here, Wright," lifting a board up onto my table, "take this drawing of mine. A duffer I fired Saturday spoiled it. Re-draw it and ink it in." . . . He wandered about some more in a haughty sort of way seeming to have no respect at all for anybody there. . . . Finally he stopped just behind me at Weatherwax's [another draftsman's] table.

"What the hell do you call that?" he said in a loud voice, without even bending to look. . . .

"What do *I* call it?" he [Weatherwax] said, evidently hot, as though struck by a lash. "Hell! It's a church, can't you see? *Christ!* What do you want?"

With trembling hands he was undoing the strings of his little black apron as he spoke. With violence he threw his pencil down on the board, grabbed the leather case of drawing instruments and deliberately walked out.

Mr. Sullivan, as though he had heard nothing, changed not a hair, looked a moment at the unhappy drawing while he blew his nose into a fresh handkerchief, then turned on his heel to the next table or two – I could see the cringing fear of him wherever he went – and walked slowly out of the room as he had come in, without another word.[33]

The Auditorium Building, finally completed in late 1889 at a cost of more than $3 million, was a triumph for the firm of Adler and Sullivan. The official opening of the Auditorium Theater on December 9, 1889, drew a glittering array of celebrities and dignitaries. Among them was recently elected President Benjamin Harrison, who had been nominated in the uncompleted theater in June 1888 under the cover of a temporary roof. In the eyes of Chicagoans, the Auditorium complex was proof that their city had come of age and was ready to challenge the economic and cultural hegemony of New York and the eastern seaboard. Wright, who drew some of the ornament for the theater, wrote later that it "was acknowledged to be the greatest building achievement of the period and to this day is probably the best room for grand opera yet built in the world, all things considered."[34]

With the completion of the Auditorium Building, Sullivan – still only thirty-three years old – was at the high tide of his life. He had money, power, fame, and a future that seemed to promise even greater achievements. He also had an office that other architects could only envy, for in late 1889 the firm of Adler and Sullivan moved into new quarters atop the 270-foot Auditorium tower, then the highest point in Chicago. Literally and figuratively, Sullivan was at the summit of his profession.[35]

The view from the tower was especially striking at night, with the lights of the great city spread out below while in the distance the huge Bessemer furnaces of south Chicago glowed fiercely in the darkness. Sullivan often worked far into the night, with Wright or Elmslie at his side. Sometimes the work was interrupted by song, for Sullivan loved to sing and was especially fond of Wagner's operas. But mostly he loved to talk. Strutting about the drafting room, his brown eyes flashing, the ever-present cigarette in his hand, he would hold forth for hours on his philosophy of life and art. Elmslie once had the temerity to ask Sullivan whether these monologues tired him out. "If you mean tired in mind — no," Sullivan replied. "My brain has never been tired; it's not made that way."[36]

The monologues were part of Sullivan's lifelong attempt to explain the ideas that obsessed him. It was no accident that when Sullivan came to write a book about his life, he called it *The Autobiography of an Idea.* Throughout his long career, Sullivan clung tenaciously to certain ideas, even when they were contradicted by the manifest evidence of his senses. He wrote about these ideas at great length. In this respect, he was following a long tradition, for great architects have felt compelled to explain themselves and their art in words. Such explanations were particularly important for Sullivan, not only because he viewed himself as a teacher but also because the weight of his ideas was simply too much for his buildings to bear. Sullivan expected more of his buildings than perhaps any other American architect (Wright included), but the message he sought to encode in brick and stone can be fully deciphered only with the help of his writings.[37]

Sullivan wrote voluminously, and to plow through the heavy, rolling seas of his ornate prose is not a task for the faint of heart. Wright, whose own prose often got the better of him, once noted that Sullivan was "always miraculous when he drew" but could be "ridiculous when he wrote." Sullivan never met a metaphor he did not like, and he also had an incurable fondness for the most stilted conventions of the romantic style. Many passages in his writings seem hopelessly antiquated now, with the result that his buildings have aged far more gracefully than his prose. Yet shining through all the excesses of his rhetoric is a luminous sincerity that glows even today, for Sullivan believed passionately in what he wrote.[38]

The ideas that moved Sullivan were as intense as those of the medieval cathedral builders. Like those builders, who sought to vault to heaven, Sullivan attempted in his buildings to express transcendent truths. But it was the spirit of nature, not that of a personal god, to which Sullivan paid homage. For Sullivan, everything began and ended with nature. In his first published work, the "Essay on Inspiration" dating from 1886, Sullivan described nature as the "deep, fluid, comprehending all" at the heart of which was "Inscrutable Serenity." In nature he saw the reconciliation of all opposites, the solution to all mysteries, the calm center of the universe. Man's task on earth, he believed, was to tap this cosmic power through a creative use of the imagination. He defined man as "a moving center of radiant energy: Awaiting his time to create anew in his proper image."[39]

Yet Sullivan also believed that man could never comprehend nature but could only attune himself to its "mysterious undulations, working freely, through marvelous rhythms, toward subtile [sic] and tremendous consummations – consummations balanced in the end by a noble decay, and the sweet oblivion of death. Whence comes the strangely complex thought of rhythm – for all is rhythm." But Sullivan was no glum fatalist. He had an abiding belief in the beauty and worth of life, which he saw as the musical unfolding of nature's mysterious design. "The utterance of life is a song – the symphony of nature," he wrote in an inscription placed on the proscenium arch of the Auditorium Theater, and he would later express that same idea in the design of the Owatonna bank.[40]

Sullivan saw himself as a poet in stone whose task was to create a universal architecture that would express the highest truths of nature. Behind this precept is the ultimate meaning of his famous, and much misunderstood, motto: form follows function. In one sense, the motto simply means that the forms of buildings should emerge organically from their functions, just as trees grow in many shapes and sizes in accord with the needs of nature. Sullivan's concept of form and function went much deeper than that, however, for he viewed their interplay as the very dance of the universe: "The interrelation of function and form. It has no beginning, no ending. It is immeasurably small, immeasurably vast; inscrutably mobile, infinitely serene; intimately complex yet simple. . . . All is form, all is function – ceaselessly unfolding and infolding – and the heart of Man unfolds and infolds with them." For Sullivan, buildings were one way to express this cosmic dance, and he believed that a building's most important function was spiritual, rather than merely practical. "I value spiritual results only. I say spiritual results precede all other results," he told a convention of architects in 1887, and he meant it. The poetry of a building – its ability to give pleasure and bring enlightenment through the artistic expression of fundamental truths – was thus always of crucial importance to Sullivan.[41]

Sullivan also believed that architecture expresses a nation's inner spirit. "Nothing more clearly reflects the status and the tendencies of a people than the character of its buildings," he wrote. "They are emanations of the people; they visualize for us the soul of our people." The true poet-architect, Sullivan said, must "function as an interpreter of the national life of his time." In Sullivan's view, this meant that the architect must seek in his buildings to express the ideals of democracy. But Sullivan's mystical view of democracy had little or nothing to do with the political realities of American life. "To envisage Democracy as a mechanical, political system merely, to place faith in it as such . . . is to foster an hallucination," he said. "The lifting of the eyelids of the World is what Democracy means." In the largest sense, Sullivan saw democracy as the inevitable outgrowth of living in harmony with nature and thus the ultimate achievement of humanity. Democracy, he argued, "is but the ancient primordial urge within us of integrity or oneness. . . . For Democracy and the oneness of all things are one."[42]

There was nothing very original about Sullivan's philosophy. The idea that form follows function, for example, goes back to antiquity and had been expounded at some length in the 1840s by American sculptor Horatio Greenough. Sullivan's rhapsodic vision of American democracy was simply warmed-over Whitman. Sullivan's philosophy also drew from such varied sources as New England transcendentalism, German idealism (especially that of Friedrich Nietzsche), the writings of English critic John Ruskin, and the mysticism of the Swedish philosopher Emanuel Swedenborg.[43]

Sullivan was not always able to translate his rather nebulous ideas into a workable style of architecture. His task was especially difficult because of the huge program he had set out for himself. "To vitalize building materials, to animate them collectively with a thought, a state of feeling, to charge them with a subjective significance and value, to make them a visible part of the genuine social fabric, to infuse into them the true life of the people, to impart to them the best that is in the people, as the eye of the poet, looking below the surface of life, sees the best that is in the people—such is the real function of the architect," he wrote, and he was foolhardy enough to believe that he could actually accomplish all of this.[44] Sullivan's self-appointed task was further complicated by the fact that almost all of his significant commissions were for commercial buildings, whose owners were not always motivated by the desire to express high ideals in their structures. Despite this handicap, Sullivan tried again and again to wring something sacred out of his commercial designs. He never quite made it—even his remarkable ornament could not turn an office building into a shrine—and this failure accounts for the peculiar poignancy of so much of his work.

Sullivan's glory days atop the Auditorium tower lasted only a few years, but he made the most of them. Designing the Auditorium Building had taken up three years of his life, and when the job was finally done, he took a rest. He traveled for several months, eventually reaching New Orleans in February 1890. There he met some friends from Chicago, who invited him along on a visit to Ocean Springs, Mississippi, on the eastern shore of Biloxi Bay. Sullivan immediately fell in love with the place and bought some property on which he built a vacation cottage. For the next eighteen years, the cottage served as a place of rest and renewal for Sullivan. Near the cottage was a huge garden where Sullivan exercised his love of nature by growing roses – one hundred varieties in all. " 'Twas here Louis did his finest, purest thinking," Sullivan wrote years later when the cottage was only a memory. " 'Twas here he saw the flow of life."[45]

By March 1890 Sullivan was back in Chicago. But his next major project, as it turned out, was to be in St. Louis. A young brewer there, Ellis Wainwright, wanted a new office building and hired Adler and Sullivan to draw up the plans. The Wainwright Building, a ten-story office block completed in 1891, was one of Sullivan's most inspired designs. Although it was not as tall as the Auditorium tower, which was an appendage to a much larger building, the Wainwright was Sullivan's first true skyscraper. Among other things, the Wainwright had an all-steel frame in contrast to the tower's old-fashioned load-bearing masonry walls. With its strong vertical emphasis, the Wainwright fulfilled in every respect Sullivan's definition of the skyscraper as "a proud and soaring thing."[46]

Sullivan has been called the father of the skyscraper, but he was more like a gifted son who took what his elders had given him and then perfected it. The skyscraper form developed in the 1870s in response to new technologies and the rising cost of land in downtown areas. Three inventions in particular were crucial to the development of the skyscraper: the all-metal structural frame, fireproofing to protect that frame, and the passenger elevator.[47]

Until the 1850s, almost all buildings of any size were built of load-bearing masonry walls. Such walls worked well for relatively low buildings but had to be tremendously thick to support a building of any height. This made extremely tall masonry buildings impractical since so much of the lower floors would be taken up by the thick outer walls. The problem was conclusively demonstrated in the sixteen-story Monadnock Building in Chicago, completed in 1891, which has outside walls six feet thick on the ground floor. The Monadnock, as it turned out, was to be the last tall masonry building in Chicago, where iron and then steel became the preferred structural material for skyscrapers.[48]

Although interior iron columns appeared in a few English buildings as early as 1780, architects did not begin using iron for large-scale struc-

Wainwright Building, St. Louis

tural framing until the mid-nineteenth century. The most dramatic demonstration of the material's potential came in 1851, when Joseph Paxton built his famous Crystal Palace in London. This gigantic structure, more than eighteen hundred feet long, featured great walls of glass supported almost entirely by iron framing. By this time, iron trusses, columns, and beams could be found in buildings in both Europe and the United States, although the material was used most extensively for decorative facades. Further advancements came in the 1860s as Henry Bessemer in England began to perfect his process for making steel, which is lighter and stronger than iron. Yet it was not until the 1880s in Chicago that architects first learned to exploit fully the technological possibilities of the metal frame for tall office buildings.[49]

Iron and steel as structural materials had at least one major drawback, however, as builders quickly discovered after Chicago's Great Fire. Both materials lose their strength and eventually melt when exposed to very high temperatures. Steel, for example, loses its strength at about 475 degrees Fahrenheit. Temperatures in the Great Fire reached an estimated 3,000 degrees Fahrenheit, which was enough to turn many of the city's cast-iron buildings into grotesquely twisted hulks. By the end of the 1870s, various inventors in Chicago had solved the fireproofing problem by developing terra-cotta tiles that could be installed around a building's metal skeleton.[50]

The last invention needed for the skyscraper was the passenger elevator, since the human spirit is generally dampened by the prospect of climbing more than five or six flights of stairs. Elisha G. Otis, an archetypal Yankee tinkerer, was the man who finally invented a safe and reliable elevator. His first models, powered by steam, appeared in the 1850s, but it was not until sometime after 1870 that elevators came to be used widely.[51]

No one quite agrees on when the first skyscraper appeared on the American scene, but the general view is that the tall office building got its start in New York City around 1870. In that year, the 130-foot-high Equitable Building was completed in lower Manhattan. Yet the Equitable, and much taller buildings that soon followed in New York and Chicago in the 1870s, usually employed an old-fashioned style of design that tended to vitiate the skyscraper's most obvious characteristic – its great height. Most of these early skyscrapers resembled giant layer cakes, one highly decorated story piled atop another, with the whole concoction typically ending in a mansard-style roof surmounted by a tower. The result was that these buildings suffered from a kind of structural schizophrenia: they were made with new materials but were clothed in old designs.[52]

Although a number of buildings erected in New York City in the late 1870s began to move away from this pattern toward a more vertical emphasis, it was not until the mid-1880s in Chicago that the modern skyscraper really began to take shape. Jenney and John Wellborn Root, designer of the astonishingly stark Monadnock Building, did notable work in this regard. But it was Sullivan who first brought high style to the skyscraper form in his Wainwright Building. In designing the Wainwright, Sullivan did two very basic things that have since become commonplace in skyscraper design. First, he allowed the building's piers to run uninterrupted from the third through ninth floors. Second, he recessed the spandrels (the area immediately above and below each window) between the piers. This made the piers stand out, thus emphasizing the vertical thrust of the building. Sullivan then gave the building a two-story base with large display windows for ground-floor shops. Finally, he crowned his creation with an elaborate cornice that seems to flow out of the tenth floor, which was largely reserved for various mechanical functions. The design of the Wainwright "was the great Sullivan moment," Wright wrote. "The skyscraper as a new thing beneath the sun . . . with virtue, individuality, beauty all its own . . . was born."[53]

Five years after the Wainwright Building was completed, Sullivan wrote an essay entitled "The Tall Office Building Artistically Considered" in which he defined all of the elements required for a proper skyscraper. Not surprisingly, Sullivan's description of the ideal skyscraper sounds suspiciously like the Wainwright. (Actually, the building fails to meet some of the practical criteria laid down by Sullivan in his essay.) Nevertheless, the essay is important because it clearly shows that the poetry of a building was always foremost in Sullivan's mind. He wrote: " 'What is the chief characteristic of the tall office building?' And at once we answer, it is lofty. This loftiness is to the artist-nature its thrilling aspect. It is the very open organ-tone in its appeal. . . . It must be tall, every inch of it tall. The force and power of altitude must be in it, the glory and pride of exaltation must be in it. It must be every inch a proud and soaring thing."[54]

Following completion of the Wainwright Building, Adler and Sullivan turned to a variety of other projects. In 1891–92 the firm had numerous commissions in Chicago, including the seventeen-story Schiller Building, a large cold-storage warehouse, a synagogue, and several houses. Other projects during this period ranged from a railroad station in New Orleans to an office building and a hotel in St. Louis. Sullivan also designed a thirty-eight-story office building that, in its use of setbacks, was far ahead of its time. But this skyscraper, which would have been the tallest building in the country, was never built.[55]

Adler and Sullivan did not remain busy for long, however, because in 1893 business quickly dried up as the nation plunged into what was then the greatest depression in its history. Banks failed, factories closed, new building came to a halt – all with stunning suddenness. The panic of 1893, more than anything else, triggered the steady decline that marked the last thirty years of Sullivan's life. Adler and Sullivan still had a few projects on the board that carried the firm through 1893. In the following year, as the depression continued to deepen, there simply was no new work, and almost all of the firm's draftsmen had to be laid off.[56]

Sullivan had other kinds of problems to contend with as well. In 1893, he provoked a needless dispute with Wright over some free-lance design work Wright had done to supplement his income. Wright's contract with Adler and Sullivan did not permit such work. Even so, a compromise could have been reached. Adler, in fact, was willing to smooth over the matter. But Sullivan would not budge. Neither, of course, would Wright, and the net result was that Wright left the firm of Adler and Sullivan for good. The falling-out was perhaps inevitable, given the gigantic egos on both sides, but the loss of Wright was certainly a blow to the firm.[57]

Wright soon set up his own office in the Chicago suburb of Oak Park and there began to design a series of long, low houses in what came to be known as the Prairie style. A diverse group of Midwest architects, the so-called Prairie School, soon followed Wright's lead. Yet even though Wright provided the immediate inspiration for the school, many of its key ideas – such as its emphasis on organic architecture – clearly came from Sullivan. Shared beliefs, however, were not enough to bring Sullivan and Wright back together after their split, and it would be seven years before they met again.[58]

The panic of 1893 was not the only event of that year which was to have a lasting effect on Sullivan. For 1893 was also the year Chicago played host to the World's Columbian Exposition, which was supposed to celebrate (a year late as it turned out) the four hundredth anniversary of the arrival of Christopher Columbus in the New World. Planned and built before the depression, the Chicago fair was one of the great events of its kind in American history. Among the fair's most impressive features was an ensemble of huge buildings that came to be known as the White City because of their dominant color. Built around a large basin connected to Lake Michigan, these buildings were devoted to exhibits in such fields as agriculture, electricity, transportation, and the fine arts. Most of them were designed in the neo-classic version of the Beaux-Arts style that Sullivan so detested. Replete with domes, columns, and pediments, the glistening buildings of the White City were a Beaux-Arts triumph, a nineteenth-century version of imperial Rome re-created on the south side of Chicago. Only citizens in togas were lacking to make the picture complete.[59]

Ten architects – five from the East, four from Chicago, and one from Kansas City – designed these buildings, almost all of which burned down or were torn down after the fair ended. Sullivan was among the ten architects chosen and was given the task of designing the Transportation Building. For the most part, this building – in the form of a Roman basilica – was nothing very extraordinary. It did feature, however, a spectacular entrance that came to be known as the Golden Doorway. Radiating out from the entrance were six arches pulsing with brilliantly colored ornament derived from Islamic sources. The arches were in turn contained within a large rectangular panel that was itself highly decorated. The Owatonna bank was to be a variant on this theme – the arch within the square or rectangle – which Sullivan used repeatedly in his work.[60]

Although the Golden Doorway drew favorable critical notice as far away as France and was considered one of the wonders of the fair, it did little to blunt the overwhelming impact of the White City on architectural tastes. Just about everyone except Sullivan seemed impressed by the majesty and grandeur of the White City. Even Henry Adams, that mordant observer of American life at the turn of the century, professed admiration for it. "As a scenic display," he wrote, "Paris [which staged a world's fair in 1889] had never approached it. . . . Honestly, he [Adams] had the air of enjoying it as though it were all his own; he felt it was good; he was proud of it."[61]

On the surface, Chicago in 1893 might have seemed about the last place in America that would produce something like the White City. After all, only a decade before the city had spawned a new style of commercial architecture largely free of historical associations. But the hard-headed, no-nonsense businessmen who helped build Chicago in the 1880s had, by the 1890s, acquired a yen for "culture." Simple, utilitarian buildings would no longer satisfy them. Like their counterparts in New York, these businessmen now wanted buildings that would give monumental expression to their newly acquired wealth and power. And when it came to a conspicuous display of riches, the Beaux-Arts architects were unexcelled.[62]

Sullivan, had he been more perceptive, might have seen this trend in his own buildings, which grew more ornate through the 1880s, culminating in the lavishly appointed interiors of the Auditorium Theater and Hotel. In fact, almost all of his buildings were themselves based on Beaux-Arts principles of design. But Sullivan, who was curiously blind about so many things, came in his old age to believe that the fair had been a great disaster for American architecture – a belief he apparently did not voice when the fair was in progress. Writing in 1923, Sullivan described the fair in some of the most sarcastic and contemptuous words ever to flow from his pen. The United States government's exhibit building, he complained, had been "of an incredible vulgarity," while he described the state of Illinois building as "a lewd exhibit of drooling imbecility and political debauchery." The style of the White City, he wrote, had eventually spread like a contagion to every corner of America: "Thus Architecture died in the land of the free and the home of the brave. . . . Thus did the virus of a culture, snobbish and alien to the land, perform its

Golden Doorway of the Transportation Building at the 1893 Chicago World's Fair (Columbian Exposition)

work of disintegration. . . . The damage wrought by the World's Fair will last for half a century from its date, if not longer. It has penetrated deep into the constitution of the American mind, effecting there lesions significant of dementia."[63]

Yet the White City and its effect on popular taste did not kill Sullivan's career, as some of his early apologists claimed. Sullivan's own intransigence, his drinking, and the depressed business climate of the 1890s were more responsible for his lack of commissions. There was one other crucial factor in his decline. After 1895 Sullivan not only found himself increasingly out of work and out of fashion, he also found himself without a partner.[64]

As a single man, Sullivan had managed to weather the first years of the depression fairly well. But Adler, with a family to support, needed a regular income. In July 1895, with little or no business in the office, Adler reluctantly dissolved his partnership with Sullivan and went to work as an engineer for an elevator company in New York. Although Adler's action clearly was dictated by financial need, Sullivan felt betrayed and the parting was not amicable. As it turned out, Adler stayed in his new job for only six months. He returned to Chicago in January 1896 and sought to re-establish the partnership. Sullivan, proud and defiant as always, refused. It was perhaps the biggest mistake of his life. Without Adler's steadying influence and business acumen, Sullivan was hard pressed to make his living as an architect.

When Adler left the firm, Sullivan had only one project under way — the Guaranty Building in Buffalo, New York. Completed in 1895, the thirteen-story building is perhaps Sullivan's finest skyscraper, its entire surface glowing with tawny terra-cotta ornament. The building had actually been designed while Adler was still in the office, but his name was removed from the plans when they were published. This act, according to Wright, "seemed to hurt the old chief [Adler] terribly." Describing a meeting with Adler during this period, Wright wrote: "I tried him in and out concerning his former partner; pleaded the master's [Sullivan's] case with him. Told him truly how much and where there was such great disappointment over their separation — we all believed each needed each other. If ever two men did, they did."[65]

In the end, Wright found that efforts to reunite the two men were "all useless." And so Sullivan remained alone atop the great tower that Adler's engineering skill had made possible. Adler finally formed a firm with his two sons in 1896 and managed to obtain a few commissions for factories, school buildings, and synagogues — all in Chicago. Still, it was not like the old days when Sullivan had been there to bring the designs alive. In late 1898, Adler apparently did rejoin Sullivan to work as a consulting engineeer on the Schlesinger and Mayer department store project. The collaboration did not last very long, however, because in April 1900 Adler died of a stroke at age fifty-six. "Adler was a man of fine mind and excellent heart," Sullivan later wrote, and it is clear that he eventually came to regret deeply the breakup of their partnership.[66]

With Adler gone, Sullivan began to rely increasingly on Elmslie to handle the day-to-day business of the office. Despite Elmslie's help, Sullivan had to struggle to stay afloat in the highly competitive world of Chicago architecture. Between 1895 and 1897 he obtained only a few minor projects in Chicago, even though the economy was beginning to revive. Nevertheless, he managed to secure a commission for a twelve-story office building in New York City. The Bayard (now Condict) Building was completed in 1898. Long since dwarfed by newer skyscrapers in lower Manhattan, the Condict Building features one of Sullivan's most lyrical cornices along with his usual terra-cotta ornament.[67]

Sullivan, besides lacking work, was plagued by personal problems during this period. In 1896 he had a falling-out with his older brother Albert, who was the general superintendent of the Illinois Central Railroad. The brothers had been close for many years and sometimes vacationed together at Ocean Springs. Their relationship began to deteriorate, however, after Albert was married in 1893. His wife, a New Orleans belle, did not get along with her temperamental brother-in-law, who apparently made no attempt to win her over. Then, in 1896, Albert and his wife had their first child, after which they decided to move into the house where Louis was living. The house had been built by the brothers for their mother, who died in 1892 and never occupied it. Louis did not appreciate being forced out of his home of four years by his own brother, and the estrangement that had begun with Albert's marriage became complete. The brothers rarely spoke to each other afterward. It was about this time that Sullivan apparently began to drink heavily. He grew moody and morose and seldom did any drawing. Most of what work there was fell to Elmslie, who was already proficient in creating the kind of intricate ornament favored by Sullivan.[68]

In the late 1890s Sullivan obtained his last significant work in Chicago when he was commissioned to design a new department store for the Schlesinger and Mayer Company. Built in several stages between 1899 and 1903, the store (now Carson Pirie Scott and Company) is often regarded as Sullivan's masterwork. The building's ten upper floors form perhaps the most powerful expression of the steel frame in all of American architecture, with each big Chicago-style window framed by bold terra-cotta ornament. The powerful simplicity of the upper stories gives way on the first two floors to an ornamental explosion in the form of an intricate cast-iron screen that in places seems to cling to the walls of the building like some huge climbing plant gone wild. A tour-de-force in cast-iron artistry, the screen is composed of plantlike forms that swirl and spiral in rhythmic patterns of incredible complexity. Display windows are positioned in the midst of the ornament, which functions as a kind of lavish picture frame. Elmslie, who designed the ornament under Sullivan's direction, said the screen was conceived to attract the eyes of shoppers and draw them into the store. Perhaps better than any of Sullivan's other buildings, the store combines structure and ornament, form and function, simplicity and complexity into that mysterious reconciliation of opposites that Sullivan saw as the ultimate expression of nature itself. In the bank he would attempt much the same thing, but on a different scale and in a different way.[69]

While the Schlesinger and Mayer store was under construction, Sullivan decided to give up his bachelor ways and get married. Unfortunately, he was no more ready for marriage than he was for running an architectural firm on his own. In his younger years, Sullivan had been known for his "fast" life style. Wright, in one of his periodic fits of sanctimony, complained that Sullivan practiced "smoking . . . drinking, whoring . . . to a dreadful extreme." The departure of Adler, whose family life he often shared, apparently made Sullivan feel the need for some domesticity of his own. In July 1899, at the age of forty-two, he married twenty-seven-year-old Margaret Hattabough, whom he had met while she was walking her dog along a Chicago street.[70]

The marriage went well at first, with the couple spending much of their time at Sullivan's cottage in Ocean Springs. But Sullivan's drinking soon got out of hand. Elmslie later recalled how Margaret Sullivan would "see me in the office, and shed tears, not knowing what to do with her Louis. She had to have assistance every night, at times, to help put him to bed." Moreover, she had literary aspirations and a taste for stylish living, both of which entailed expenditures her husband could ill afford. By the time Sullivan came to Owatonna in 1906, his marriage was on the verge of breaking up, although Margaret did not leave him for good until 1909.[71]

In the first years of the new century, Sullivan still had very little work. Aside from the Schlesinger and Mayer store, he had only two commissions of any note from 1900 to 1906. One was for a five-story office building, the other for a small store. He spent most his time writing. The *Kindergarten Chats,* probably his best literary work, appeared in installments in a small trade magazine in 1901–02. Soon after, Sullivan began writing *Democracy: A Man Search,* which he believed to be his masterpiece. But the manuscript — much of it in Sullivan's densest, most forbidding prose — came to 180,000 words. No publisher would touch it.[72]

By 1906 Sullivan was at one of the low points of his life. He had no work and few prospects. He had alienated the two people closest to him — his wife and his brother. He suffered from frequent bouts of depression and was drinking heavily. Yet "he held his handsome head high," one of his draftsmen recalled. He would not give up because that simply was not part of his nature. And, of course, there was still the matter of a small-town banker in Minnesota who wanted something special in the way of a new building. Sullivan, with help from Elmslie, would try to give the man from Owatonna what he wanted.[73]

Margaret Hattabough Sullivan

3

DESIGN AND CONSTRUCTION

The layout of the floor space [of the bank] was in mind for many years, but the architectural expression of the business of banking was probably a thing more felt than understood. — Carl Bennett[1]

DIRECTLY ACROSS BROADWAY STREET from the bank is a small patch of greenery called Central Park. Shaded by elm trees and with a fountain at its center, the park has always been the focal point of downtown Owatonna. It was to this pleasant little park that Sullivan may well have come one day, probably in early October of 1906, to create the outlines of a masterpiece. Although there is no way to know for certain whether Sullivan indeed visited the little park, it was his usual procedure to study a site, sometimes for several days, before making a quick sketch. Sitting in the park, doubtlessly smoking the particularly cheap and vile cigarettes he favored, he would have had ample time to study the challenge confronting him. In particular, the park would have offered him an excellent vantage point from which to ponder how the site would look once the old bank building had been razed to make way for his creation.[2]

The park would also have been an ideal place for Sullivan to wait for inspiration, which he considered to be a vital element in the creative process. Sullivan did not believe in making sketch upon sketch of a project in search of final perfection. Instead, he preferred to "commune" with the problem until a vision of the building would flow into his mind. That is how the Wainwright Building had come to him. He had been strolling down Michigan Avenue in Chicago when the basic design of the Wainwright struck, and then it had been simply a matter of sketching it out in a few quick strokes. "Sullivan was a marvelous object lesson in his methods of arriving at a solution," Elmslie remembered. "All of his integrations . . . were primarily mental conceptions and fairly complete in detail before transfer to the necessary paper. . . . Very accurate, very quickly done and complete in all essentials were his original drawings."[3]

If Sullivan did indeed spend some time in Central Park that October, at least two of its traits might have caught his eye almost at once. First, there were the park's trees, which at that time of the year would have been at or near the height of their autumn colors. The bank's exterior — predominately red and brown — certainly has an autumnal look that may well reflect what Sullivan saw in the park in the slanting sunlight of an October afternoon. Then there was the shape of the park itself. Central Park is now a rectangle, but in 1906 it was oval shaped, so that the streets around it featured sweeping curves. The elliptical roadway around the park may have suggested to Sullivan a suitable motif for the new bank in the form of large arched windows. To what extent, if any, these sights may have influenced Sullivan's scheme for the bank is impossible to determine. Moreover, it appears that some elements of the design came from Sullivan's previous work, while Elmslie supplied others. But regardless of the source of his inspiration, Sullivan probably needed only a few days of thought and study in Owatonna before making the basic sketch from which the bank would be built.[4]

When Sullivan visited Owatonna — and he was to be there often between 1906 and 1916 — he always stayed with Carl Bennett and his family. In 1906 the Bennetts lived in a big, white house just three blocks from the bank. It was a handsome, comfortable home, with fine woodwork, large rooms, and a nice porch to catch the summer breeze. Sullivan and Bennett became friends almost at once, even though they appeared to have little in common. Bennett was a dedicated family man; Sullivan, although he had finally married, was known for his nocturnal escapades. Bennett was a faithful Baptist; Sullivan was an agnostic who believed that "the personal God has been a twilight phantom by the door of truth." Bennett neither drank nor smoked; Sullivan did both, frequently to excess. Bennett, except for four years at Harvard, had spent his entire life in the cloistered society of a small midwestern town; Sullivan was thoroughly cosmopolitan in his tastes and style. Bennett was a quiet, eventempered man; Sullivan had a volatile personality and was capable of titanic fulminations. Bennett was born to wealth and comfort; Sullivan had risen from unpretentious beginnings on sheer talent and was plagued by money problems almost all of his life.[5]

Despite these differences, Bennett and Sullivan did share a common philosophy, particularly as it related to architecture, for both men were idealists who believed that buildings could express their culture's highest aspirations. The two men also shared another passionate interest — music — and that may have been what cemented their relationship. The grand piano in the living room of the Bennett home was seldom silent during Sullivan's frequent visits. Lydia Bennett was, like her husband, a fine pianist, and the couple would often entertain Sullivan by playing four-hand arrangements of classical pieces. Sullivan himself had no formal musical training, but he played the piano quite well and claimed to have a repertoire of four hundred songs.[6]

Sullivan also loved to give readings of his latest literary effusions, and in the Bennetts he had an interested, if perhaps captive, audience. From 1906 to 1908 Sullivan was hard at work on his magnum opus, *Democracy: A Man Search*, and in the evening he would often read his latest chapters to the Bennetts. It must have taken considerable forbearance on their part to sit through the great man's readings because *Democracy: A Man Search* contains some of Sullivan's most ornate and impenetrable prose. But the Bennetts clearly enjoyed their visits from Sullivan. "We had very happy times together when he would come to our house," Mrs. Bennett recalled many years later. "He seemed very happy there."[7]

With his own wife about to leave him, Sullivan must have found the calm and amiable domesticity of the Bennett home a refreshing change of pace. The couple had one daughter in 1906 (three more would be born later), and Sullivan in his many letters to Bennett would often inquire about the girls' health. Besides good music, the Bennett home offered two other things Sullivan loved: good food and good conversation. Lydia Bennett arose early every morning to begin fixing elaborate meals for her husband and Sullivan. "I gave these men five course dinners every day as well as their lunches and breakfasts and Mr. Sullivan found great pleasure, as we always did, in visiting over demitasses of coffee for sometimes as long as an hour."[8]

Much of this conversation over coffee must have focused on the new bank Sullivan was to design. It appears that Bennett and Sullivan did not always agree when discussing plans for the building. Oskar Gross, who painted the bank's murals in 1908, recalled that Bennett "was a man that wanted simplicity and Sullivan was too complicated for him." Yet Bennett was in many ways an ideal client. He was well versed in architectural theory, he knew the bank's needs, and he was thus able to give Sullivan specific suggestions about how the new building should be laid out. However, Bennett's comment that "the architectural expression of the business of banking was probably a thing more felt than understood" suggests that he was willing to defer to Sullivan's expert judgment when it came to specifics of design. Bennett probably had little choice in this regard, since Sullivan demanded and expected a free hand in designing his buildings. "He [Sullivan] was a very stubborn man. . . . He wouldn't change one of his ideas," Mrs. Bennett recalled. But she also noted that her husband "had complete faith in Sullivan," and it is clear that the two men quickly developed a mutual respect that made their relationship an unusually harmonious one.[9]

Bennett and his board of directors were expecting much from Sullivan. They were about to spend the unheard of sum of $125,000 for their new bank and office building, and they wanted something extraordinary in exchange for all that money. For Sullivan, the bank presented a new kind of challenge. He had spent most of his career designing very large commercial buildings in Chicago. Now he was being asked to scale everything down to small-town size, yet at the same time he was expected to produce a building so strong and distinctive that it would attract new customers to the bank. It was also very important for the bank to convey a sense of invulnerable security, so that depositors would feel their money was safe. Finally, Bennett had insisted that the bank be "modern." Bennett did not want a Roman temple, nor would Sullivan have given him one had he asked for it. Sullivan, in fact, once suggested that if a banker wanted a Roman temple, then he should "wear a toga, sandals, and conduct his business in the venerated Latin tongue – oral and written."[10]

What Sullivan was being asked to do, in effect, was to create a whole new image for one of the basic institutions of American life: the small-town bank. "The bank was a prominent architectural feature of every midwestern town," notes historian H. Allen Brooks. "Only civic buildings, those associated with democracy, took precedence over banks." This was exactly the case in Owatonna, for the bank would occupy a strategic downtown corner almost directly across Central Park from the Steele County Courthouse.[11]

In arriving at a suitable design for the bank, Sullivan had little to guide him. Almost from the beginning days of the nation, when Benjamin Latrobe designed his Greek-inspired Bank of Pennsylvania in Philadelphia, American banks had tended toward the classical style so despised by Sullivan. During the mid-1800s, banks had also been built in various of the revival styles, but these, too, were anathema to Sullivan. Nor did Sullivan's own work provide any precise models for the bank. Although he had designed several small stores in the 1880s, his only recent building comparable in size to the Owatonna bank had been the Felsenthal Store in Chicago, completed in 1906. The store showed that

Sullivan could do very well by a small building. But the store, a relatively inexpensive building, was not nearly as demanding a project as the bank.[12]

There were, however, three bank designs — none of them ever built — that may have exerted some influence on Sullivan's thinking as he pondered his problem that autumn in Owatonna. The first was a bank project drawn in 1891 by Harvey Ellis for Minneapolis architect Leroy S. Buffington. Ellis's design was for a long, low building with heavy, windowless walls pierced only by a large arched doorway set between two small niches. The design also called for a good deal of terra-cotta ornamentation and a frieze running along the top of the building for its full length. In addition, the building was to have a shallow dome, not visible from the street, that would provide interior light through bulls-eye windows at its base. The whole design had a strong, solid look to it that was very appropriate for a bank.[13]

The other two noteworthy bank designs of this period came from the fertile imagination of Frank Lloyd Wright. In 1901 Wright published plans for "A Village Bank" in *Brickbuilder* magazine. Wright's proposed bank was a small cubic mass with an enframed area in front containing decorative terra-cotta panels and clerestory windows above two bronze doors. This enframed area was divided into bays by pillars emerging from battered (inwardly slanted) walls. The bank, as rendered by Wright, had an almost tomblike appearance — very solid and monumental. In 1904 Wright produced another interesting design, this one for a small bank in Dwight, Illinois. The Dwight bank was to be a rather tall, narrow building with heavy corner piers supporting a high attic. Between the piers were two recessed columns on either side of the main entrance. Above the entrance were large windows taking up all the space between the piers and columns.[14]

Sullivan and his chief draftsman, George Elmslie, were undoubtedly aware of these designs. Elmslie, who contributed so much to the design of the Owatonna bank, reputedly kept a sketch of the Ellis project over his drafting table. Yet the projects by Ellis and Wright, while showing some similarities to the Owatonna bank, can hardly be classified as its inspirations. In fact, the design of the Owatonna bank seems to have sprung out of Sullivan's own work, rather than that of others. The basic form of the bank — a cube punctured by large semicircular arches — is one that Sullivan had used again and again in his work. The huge portal arch of Sullivan's Transportation Building at the 1893 Chicago Fair certainly anticipates the bank, as do a number of his large commercial buildings that feature arched entrances.[15]

The bank, however, most closely resembles in its general form a tomb designed by Sullivan in 1890 for Carrie Eliza Getty, the wife of a Chicago lumber merchant. Like the bank, the tomb – in Graceland Cemetery in Chicago, not far from where Sullivan himself is buried – has a base of plain stone that gives way to a highly decorated upper section. The whole creation is then capped with a beautifully detailed cornice. Moreover, the tomb has a single arched window on each side, with the arch springing from the line that separates the unadorned base from the decorated wall above. The huge arched windows of the bank are positioned in exactly the same manner. It is perhaps no coincidence that the bank resembles

Tomb for Carrie Eliza Getty,
Graceland Cemetery, Chicago

a tomb, since the building seems to have been conceived at least in part as a monument to the Bennetts.[16]

By the time Sullivan left Owatonna in October of 1906, he had sketched for Bennett the general design of the bank and the shop and office building that was to adjoin it on the east. He also must have decided what kind of materials would be used for the two buildings because it was his practice to give clients a cost estimate before drawing up any plans. Sullivan was back in Chicago by October 16, when he received a letter from Bennett giving the exact dimensions of the new buildings' site. Four days later, a Chicago builders' magazine reported that Sullivan was at work on a bank and office building in Owatonna which was to cost one hundred thousand dollars. The story said the bank was to be built of brick, stone, and terra cotta, along with oak woodwork, maple floors, and nickel plumbing, among other items. This article provides solid evidence that Sullivan, by the time he left Owatonna, had been able to provide fairly detailed plans for the bank and adjoining office building.[17]

Although Sullivan was clearly in charge of the bank project, it was another man – George Grant Elmslie – who did much of the actual work. That Elmslie played a vital role in designing the bank is indisputable. The six original drawings for the bank that have survived are all in Elmslie's hand, and it appears that Elmslie drew virtually all of the bank's famous ornament. Elmslie himself took a great deal of credit for the bank, and his claims must be given considerable weight, because he was by nature a self-effacing man not usually given to braggadocio. In a letter to Bennett dated December 7, 1909, Elmslie wrote: "He [Sullivan] did none of the work you see on your building, none whatever. That may surprise you but it is quite true. I made every drawing that enters into the fabric of your building, every design from your stenciled walls to your stained glass, your clock, electroliers, grilles, everything. I never meant to say anything of this kind, but at the parting of the ways surely no harm is done. Even the big arched windows was [sic] first brought out by me. He [Sullivan] came back from Owatonna with a scheme for 3 arches."[18]

This letter was sent shortly after Elmslie had been fired by Sullivan. Coming as it did after a bitter parting, Elmslie's letter may appear to be an act of revenge. And, in fact, Elmslie did go a bit overboard in his claims. He acknowledged in a letter written many years later that Sullivan himself had designed the cornice of the bank, although Elmslie could not resist remarking that it was "a wee bit out of scale." Elmslie also admitted later that Sullivan had designed at least one of the ornamental motifs in the banking room. Yet there is much truth to Elmslie's

Elmslie's working drawing for the
terra-cotta clock

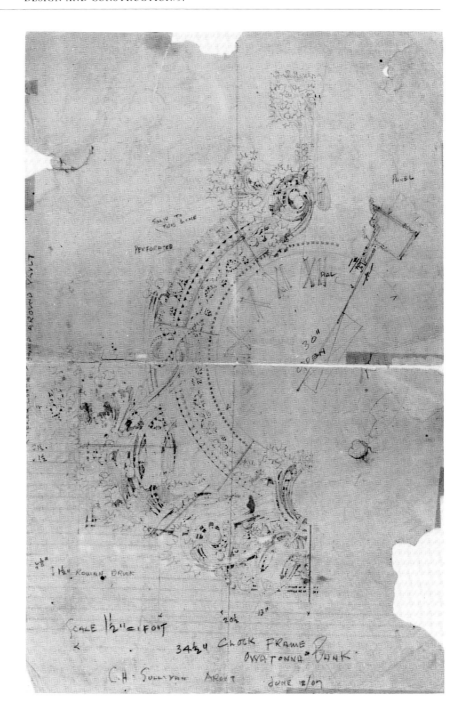

claims concerning the design of the bank, for he was far more than a mere draftsman in Sullivan's office. He was, in fact, a great artist in his own right who spent much of his life laboring in the giant shadow cast by Sullivan.[19]

For two decades, through good times and bad, Elmslie was the indispensable man in Sullivan's life. When Sullivan was too drunk or too ornery to deal with clients, Elmslie would step in to smooth things over. When Sullivan had one of his legendary temper tantrums, Elmslie would pick up the pieces, sometimes quite literally. "He [Sullivan] had destroying spells at times, especially when a 'bit under.' Tore up all his life insurance policies one day," Elmslie recalled. "Quite a chore to reconstitute." When Sullivan needed a sounding board for his latest ideas, Elmslie would sit patiently in the Auditorium tower and listen as the great man droned on, sometimes for as much as seven hours at a stretch. And when work needed to be done, it was usually Elmslie who ended up doing it because Sullivan was often absent from the office for long periods. "I got so frightfully lonesome at times," Elmslie remembered, "especially when the master came in late in the day very glazed in the eye. Unhappy man!"[20]

Yet Elmslie was often an unhappy man himself and in many ways as puzzling a character as Sullivan. Perhaps the biggest puzzle of all is why Elmslie stayed with Sullivan as long as he did. To be sure, he genuinely admired Sullivan and believed him to be a great genius. Their relationship, however, seems to have been decidedly one-sided because Elmslie received very little appreciation or recognition in return for his long years of devoted service. It seems likely, for example, that Elmslie hoped at some point to become Sullivan's partner in name as well as fact. But Elmslie, by his own admission, "never had the courage" to ask for a partnership, and Sullivan never offered one. Nor did Elmslie ever make much money working for Sullivan. For many years, in fact, he worked for half of his regular salary because that was all Sullivan could afford to pay him. The result was that Elmslie often had barely enough money to meet his own needs.[21]

Despite being treated poorly, Elmslie stayed on with Sullivan year after year, and when the two men finally severed their ties, it was Sullivan who did the cutting. In a letter written in 1944, twenty years after Sullivan's death, Elmslie complained: "If ever in all his [Sullivan's] life he did a disinterested thing for me, tell me about it. 'I am keeping you, George, [Sullivan is quoted as saying] because I don't want anyone else to get you.' Naive to be sure to make such a comment but truth will out. Selfish, what?" Yet in many of his other writings, Elmslie fiercely defended Sullivan and spoke glowingly of his fine character.[22]

Elmslie, it appears, stayed on with Sullivan year after year, at great personal cost, simply because he was not ready to take on the world by himself. He was by nature an extraordinarily diffident man who seldom made his feelings or desires known to others. He was also inclined toward melancholia, and his letters to Purcell are full of moody ruminations on the futility of life. His letters often end with the words "Ho hum," which was his favorite way of expressing the sense of resignation that was so much a part of his character. Wright, who in his various memoirs never ran out of bad things to say about other architects, depicted Elmslie as a timid, slow-witted man who clung to Sullivan with almost animal-like devotion. "George wasn't a minister's son but ought to have been," said Wright, who was fond of referring to Elmslie as "the faithful George" in a condescending sort of way.[23]

But Elmslie was not the silent churchmouse described by Wright. "He [Elmslie] was not a long-distance talker," said his partner for many years, William Purcell, "but he was by no means a silent person." Nor was Elmslie at all slow of mind. His letters, in fact, reveal that he possessed a remarkably wide-ranging intellect. And as those letters also make clear, he was no fawning devotee of Sullivan. His attitude toward Sullivan actually was highly ambivalent, oscillating between love and hate, fondness and disgust.[24]

Although he was every bit as passionate and romantic as Sullivan, Elmslie was reluctant to show this side in public, and it was only in his magnificent ornament that he expressed his inner spirit. His work in the Owatonna bank and on other projects earned him recognition only after his death as one of the great ornamentalists in the history of American architecture. Because he lacked Sullivan's supreme self-confidence and had none of Wright's talent for self-advertisement, Elmslie was never really able in his lifetime to win the laurels that might have been his. In his later years Elmslie became a bitter man, nursing a cancerous resentment fed by thoughts of what might have been. He believed that others — first Sullivan and later Purcell — took credit for achievements that were rightly his. In both cases, Elmslie was probably right. But if Elmslie failed to achieve the recognition he deserved, it was largely because of his own inability to assert himself.[25]

Of the men who made the Owatonna bank, Elmslie is in some ways the most intriguing because of his background. Sullivan came from an artistically inclined family. Carl Bennett was born to wealth and thus had ample opportunity to pursue his artistic impulses. By contrast, Elmslie grew up in the hardscrabble world of the Scottish hills, where opportunities for a budding artist were limited. Elmslie was born in 1871 on a farm in Aberdeenshire in the northeastern part of Scotland. "I wore a cute tartan kilt until about [age] 6 or 7," he remembered many years later. His father, John Elmslie, was a weaver by trade who had turned to farming in an effort to support a family of eight children. Aberdeenshire was a romantic sort of place, full of swift streams and deep valleys, and there was even the ruin of an ancient castle near the Elmslie family farm. In his old age, pent up in a house on the south side of Chicago, George Elmslie could still vividly recall the homeland of his youth:

George Elmslie in about 1908

Heather clad hills and rippling streams, deep water pools and grassy banks on which the boys lay and fished with their hands for the quick-witted trout. A very ticklish and skilled occupation it was and such fun. . . .

Our farm was partly on a hillside and therefore poor, facing west, and one of my earliest memories was watching the sunlight creep across the valley eventually flooding all in sunshine. On clear days might be seen the North Sea from the top of our hillside. Our summer evenings are still fresh in memory, long sweet twilights in which, in midsummer, we could read out-of-doors until ten-thirty.

A stable countryside nurtured in the finer values of human intercourse, facing storm and stress with a smile and leaving for foreign parts with a smile, perhaps a sad one, and never forgetting the essential romance and glamour of the homeland wherever they might be. In far-off Chicago it lingers with us who were born there. . . .

There was much singing in our country of the simple songs and ballads. Hardly a farm hand in the fields remained inarticulate — with the lark singing aloft in the sweet sky. This whole background fed the imaginative youth with unforgettable memories. . . .[26]

But there were other, less idyllic memories of shortages of food and clothing, for John Elmslie could barely eke out a living for his family on his small farm. By 1883 John Elmslie had had enough. He immigrated to the United States and found a managerial job in a Chicago meatpacking plant. His family followed him in 1884. George had shown a gift for drawing as a student at the Duke of Gordon Schools in Scotland, and he decided to pursue that interest. He began as an apprentice in the office of William LeBaron Jenney, Sullivan's old employer. By the time he turned seventeen in 1888, Elmslie was a good enough draftsman to obtain a job with Joseph Lyman Silsbee, a prominent Chicago architect who specialized in designing Queen Anne style houses. It was in Silsbee's office that Elmslie met Wright, who soon left to go to work for Sullivan. Elmslie, however, stayed with Silsbee until early 1889. At that time, Sullivan was preparing final drawings for the Auditorium Building and needed more good draftsmen. Wright suggested Elmslie, who was promptly hired by Sullivan.[27]

When Wright left the office in 1893, Elmslie became Sullivan's chief draftsman. As Sullivan's decline accelerated in the late 1890s, Elmslie took over more and more of the responsibilities of the office and began to function as a virtual partner in design. During this period, he played a major role in the design of some of Sullivan's most famous works, including the Guaranty Building and the Schlesinger and Mayer store. "Beginning in 1895 and until 1909 I did 99 3/5% of it [the design work coming out of Sullivan's office]," Elmslie once claimed. "When I left[,]

some knowing people wondered what had happened to Sullivan's ornament. This happened – he went back to the things he had been doing
before 1895."[28]

Elmslie also handled most of the day-to-day business of the office,
such as dealing with clients and contractors. Six feet tall, slim, with
sandy hair, sharp blue eyes behind wire-rim glasses, thick eyebrows, and
a brushy mustache, Elmslie could be a most charming man, and clients
usually enjoyed working with him. He was a model of tact and patience –
two virtues Sullivan seldom displayed. In fact, Elmslie was in his quiet
way a much more likable man than Sullivan, if only because he was so
much easier to get along with. Lydia Bennett remembered Elmslie as "a
delightful personality," and other clients also recalled him fondly, citing
his quiet competence and wry sense of humor.[29]

When the Owatonna bank commission came along, Elmslie was just
thirty-five years old and at the peak of his creative powers. Yet even
though he had already demonstrated his skill as a designer, he still very
much needed Sullivan, just as Sullivan needed him. Elmslie was the
Chopin of American architecture, a brilliant miniaturist who had trouble
orchestrating the larger forms of buildings. He needed a guiding hand,
and when he got it – first from Sullivan and later from Purcell – he produced his finest work. By the same token, both Sullivan (after 1900) and
Purcell did their best work when teamed with Elmslie. And of all the
buildings Sullivan and Elmslie worked on together, it was the Owatonna
bank that perhaps offered them the best opportunity to display their com-
plementary talents.

Elmslie's claim that he designed virtually every detail of the bank is
thus misleading, though perhaps not intentionally. The fact is that
Sullivan was very much involved in designing the bank even though he
did virtually none of the working drawings. The basic idea of the building as a kind of giant jewel box was Sullivan's. Sullivan, as at least one
of his letters to Bennett makes clear, also was intimately involved in
working out the bank's unusually rich color scheme and in selecting the
materials to be used. And while Sullivan clearly gave Elmslie a free hand
in designing the ornament, he undoubtedly had considerable say as to
where the ornament should be placed and how it should relate to the total
design of the building. There is also the simple fact that, in the day-to-
day workings of a small architectural office such as Sullivan's was in
1906, everyone takes a hand in the work.[30]

Moreover, the question of who should get credit for the bank does not
really come down to a choice between Sullivan and Elmslie. The bank
was, in fact, the creation of many skilled hands who together formed a
kind of all-star team of artisans and craftsmen that Sullivan had as-

sembled over the years. Elmslie was the most vital member of this team, and there can be no question that he contributed immensely to the bank's final excellence. But the Sullivan-Elmslie debate that has sometimes been carried on in scholarly circles seems pointless. It takes nothing away from Sullivan's achievement to say that Elmslie had a large hand in the bank; nor does it detract from Elmslie's reputation to suggest that he needed Sullivan's guidance in working out the building's details.

After Sullivan's return from Owatonna in October 1906, he and Elmslie spent the next few months preparing plans for the bank and the adjoining shop and office building. The plans, which did not include a final working out of the bank's complex interior color scheme, were finished in January 1907. Sullivan and Elmslie's design called for a building simple in its basic form but uncommonly rich in its detailing. The bank itself was to be almost a cube – sixty-eight feet square and forty-nine feet high. The exterior was to feature a nine-foot-high sandstone base punctured by sixteen small, square windows placed at eye level. These windows, arranged in horizontal bands to reflect the interior plan of the bank, were to be deeply recessed in the wall like oversized gunports. At the southwest corner of the bank, where L. L. and later Carl Bennett were to have their offices, the plan called for two much larger windows set very low in the wall so that the president could look out over the community while sitting at his desk. The main entrance to the bank was to be on the west or Cedar Street side, and it was to be recessed into the sandstone base, thereby contributing to the bank's fortress-like appearance.[31]

Above the base, which was intended to give the bank an intimate human scale, Sullivan and Elmslie's design called for something more heroic and monumental. Much of the dramatic effect was to be provided by two huge semicircular stained-glass windows, one facing south and the other west. Springing from the sandstone base, each of these windows was to have a diameter of thirty-six feet, making them in their day among the largest ever shipped west of Chicago. It was Elmslie who conceived of these great windows, as he recalled years later:

L.H.S. [Sullivan] was sitting at the drawing board drawing in three arches for the leading forms.
   "What do you want, George," said he, as I seemed to demur at the three.
   "One great arch," said I. "About 35 feet."
   So he drew in a 36-foot one, and said, "Is that what you want?"
   "Yes, sir," said I.[32]

The windows were to be set in a wall of richly textured brick designed to contrast but not conflict with the lighter colored base. Each window was to be framed by a wide band of colorful terra-cotta ornament accented by a much narrower band of glass mosaic. The upper corners of these frames were to contain large, oddly shaped ornaments that are sometimes called cartouches. Capping the bank there was to be a simple stepped-out cornice defined at top and bottom by bands of terra-cotta ornament.[33]

For the interior of the bank, Sullivan and Elmslie created a large lobby, around which were distributed offices, tellers' cages, vaults, and various special meeting rooms. The lobby was to be reached through a low vestibule designed to provide a dramatic entryway to the forty-foot-high banking room. Among other things, the banking room was to feature arches set in the north and east walls. These arches, identical in size to those of the windows, were to have no structural purpose but were created purely for symmetry. Two large murals of agricultural scenes were to be painted beneath these arches to underscore the bank's dependence on its farm customers. The banking room was also to be ornamented in plaster, terra cotta, and cast iron and was to feature an extremely complex color scheme. Lighting was to be provided by the two big arched windows, a stained-glass skylight, and four gigantic light fixtures or electroliers, as Sullivan liked to call them.

The design themes of the bank were carried through into the shop and office building that was to adjoin it to the east along Broadway Street. In designing this building, Sullivan and Elmslie sought to complement but not to compete with the bank's monumentality. The building was to be two stories high (one story less than the bank) so that it would serve as a transition between the bank and the many two-story commercial buildings found in Owatonna. Designed to house a small shop and a newspaper plant on the first floor and offices above, the building was to have the same sandstone base as the bank and the same kind of bricks above. There was to be an ornamental cast-iron panel above first-floor display windows and an elaborate arched entryway over an alley separating the shop from the newspaper office. The second floor was to have eight arched windows, separated by terra-cotta capitals. Terra cotta was also to be used to decorate the areas, called spandrels, between the window arches. In addition, there was to be a terra-cotta band, much like that used on the bank, to enframe the windows. Large "B" crests, denoting the Bennett family, were to anchor each corner of this frame. The interior of this building was to be very plain, however, with none of the lavish decoration that was to go into the banking room.

The first set of plans for the bank and commercial building are dated

January 15, 1907. Later that month or possibly early in February, they were presented to Bennett and his board of directors. The bank plans were approved without change, but the board balked at the design of the shop and office building because of its cost. The board was already spending a small fortune on the project, and the ornate shop and office building was simply more than the bankers could afford. Sullivan and Elmslie were told to simplify the building. This process was completed by March and the revised plans were quickly approved by the board. Among other things, the new plans eliminated much of the decorative terra cotta around the second-floor windows, replacing it with a beautifully articulated band of brick. The terra-cotta "B" crests were kept, however. The ornamental cast-iron panel above the first-floor windows was also eliminated, as was the arched entryway to the alley, which gave way to a simple rectangular opening. In addition, common brick was substituted for the more expensive tapestry brick except on the street facade. As it turned out, the revised plan may have been one of those cases of less being more, because the simplified facade of the shop and office building harmonizes but does not conflict with the more ornate elevations of the bank.

On March 15, 1907, the bank – in a large, three-column notice placed in both of Owatonna's newspapers – announced its building plans. The first public description of the project came on March 22 in a front-page story in the *Owatonna Journal-Chronicle*, whose offices were to be located in the building adjoining the bank. The story carried no by-line, but it was doubtlessly prepared with the help of Bennett, who sat on the newspaper's board of directors. "It is at last possible for the Journal-Chronicle to make public the announcement that during the coming year there will be erected in Owatonna not only the largest and most imposing building in the city but also probably the most beautiful building in this part of the state," the story began. "It may also be confidently declared that this building will contain probably the most complete and well arranged banking offices in this part of the country." The story went on to give a detailed and very accurate description of the new bank and described Sullivan as "a man of national reputation whose designs are even on exhibition in great European museums." Owatonna's other newspaper, the *Daily People's Press,* did not get around to running a story on the new bank until April 19, perhaps because it had been scooped by its rival the month before. The *Daily People's Press* story also hailed the new bank as a great step forward for the town but made no mention of the architect.[34]

Construction began almost immediately after the project was announced. Bennett wanted the bank finished within a year, which meant that most outside work had to be completed by the end of November

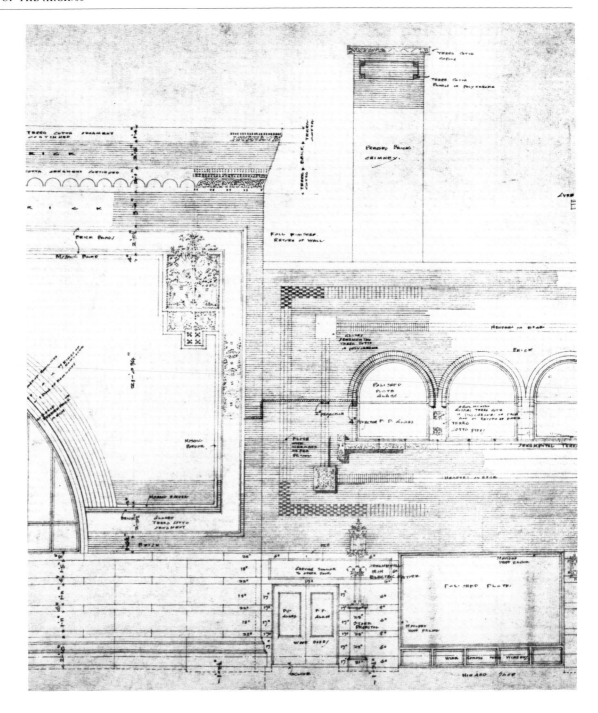

Part of an elevation drawing, undoubtedly made by Elmslie, showing exterior details of the bank and adjoining shop and office building

before really cold weather set in. An Owatonna construction firm, Hammel Brothers and Anderson, had already been selected as general contractor, and various subcontractors were quickly lined up as well. The project was complicated by the fact that the bank's existing building had to be razed before the new bank could be built in its place. As a result, the bank would need temporary quarters while awaiting completion of its new home. The problem was solved by constructing the shop and office building first, so that it could be used initially as the bank's temporary quarters. At the same time, demolition work began on the bank's existing building, only part of which was occupied by bank offices. A temporary roof was placed over these offices while the rest of the old building was razed.[35]

Meanwhile, work moved ahead rapidly on the shop and office building, which was to be a much larger structure than its appearance from the street might indicate. The building was designed to have two distinct parts—a long, narrow section on the east extending about 130 feet back from Broadway and a smaller section to the west adjoining the bank. The east part of the building, to be occupied by the *Journal-Chronicle,* included offices as well as a large, two-story-high room for the newpaper's presses. The west section of the building was designed to house a small shop and offices. The two parts of the building, separated by an alley on the ground floor, were neatly tied together on the second floor by a bridge of offices spanning the alley. Through this device, Sullivan and Elmslie were able to provide a unified facade for the building. Apparently for security reasons, there were no doorways connecting the shop and office building to the bank on either the first or second floor. But the two structures did share a common heating system, located in the basement of the shop and office building. Construction of the shop and office building went ahead so rapidly that the bank was able to move its offices there by mid-August. What remained of the old bank building next door was then demolished, clearing the way for construction of the new bank.

The bank building itself took far longer to complete, mainly because of the intricate decorative work in the banking room. The exterior of the bank went up quickly, however, and presented no really formidable construction problems. The outer walls were made of common brick, which was then faced with the sandstone, tapestry brick, terra cotta, and glass mosaic that form the bank's facades. The two huge window arches that cut into the south and west walls were also built with common brick in a technique that has changed little since antiquity. The first step in building the arches was the construction of wooden centering. Elmslie made a drawing for the construction of this centering, which was required because brick arches do not become self-supporting until all the bricks are in place. Once the centering was complete, the arch was built over it, after which the centering was removed.

Helped by unusually mild autumn weather, work on the bank exterior moved along ahead of schedule. Workers began installing the exterior terra cotta and glass mosaic in late September and finished the job in November. It was also in November that the roof was completed. The roof structure posed some special problems in part because the bank — basically one large room more than sixty feet across — could not be readily spanned by the kind of wooden rafters available at that time. As a result, two steel-plate girders were placed atop the banking room, along the east-west axis, to provide cross support for the rafters. These I-shaped girders, more than four feet high where they bow toward the middle, were designed to support far more than the weight of the roof, however. Their main function, in fact, was to hold up the four huge cast-iron electroliers, weighing fifty-five hundred pounds and carrying twenty-four globes each. Two electroliers were to be suspended by steel cables from each girder, which thus had to be strong enough to support not only part of the roof but more than five tons of decorative cast iron as well. Because of this, the girders are unusually strong and heavy for a building of the bank's size.[36]

Constructing the bank required complicated wooden falsework centering to create the arched windows. This is the only known picture of the bank under construction.

The construction of the bank must have attracted considerable attention in Owatonna. It was, after all, both the costliest and most unusual building in the city's history, and it used many materials – such as tapestry brick and polychromed terra cotta – that had never been seen in Owatonna before. Carl Bennett was well aware of this interest, and he attempted to capitalize on it by means of a shrewd advertising campaign in the local newspapers. For all of its elegance and art, the new bank was still a commercial proposition. Bennett believed – perhaps wrongly as it turned out – that the bank presented an opportunity for art to serve commerce. He tested this thesis in a number of large display advertisements that began appearing in the Owatonna newspapers as soon as construction was underway on the bank. These advertisements, quite possibly written by Bennett himself, were carefully timed to coincide with various stages of work on the building. For example, an advertisement that appeared on September 20, 1907, as workmen were laying the tapestry (or Oriental) bricks of the bank's facades, concluded: "Oriental bricks are new in this vicinity and should be studied to be wholly appreciated. We study the wants of all our customers and respectfully solicit your banking business." Another advertisement, two weeks later, used the bank's polychromed terra cotta as the starting point for a similar message: "Our terra-cotta is exceedingly strong and enduring like the friendship which we endeavor to build up with each one of our customers among whom we desire you to be numbered."[37]

Bennett had hoped to have his new bank completed by February 1908. But work on the banking room fell behind schedule, apparently because Sullivan and his decorator, Louis J. Millet, needed additional time to work out the intricate color scheme. It was not until April that workmen finally began applying the final touches to the interior, according to a notice that appeared in the *Journal-Chronicle:* "We have now begun on the last big job in connection with the completion of our new banking room. This is the painting and ornamental color work of the plaster walls . . . and the placing of the leaded glass skylight and the leaded glass in the two big windows. This work is under the direction of Mr. Louis J. Millet, a colorist of national reputation. Although such work requires time for its proper execution, Mr. Millet assures us that our job will be finished in about eight weeks. While this painting is going on we will be able to finish up the wood work, install the steel lined vault and big door, and generally to finish up the other last details."[38]

Millet was in Owatonna for virtually all of May and June to supervise work on the banking room. Sullivan, who had made it a practice to visit Owatonna at least once a month during construction of the bank, also was in town frequently. The two men were old friends and shared a fondness for the pleasures of the saloon. At that time there were no fewer than four saloons distributed around Central Park within a block of the bank, and Sullivan and Millet became regular patrons. According to Oskar Gross, the two comrades usually began their circumambulation of the park in the morning and would visit all four drinking establishments before the day was done. Bennett, of course, did not frequent saloons, nor did Gross, so they would sometimes hitch up two of Bennett's fine horses

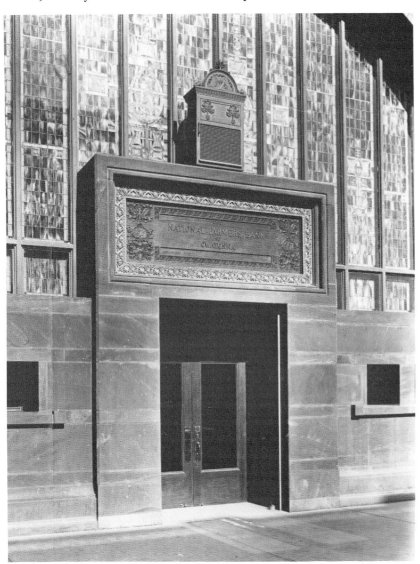

The original cast-iron sign over the bank's entrance was probably designed by Elmslie, but only Sullivan's name appears on it. The object above the sign is a burglar alarm.

and go for long rides in the country while Millet and Sullivan did their imbibing.[39]

On July 14, 1908, five months behind schedule, the National Farmers' Bank officially opened for business in its new home. The building was essentially complete, and about all that remained to be done were the two murals on the north and east walls of the banking room. During its opening week, the bank was kept open at night so that everyone in town would have a chance to see it. Under the soft light of the great electroliers, the banking room must have struck those early visitors as a magnificent fantasy, mysterious and colorful and utterly unlike anything they had seen before. Yet the farmers and tradesmen and shopkeepers who came to see the bank discovered that, for all of its splendor, it had been built with them in mind because it was very practical and down-to-earth in its layout. The bank is, in fact, perhaps the ultimate demonstration of Sullivan's belief that architecture serves human needs by unifying the practical and the spiritual in a kind of higher functionalism.[40]

The bank and shop and office building as completed in 1908

4

THE FINAL AND LOGICAL FLOWERING

I want a color symphony and I am pretty sure I am going to get it. . . .
There has never been in my entire career such an opportunity for a color tone
poem as your bank interior plainly puts before me. — Louis Sullivan[1]

THE BANK IS A BUILDING that neither climaxed nor inaugurated a
tradition. Throughout his career, Sullivan sought to forge a uniquely
American style of architecture that would one day flourish throughout
the land. But what he and Elmslie actually created in Owatonna was an
exotic building that has always been firmly outside the mainstream of
American design. Although the bank is usually considered to be an example of Prairie School architecture, it is an extreme example at best, for
it combines monumental simplicity of form with incredible complexity
of detailing in a way that few other Prairie School buildings can match.
The bank's exotic qualities – from its unique and instantly recognizable
elevations to its fantastic interior ornamentation – account for much of its
appeal and its enduring place in the architectural history books.

The bank's originality in and of itself, however, does not explain why
it has come to be recognized as one of the indisputable masterpieces of
American architecture. Rather, its high status comes from the fact that,
as designed by Sullivan and Elmslie, it was a fully integrated work of art
in which every part contributed to the effect of the whole. The elements
of this integration included its practical and efficient floor plan, its magnificent ornamentation, its beautifully conceived color scheme, and the
superb craftsmanship of its builders and decorators. The integrated qual-

ity of the bank's design is less evident now than it once was because the banking room has been drastically altered by several remodelings. Yet even though the opportunity to experience the bank in all of its original splendor is now lost forever, it remains an endless visual feast for those who would take the time to look.[2]

Although the banking room was clearly a space designed to inspire a kind of secular awe, it was also geared toward meeting the practical needs of the bank and its customers. The banking room's original layout was quite simple. It consisted of a forty-foot-high, skylit lobby around which were clustered tellers' cages, offices, and customer-service rooms. These areas were separated from the lobby by a brick enclosure, nine feet high in most places. The lobby itself provided a spacious, comfortable place for business and included two specially designed check desks at which customers could fill out bank forms.[3]

The rooms grouped around the lobby were also carefully planned, with each serving a clearly defined function. The best description of these spaces was provided by Bennett himself in his article for *The Craftsman*. To the left as customers entered the lobby was the farmers' exchange room, located in the northwest corner of the bank. This area, Bennett wrote, "is finished with white glazed tile walls, green tile floor, and a ceiling of leaded glass panels set between heavy oaken beams. Along the walls are comfortable built-in seats covered with Craftsman [a popular furniture style of the time] cushions. This room is intended for the private use of farmers in their business meetings and is used also as a convenient meeting place for business or social engagements." Segregation of the sexes, or at least some rather strong feelings that they required different treatment, explains the next area in the bank, which was called the women's room. Located next to the farmers' room along the bank's north wall, this chamber was supposed to provide "a rest room for the farmers' wives and children," according to Bennett, who noted that it was designed to be "somewhat more homelike than the room for men, as it shows a warmer and richer color scheme and is provided with high-back settles, low rocking-chairs and small tables and writing desks." Both the men's and women's rooms had adjoining lavatories, an uncommon amenity at the time. Next to the women's room was the savings department and past that were small cubicles for customers wishing to use their safe-deposit boxes.

To the right, or south side of the lobby, was the president's office, which took up the entire southwest corner of the bank. Paneled in quarter-sawn white oak, the office was comfortable and dignified. Moreover, the two large windows allowed L. L. Bennett, and later Carl, to keep in touch with the community around them even as they conducted bank business. Next to the president's office, along the south side of the bank, was a conference room. It, too, was paneled in oak, but unlike the president's office it had a large window overlooking the lobby. Farther along the south wall was a large open area, separated from the lobby by a low brick wall, which provided desk space for bank officers other than the president. In 1908 four officers worked there, including Carl and Guy Bennett. So many changes have been made in the banking room since 1908 that only the president's office (restored in 1982) remains in its original position, although for many years even it was located elsewhere in the bank.

Along the room's east wall, directly across from the main entrance, were the money and bookkeeping vaults. Above the vaults, mounted on a brick parapet, was a large clock enframed by elaborate terra-cotta decoration. The clock, which has survived all of the remodelings, was designed to serve as a focal point amid all the color and ornament of the

The women's room was on the north wall of the bank and had a teller's wicket into the Savings Department.

The bank officers, including Carl and Guy Bennett, sat at desks overlooking the banking room floor.

The clock (east) wall of the newly opened bank was photographed before the murals had been installed. The vault door is clearly visible (left center).

banking room. The door to the money vault (relocated in 1929) was clearly visible behind a brick tellers' enclosure that jutted out into the lobby. Sullivan may have placed the vault door in clear view of the front entrance in order to discourage thieves by ensuring that their activities could be seen from the street. Banks around the turn of the century were almost fanatical about security, and bankers' magazines from the period often featured lengthy articles on the latest developments in locks and vaults. It is more likely, however, that Sullivan put the vault where he

did simply because it was a way to emphasize the bank's chief function, which was to store and protect valuables.[4]

The offices and rooms clustered around the lobby created a nice division of scale in the banking room: a lower level for business and an upper level for what might be called pleasure. The most colorful and eye-pleasing ornament was placed on the upper walls of the room, above the brick enclosure that defined the business space. This ornament, by and large designed by Elmslie in accord with principles developed years before by Sullivan, is the bank's most famous feature.[5]

For Sullivan and Elmslie, ornament was not mere decoration but rather an outward expression of a building's inner spirit. It was not the icing on the cake; it was the essence of the cake's flavor given physical form. Sullivan himself once described ornament as "the last line in the sonnet," a metaphor that neatly expresses the vital role ornament played in his buildings. Throughout his career, Sullivan sought to combine the organic and the inorganic, the emotional and the rational, in his designs. Ornament, he believed, could accomplish this by providing a flowing, organic counterpoint to the inorganic, blocklike masses of his buildings. "Bring it alive man! Make it live!" Sullivan would tell his draftsmen as they struggled to master his intricate style, for above all he saw ornament as a way to breathe vitality into his creations.[6]

Sullivan gave a full statement of his theory of ornament as early as 1892. In an article that year in *Engineering Magazine,* Sullivan readily admitted that it is possible to produce buildings "well formed and comely in the nude," that is, without ornamentation. But he argued that ornament, if done properly, could be an integral part of a building and add greatly to its effect. "We feel intuitively that our strong, athletic and simple forms [of buildings] will carry with natural ease the raiment of which we dream, and that our buildings thus clad in a garment of poetic imagery . . . will appeal with redoubled power, like a sonorous melody overlaid with harmonious voices," he wrote. Moreover, he insisted that ornament must appear to be a part of the building rather than as something "stuck on" the surface. "It should appear, when completed, as though by the outworking of some beneficent agency it had come forth from the very substance of the material and was there by the same right that a flower appears amid the leaves of its parent plant."[7]

Another important aspect of Sullivan's theory was his belief that ornament should serve as a means of personal expression, a kind of signature in stone (or, more often in Sullivan's case, in terra cotta). Ornament was, therefore, a way for the architect to give individuality to buildings: "It

The 1908 floor plan shows the relationship of the bank to the two-story office and shop building. The *Owatonna Journal-Chronicle* occupied the long section to the right.

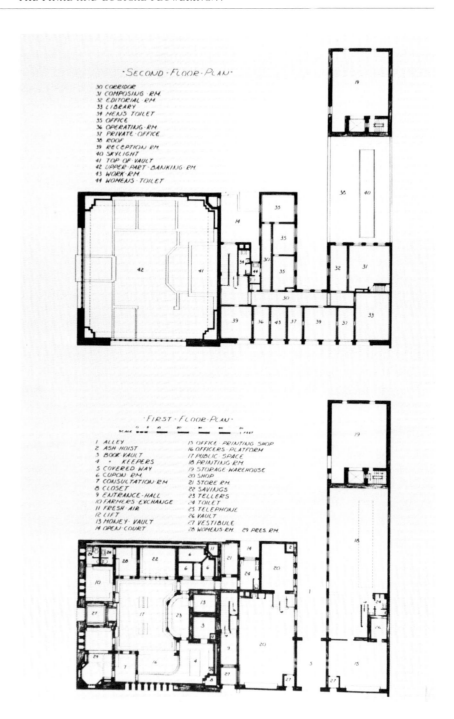

·SECOND·FLOOR·PLAN·

30 CORRIDOR
31 COMPOSING·RM
32 EDITORIAL·RM
33 LIBRARY
34 MENS TOILET
35 OFFICE
36 OPERATING·RM
37 PRIVATE·OFFICE
38 ROOF
39 RECEPTION·RM
40 SKYLIGHT
41 TOP·OF·VAULT
42 UPPER·PART·BANKING·RM
43 WORK·RM
44 WOMENS·TOILET

·FIRST·FLOOR·PLAN·

1 ALLEY
2 ASH·HOIST
3 BOOK·VAULT
4 " KEEPERS
5 COVERED·WAY
6 COUPON·RM
7 CONSULTATION·RM
8 CLOSET
9 ENTRANCE·HALL
10 FARMERS·EXCHANGE
11 FRESH·AIR
12 LIFT
13 MONEY·VAULT
14 OPEN·COURT

15 OFFICE·PRINTING·SHOP
16 OFFICERS·PLATFORM
17 PUBLIC·SPACE
18 PRINTING·RM
19 STORAGE·WAREHOUSE
20 SHOP
21 STORE·RM
22 SAVINGS
23 TELLERS
24 TOILET
25 TELEPHONE
26 VAULT
27 VESTIBULE
28 WOMENS·RM   29 PRES·RM

follows then, by the logic of growth, that a certain kind of ornament should appear on a certain kind of structure, just as a certain kind of leaf must appear on a certain kind of tree." Sullivan heeded his own counsel in this regard, for each of his buildings has its own individualized ornament. Elmslie, who learned his ornamental style from Sullivan, offered similar theories in his writings on the subject, calling ornament the "final and logical flowering of the building."[8]

Although Sullivan's theory of ornament may sound a bit abstruse, it really is not. For both Sullivan and Elmslie understood that the ultimate function of their ornament was to add beauty and grace to the human enterprise. "I suppose I was a transmitter of some kind to add a little beauty to this old earth," Elmslie once wrote, and that perhaps explains his love of ornament as well as anything. And, of course, there was also the fact that both men found the creation of ornament to be a source of endless delight. "It is the play work in the architect's day," Elmslie said, "his hour of refreshment."[9]

Sullivan's ornament – usually done in terra cotta, cast iron, plaster, or wood – went through several periods. The ornament of his early years, consisting almost exclusively of stylized plants and flowers, showed the influence of Victorian Gothic. But by the time of the Auditorium Building, Sullivan had devised his own highly personal style based on flowing, naturalistic botanical motifs. Later, as with the Getty Tomb of 1890, he began mixing in geometric patterns, sometimes as the dominant motif and other times as a backdrop for his swirling, plantlike ornament. The chief characteristic of all of Sullivan's ornament is its driving, rhythmic energy. His best buildings seem almost to pulsate as the ornament dances along the surface, bringing the block to life. And yet the ornament is always contained within the larger framework of his buildings. This quality of barely contained energy, which Sullivan described as "mobile serenity," is the hallmark of his ornamental style.[10]

A number of critics have likened Sullivan's ornament to that produced by contemporaneous Art Nouveau architects in Europe. If Art Nouveau is defined broadly enough, then the comparison probably has some validity. But the ornament of many of the better known Art Nouveau architects, such as that of Belgian-born Victor Horta, differs markedly from Sullivan's in that it is usually asymmetrical, often projects out into the space of a room, and tends toward a rather languid artiness. By contrast, Sullivan's ornament is almost invariably symmetrical, is usually confined to wall surfaces, and has a kind of four-square heartiness seldom found in the more precious and mannered European style.[11]

Elmslie claimed that the "real source of [Sullivan's] ornament, one may say its inspiration, was [Asa] Gray's *Botany* and little else." Scholars, however, have labored to trace Sullivan's ornament to a variety of sources, including Frank Furness, Gothic design, the Moorish architecture of Spain, and the work of nineteenth-century English and French designers. Sullivan undoubtedly drew on these and other sources simply because, as is true with all artists, he did not work in a vacuum. But in the end his ornament was uniquely his own. There had been nothing quite like it before. Nor has there been anything quite like it since.[12]

Yet in the case of the Owatonna bank, there can be no doubt that virtually all of the ornament came from the hand of George Elmslie. Only one ornamental motif in the main banking room – a pattern on the underside or soffits of the arches – apparently was drawn by Sullivan himself. "Sullivan did not seem to like the ornament I had designed for the soffits," Elmslie recalled. "It is the only one he touched of the scores [of drawings for the bank's ornament] and it is the only one that is not in tune with the rest. He modified some of the curves. . . . As it stands

Elmslie asserted that the design on the underside of the arch was the only one that could be attributed solely to Sullivan.

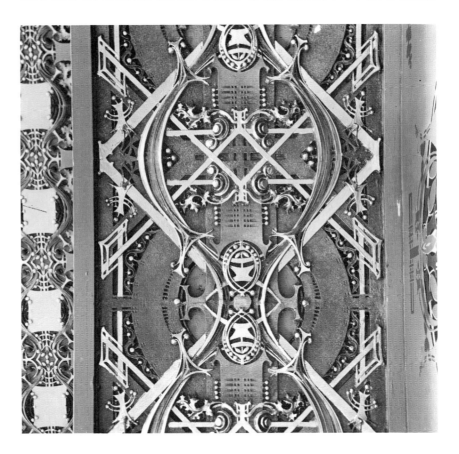

it is really a bad ornament, a conflict of two ideas." Nor does it appear that Sullivan did any of the bank's exterior ornament. Although Elmslie learned his ornamental skills under Sullivan's tutelage, he gradually developed his own method and style of ornamentation. "We had a different way of arranging ornamental forms," Elmslie wrote. "I couldn't do as he did. I never copied any of it [Sullivan's ornament], strange as it may seem." Sullivan, in fact, would sometimes tease Elmslie about his ornament, telling him it was "too beautiful and serious for a Presbyterian to draw."[13]

By the time the bank commission came along, Elmslie had matured into an artist of the first rank. The ornament he designed for the bank tends to be less flowing than Sullivan's and more curvilinear, in this respect showing some resemblance to the Art Nouveau style. Yet it would be a mistake to consider Elmslie's ornament for the bank as being a wholly independent creation. Elmslie's work clearly grew out of Sullivan's and the differences between their styles are often quite subtle. Moreover, it is likely that Sullivan had a large role in determining the general ornamental scheme of the bank. "The presence or absence of ornament should, certainly in serious work, be determined at the very beginnings of the design," Sullivan once wrote, and his initial sketch of the bank probably included a general indication of where ornament should be placed. Still, Elmslie is entitled to his just due, for the bank's ornament is largely the handiwork of his pencil, regardless of how much inspiration and guidance Sullivan may have provided.[14]

The basic theme of the bank's ornament, as of the whole building, is the unifying power of nature – the dance of the organic and inorganic in which Sullivan and Elmslie saw the fundamental rhythm of life. Much of the ornament is based on the seed pod, which Sullivan called "the seat of identity. Within its delicate mechanism lies the will to power; the function which is to seek and eventually find its full expression in form." This theme is expressed time and again in the ornament that survives in the banking room.[15]

As originally built, the banking room contained about sixty different kinds of ornament. Walls, moldings, doors, windows, signs, furniture, tellers' wickets, light fixtures, even the small grille over the heating vent in Bennett's office – all were incorporated in the ornamental scheme. Especially lavish ornament was designed for the room's upper walls, which were perhaps intended by Sullivan and Elmslie to be their version of a heavenly vision – nature in all its rhythmic abundance of form set aglow by the light of the great stained-glass windows. At floor level, however, the ornament was less flamboyant as befitting the down-to-earth activities of a banking business. Thus, the Craftsman furniture specified by Sullivan and Elmslie was simple and unadorned, like that which might well have been found in the farm homes of the bank's customers.[16]

Although the ornamental scheme of the banking room at first seems to be overpowering in its rich complexity, a closer look reveals a consistent pattern to it all. Much of the room's ornament is based on a sophisticated interplay of the square (or rectangle) and the circle, which are the leading forms of the building itself. In some cases, the relationship of ornament to building is made explicit, as in a number of light fixtures that are miniature versions of the bank itself.[17]

A duplicate of the terra-cotta piece over the interior main entry is in the collections of the Louvre in Paris. The benches inside the doorway are in the Craftsman style.

The four great electroliers, which if nothing else are magnificent pieces of cast-iron craftsmanship, provide a good example of how ornament functions – both practically and symbolically – in the bank. Designed in Elmslie's most lavish style, the eighteen-foot-long electroliers drop down into the lobby like huge plants ready at any moment to entangle the room in their exuberant growth. (The electroliers have remained untouched through all of the remodelings, probably because no one wanted to go to the trouble of trying to remove them.) Each electrolier is linked to a corner of the lobby skylight by a narrow rootlike strip of ornament. This strip, which gives the illusion that the electrolier is growing out of the skylight, swells into an ornamental base attached to the ceiling. Dropping down from this base is the electrolier's long octagonal shaft, each of its eight sides aswirl with identical ornament. Toward the bottom of the shaft is a ring of globed lights, below which emerge four snail-like shapes that display rich botanical ornament at their outer edges. In the middle of each of these snail-like shapes is an ornamental motif that Sullivan and Elmslie used again and again. It is an elongated shape with four concave sides created by the arcs of four nearly tangent circles. This shape appears throughout the bank's ornament and possibly represents the linking of the organic and inorganic. Below the snail-shaped protrusions, the shaft of the electrolier narrows briefly, then widens before ending in a point from which a final burst of foliate ornament appears, like a small green shoot growing from a plant. The whole creation is simple in its basic geometric forms, yet incredibly intricate in its detailing. "Simplicity in complexity, complexity in simplicity," Sullivan called this quality, and he and Elmslie saw it as a way to express the deepest mysteries of nature itself.[18]

Perhaps the most glorious objects in the original banking room were seven identical tellers' wickets made of bronze-plated cast iron. Although Elmslie later complained that the wickets (or grilles, as he called them) were "overlyrical," they are now regarded as among his greatest achievements as an ornamentalist. Four of the wickets were used for the tellers' enclosure in front of the vault, two were along the north side of the banking room, and the other was between the women's room and the savings department. The wickets, which served the practical function of separating tellers from customers as a security precaution, were superb examples of how Sullivan and Elmslie sought to glorify utility by making everyday objects beautiful. "I remember drawing it [the design for the wickets] full size in the end room [of Sullivan's Chicago office] overlooking the lake," Elmslie wrote years later. "I don't remember whether LHS saw it or not; probably he did. Anyway, he admired it in place in the bank and said so." The wickets were removed in 1940. One is now in a museum, another

The octagonal electrolier with its snail-like swirls seems to grow out of a corner of the skylight.

The cast-iron teller's wicket designed by Elmslie

is in a church, and the others apparently are in the hands of private collectors. An eighth, however, was donated at the time of its manufacture to the Art Institute of Chicago, where it remains today.[19]

Although Sullivan for the most part left the ornamentation of the bank up to Elmslie, he had a direct hand in planning the building's intricate color scheme. Sullivan, who had long been fascinated with color in architecture, conceived of the bank as a "color symphony" and worked closely with Millet to achieve the effects he desired. In a letter to Bennett dated April 1, 1908, when final work was about to begin on the banking room, Sullivan described his intentions:

This is to let you know that I arrived right side up and ok [in Chicago]; after a 5 o'clock adventure studying the color effects of the lovely grass, of very early skies, as seen along the valley of the Illinois River. My whole Spring is wrapped up just now in the study of color and out of doors for the sake of your bank decorations – which I wish to make out of doors-in-doors if I can. I am not sure that I can, but I am going to try. I am almost abnormally sensitive to color just now and every shade and nuance produces upon me an effect that is orchestral and patently sensitive to all the instruments. I know in my own mind what I am trying to achieve for you and I have in Millet the best chorus master that could be found. I want a color symphony and I am pretty sure I am going to get it. I want something with many shades of the strings and the wood winds and the brass, and I am pretty sure I am going to get it. There has never been in my entire career such an opportunity for a color tone poem as your bank interior plainly puts before me. It is not half so much a matter as whether Millet is equal to it as whether I am equal to giving him the sufficiently delicate initiatives. I don't think I can possibly impress upon you how deep a hold the color symphony has taken upon me. And what I have in mind to accomplish – if accomplish I can. Suffice it to say that Millet is the greatest of colorists extant, and suffice it further to say that I am wrapped up in your project to a degree that would be absurd in connection with anyone but yourself.[20]

Sullivan's interest in color was part of his romanticism and his abiding love of nature. He had always been fascinated with the subtle colors of flowers, an interest that went back to his childhood days on his grandfather's farm in Massachusetts. Moreover, Sullivan's brief stint as a draftsman for Frank Furness had exposed him to an architect who delighted in creating vividly polychromed buildings. From the beginning of his career as an independent designer, Sullivan had experimented with color relationships, and color played a vital part in some of his best-known works before the turn of the century. The interiors of the Auditorium Building (1889), the Schiller Theater and McVicker's Theater (both from the early 1890s), and the Chicago Stock Exchange (1894) all featured carefully worked out color schemes. And, of course, the famous golden doorway of his Transportation Building at the Chicago World's Fair had been the brightest swatch of color in the White City.[21]

The "color symphony" Sullivan spoke of when describing the Owatonna bank has two distinct but interrelated movements, one for the outside and one for the inside. The bank's exterior, dominated by the reddish tapestry bricks, has a decidedly autumnal feeling, while on the inside a more springlike bluish-green predominates. Yet there is more than a hint of autumn in the burgundy bricks used in the lower part of the banking room, just as the green and blue terra cotta and glass mosaic give a touch of spring to the exterior elevations. The color of the exterior is largely determined by its materials, while on the inside Sullivan relied to some extent on painted and gilded plaster, as well as stencil work, to achieve his effects. In working out the bank's color scheme, Sullivan (along with Millet and Elmslie) left no detail overlooked. For example, they even tried to find green mortar for the building's brick facades. But a chemist who was engaged to work on the problem was unable to come up with anything satisfactory.[22]

Bennett, in his article for *The Craftsman,* provided an excellent description of the exterior of the bank and its adjoining building, both of which have remained virtually unchanged through the years. Bennett wrote:

Reddish brown sandstone [called Port Wing and quarried near Superior, Wisconsin] forms the base of the entire building; above this, Oriental bricks in soft and variegated colors are used for the walls. . . . A wide band of polychromatic terra cotta (chiefly Teco green) and a narrow band of glass mosaic in high color [predominately blue] "frame in" the bank exterior, which is further enriched by corner ornaments [the cartouches] and a cornice of brown terra cotta. The two massive brick arches enclose stained glass windows which have a general effect of rich variegated green. The shop and office portion of the building is notable for its piers of rich brown terra cotta, enlivened with ornaments of Teco green and bright blue. The color effect of the exterior is hard to describe for it has something of the color quality of an old Oriental rug, — that is, all the colors, when seen from a distance, blend into a general impression of soft red and green, while at close range they maintain their strong and beautiful individuality.[23]

Sullivan was especially fond of Oriental or tapestry brick. This type of brick, which Sullivan helped to popularize around the turn of the century, is made of variously colored clays and then given a rough cut so that the brick face has a rich texture. The Owatonna bank was one of the first buildings for which Sullivan used tapestry brick. In an article published in 1910, he described its color effects:

Inasmuch as the color scale varies from the softest pinks through delicate reds, yellows . . . through the light browns, dark browns, purples and steel blacks — each of these colors with its own graduations and blendings — the possibilities of chromatic treatment are at once evident. When laid up promiscuously, especially if the surface is large, and care is taken to avoid patches of any one color, the general tone suggests that of a very old oriental rug and the differing color values of the individual bricks, however sharply these may seem to contrast at close view, are taken up and harmonized in the prevailing general tone.[24]

The exterior of the bank and shop and office building are also notable for their polychromed terra cotta. Sullivan had always been attracted to terra cotta, a type of fired clay, because it could be molded into an infinite number of ornamental patterns. "All materials were only one material to him [Sullivan] in which to weave the stuff of his dreams," Wright wrote. "Terra cotta was that one material. Terra cotta was *his* material, the one he loved most and served best." Wright, as usual, was exaggerating a bit, because terra cotta was not the only material Sullivan used effectively. But there is no question that terra cotta was his favorite, and it can be found in or on almost all of his buildings.[25]

The outstanding terra-cotta work on the bank is the band of plantlike ornament, predominately green in color, that enframes the two big arched windows. This green band was perhaps intended by Sullivan and Elmslie to symbolize the agrarian wealth upon which the bank depended. The agrarian theme is further suggested by the band of blue glass mosaic that flows alongside the terra cotta like a life-giving river. The terra cotta is in a color called Teco (from TErra COtta) green, which was introduced in 1902 by the American Terra Cotta and Ceramic Company. American Terra Cotta had spent more than a decade developing and perfecting Teco green, primarily for use in the company's line of art pottery. Sullivan was one of the first to find architectural uses for the color, which can range from a pale to a deep green and has a rather silvery look to it.[26]

For the banking room itself, Sullivan (with a great deal of help from Millet) created a color scheme of extraordinary richness and subtlety. The room has more than two hundred shades of color, ranging from deep black and red to delicate blues and greens. Bennett described the color scheme of the original banking room this way:

Within, a floor of plain green tile is laid over all. The wainscoting is made of Roman bricks of a rich red color, capped with an ornamental band of green terra cotta. The counters and partitions are of these same red Roman bricks capped with green terra cotta, and the counter tops and deal plates are of Belgian black marble. Above the wainscoting the walls and ceiling are a glory of luxuriant color and form. The colors of early spring and autumn predominate, with a steadying note of green throughout the entire scheme. The woodwork is all of quarter-sawed white oak, laid in broad smooth surfaces and panels and finished in Craftsman style, which gives the wood a soft brown tone in which there is a subtle undertone of green.[27]

The ultimate mediator of color in the banking room is the natural light that pours through the huge semicircular windows and the skylight above. Filtered by these great expanses of stained glass, the light as it enters the banking room has a peculiar and strikingly beautiful quality. Hugh Morrison, Sullivan's first biographer, likened it to "sunlight passed through sea-water." The quiet blue-green glow created by this interaction of sunlight and colored glass gives the room an ethereal aura not usually associated with the down-to-earth business of banking. It took remarkable skill on the part of Sullivan and Millet to build the room's color relationships around this magnificent light, which is so dominant that colors in the bank are never quite what they seem. Thus, ornament on the upper walls that appears green turns out to be blue when viewed in more neutral light. The light also changes with the movement of the sun across the sky, with weather conditions, and with the time of year. As a result, the ornament that fills the bank goes through subtle shifts in color from hour to hour, day to day, and season to season. By bringing indoors and outdoors together in the banking room through the manipulation of light, Sullivan was thus able to compose his "color symphony" – a symphony conducted by the sun itself.[28]

At the time the bank was designed, Sullivan had been an architect for about thirty years. During that period he had assembled a talented team of Chicago artists and craftsmen to work on his buildings. The high quality of the bank's terra-cotta, cast-iron, and stained-glass ornament testifies to the skill of these craftsmen, who shared Sullivan's vision of an organic and uniquely American architecture. Among these men, the most noteworthy were William Gates, founder of the American Terra Cotta and Ceramic Company; Kristian Schneider, a sculptor who made all the models for Sullivan and Elmslie's terra-cotta, cast-iron, and plaster ornament; William Winslow, whose firm produced the electroliers, tellers' wickets, and other ornamental ironwork in the bank; Louis Millet, who executed the bank's stained glass and did much of the interior decorating; and Oskar Gross, who painted the two large murals in the banking room.[29]

Terra cotta, which is Latin for "burnt earth," has been employed as a building material since antiquity. But it was not until the 1870s in Chicago that it began to be used for that purpose in the United States. At first, architects used terra cotta largely for decorative cornices on buildings. By the 1880s it was also being widely used to fireproof the metal frames of tall office buildings. Sullivan and other architects of his time turned to terra cotta because it weighed about half as much as most stone, was virtually indestructible if properly installed, and — most importantly — could be made into extremely elaborate and easily replicated patterns without the kind of costly piece-by-piece carving often required for stone ornament.[30]

By the 1890s, there were half a dozen terra-cotta manufacturers in the Chicago area. The two largest were Northwestern Terra Cotta Company and American Terra Cotta. Both firms specialized in producing decorative architectural terra cotta. From 1880 to 1906, most of Sullivan's terra-cotta work was done by Northwestern. The firm's chief modeler during much of this time was Kristian Schneider, a talented Norwegian-born sculptor. Sullivan had personally trained Schneider to model his ornament and would let no one else do the work. In 1906 Schneider left Northwestern to become a partner with another modeler in a small firm. As an independent contractor, Schneider worked with Sullivan and Elmslie to make the models used by American Terra Cotta in manufacturing the bank's ornament.[31]

American Terra Cotta had been founded by William Day Gates, a remarkable character who presided over the firm for almost half a century. A lawyer by training, Gates in 1881 inherited a large tract of land near Crystal Lake, Illinois, about forty miles from Chicago. He developed his terra-cotta firm on this property, using water power from an old mill site. Initially, the company produced drain tiles, but it quickly expanded into a wide range of other terra-cotta products. In 1887 Gates began experimenting with art pottery and was particularly interested in developing new colors. This work, which Gates apparently did for his own pleasure, culminated in 1902 with the introduction of the Teco line of pottery. The firm hired many sculptors and even a few architects (though apparently not Sullivan) to make designs for the Teco line. Gates, a man of many skills, designed some of the pottery himself, including a seven-foot-high vase that became something of an attraction at the 1904 World's Fair in St. Louis. Teco green and other new colors that Gates created for his pottery were then used for the company's architectural terra cotta. By 1906, Gates's firm had become one of the country's largest terra-cotta producers and was at the forefront of ceramics technology. Meanwhile, Gates had provided an impressive demonstration of his product's versatility by building for himself in suburban Chicago a large house that was made entirely of terra cotta.[32]

The terra-cotta ornament created for the Owatonna bank was the result of a complex process that required a high level of craftsmanship every step of the way. It began with drawings made by George Elmslie, whose two-dimensional dreams had to be transformed into the three-dimensional reality of terra cotta. Elmslie's drawings showed the pattern, shape, size, and location of all of the terra-cotta ornament to go into the bank. Using Elmslie's drawings, draftsmen at American Terra Cotta then prepared shop drawings, which indicated exactly how individual terra-cotta pieces were to be joined and how they were to be anchored to the walls of the bank. It is also probable that some of Elmslie's designs were slightly modified in the shop drawings to help reduce manufacturing costs.[33]

After the shop drawings were completed, Schneider began working on clay models of the ornament. Schneider actually made his models slightly larger than indicated by the drawings because terra cotta shrinks when it is fired. Either Sullivan or Elmslie usually sat in on modeling sessions to direct Schneider. Wright, who had often attended similar sessions with

William Gates (left) and Kristian Schneider (right) conferring over a piece of terra cotta

Kristian Schneider posed next to a
terra-cotta cartouche destined for an
upper corner of the bank's exterior.

Sullivan, wrote: "In the primal plastic — clay — his [Sullivan's] opulent energy could triumph, and did so. . . . If he attended to the modeling himself (he usually did): perfection! His own soul's philosophy incarnate. Music its only paraphrase and peer." Elmslie also recalled these modeling sessions. "How many times with a modeler at his clay . . . I have watched the third dimension appear and what high grade pleasure it was. 'Emphasize this more! too deep here! raise this part of the foliage! Subdue here.' Finally ok, and *just* as desired and impossible to show on a drawing." After completing a clay model of a particular piece of ornament, Schneider made a plaster and cement mold from it. Since terra cotta was normally used in a repetitive pattern or band, a mold provided an easy way to make as many individual pieces of a particular design as necessary.[34]

Once the mold was completed, the next stage was to cast the piece. Casting was done by firmly pressing clay into the mold. The clay was then carefully hollowed out from the back to reduce the weight of the piece and to provide for even firing without warpage. Next, the piece went through a drying process, after which it was ready for coloring. There were at least two methods by which a piece could be colored. The brown terra cotta on the bank's cornice was created by applying a "slip" of colored clay to the surface of each piece before firing. Slips, which consisted of finely strained and liquified clay, could be applied in a wide variety of colors. Another coloring technique, used for the bank's green and polychromed terra cotta, involved spraying a tinted glaze on the clay prior to firing. Additional colors, if desired, could be added with a brush once the glaze had dried. Whereas pieces colored by use of slips usually had a matte finish, those treated with glaze had a more glass-like finish similar to that found on porcelain.[35]

When the coloring was completed, pieces were ready for firing in one of American Terra Cotta's large kilns. This delicate process required precise control of the kiln's temperature so that the pieces would shrink at a predictable rate and thus avoid cracking or splitting. The firing process usually took about two weeks. During the first week, the temperature in the kiln was gradually raised to about two thousand degrees Fahrenheit. Then the temperature was slowly lowered for a week until it finally matched that of the air outside the kiln.

Once out of the kiln, pieces were inspected, tested to ensure tight-fitting joints, and then assigned an identifying number keyed to the assembly shop drawings. Some sample pieces were also photographed for insurance purposes. The pieces used in the bank were shipped by rail, carefully cushioned with hay and packed in wooden frames. Even so, damage during shipment was fairly common, and the usual practice was to send along extra pieces as a precaution. Although the terra cotta produced for the bank was very durable, it was susceptible to damage or deterioration if installed improperly. To avoid such problems, American Terra Cotta recommended that its own staff of specially trained masons be used for most projects. It appears, however, that a local mason installed the bank's terra cotta, and he did excellent work because the terra cotta has worn exceptionally well through the years.[36]

The bank's intricate cast-iron ornament was manufactured by the Winslow Brothers Ornamental Iron Company, a firm that had first begun doing work for Sullivan in 1889. The driving force behind the company was William Herman Winslow, a man who shared Gates's talent for mixing shrewd business sense with high standards of craftsmanship. Like Gates, Winslow was a lawyer by training who found his

William Winslow

niche as a businessman. Born in Brooklyn in 1857, Winslow started his career with a New York ornamental iron firm in 1881. Four years later, he was lured away by the opportunity to become a partner in an ornamental iron and bronze company in Chicago. His partner soon retired, however, and Winslow recruited his brother Francis to help manage the company. The firm quickly expanded by opening offices around the country, including one in Minneapolis. Known for its high quality ornamental ironwork, the company specialized in made-to-order architectural ironwork such as elevator grilles, stair railings, and decorative panels. Perhaps the company's most famous creation is the intricate iron screen that wraps around the first two stories of the Carson Pirie Scott store in Chicago.[37]

Winslow himself was one of those marvels of Victorian energy who was adept at many things. He was a skilled cabinetmaker, an inventor (best known for a new kind of window sash he and his brother devised), a printer, a photographer, and an accomplished violinist. And in 1893, Winslow assured himself of at least a footnote in the history books when he hired a young architect named Frank Lloyd Wright to design a new house in the Chicago suburb of River Forest. The Winslow house, which still stands, was Wright's first major commission as an independent architect.

Like Gates, Winslow took a great interest in the technical side of his business. Under his direction, Winslow Brothers became one of the nation's most innovative architectural metal foundries and pioneered techniques for mass production of extremely high quality castings. The ironwork for the bank, especially the electroliers and the tellers' wickets, was as intricate as any Winslow Brothers ever cast for Sullivan. But Winslow was used to such technical challenges. Elmslie recalled that Sullivan had a way of making Winslow and other craftsmen "do things they said could not be done." On one occasion, Elmslie wrote, Sullivan wanted Winslow's firm to do some especially intricate castings for a project in Chicago. Winslow, according to Elmslie, responded: " 'We can't cast such fine ornamental work, Mr. Sullivan. It can't be done.' 'Winslow, I want 3 castings of that. Go ahead and make them.' 'All right (sighing deeply) we will try.' " The result, Elmslie said, was "3 perfect castings and no breakages."[38]

For the stained glass and other interior decoration of the bank, Sullivan turned to Louis J. Millet, an old friend from his student days in Paris. Millet was almost exactly a contemporary of Sullivan's. Born in New York City in 1855, Millet was the son of a musician and the nephew of

Aimé Millet, a well-known French sculptor of the mid-nineteenth century. Millet and Sullivan met at the École des Beaux-Arts in about 1874 and formed a friendship that lasted a lifetime. Unlike Sullivan, Millet stayed in Paris for the full course – six years in all. When he finally left the École in 1879, Millet came to Chicago to begin a long career as a designer and decorator.[39]

In 1880 Millet formed a partnership with George Healy, another of his Paris friends, and set up business in the Chicago Loop. After 1886, Millet was also an instructor at the Chicago Art Institute, where he was a founder of the Department of Decorative Design and later head of its School of Architecture. In his courses at the institute, Millet championed

Louis Millet

an organic style of ornament that would flow from the very nature of the object or structure to be decorated. In this respect, his thinking was perfectly in line with Sullivan's and may well have been influenced by it.[40]

Millet also played an important role in spreading the gospel of the Arts and Crafts Movement, which was an important cultural force in Chicago around the turn of the century. This movement attempted to revive interest in the home handicrafts, and many of its adherents in Chicago followed design principles laid down by Millet in his classes at the institute. When not teaching, Millet was busy with his partner Healy carrying out various commissions, mainly in Chicago. The firm began working with Adler and Sullivan in 1884 and helped to decorate some of their major buildings, including the Auditorium, McVicker's Theater, the Transportation Building, and the Chicago Stock Exchange.[41]

Although Millet worked in frescoes, stenciling, and other related arts, he was best known for his stained glass. Among other innovations, he and Healy in the 1880s devised what eventually became known as "American glass." Whereas European stained-glass artists generally used paint to create background effects on their windows, Healy and Millet instead employed small fragments of glass for this purpose, thereby creating a mosaic effect. Two windows made in this way by Healy and Millet drew critical acclaim at the 1889 Paris Exposition, and their technique was later adopted by some European designers. Louis Tiffany in New York City also used this process for some of his stained-glass windows.[42]

Healy and Millet remained partners for eighteen years and received numerous commissions for stained glass and other decorative work in office buildings, churches, and homes. Most of their business continued to be in Chicago, but they decorated a number of buildings elsewhere, including the old Metropolitan Opera House in St. Paul. Healy and Millet dissolved their partnership in 1899. Millet then continued on his own, designing stained glass for several major Chicago buildings, among them the Ryerson Library at the Chicago Art Institute. In 1904 Millet's reputation was further enhanced when he was named chief decorative painter for the St. Louis World's Fair.[43]

The precise extent of Millet's contribution to the bank is uncertain, although there can be no doubt that he had a large hand in creating the intricate color scheme of the banking room. It is known that he personally supervised final decorative work in the bank under Sullivan's direction. In his letter to Bennett in April 1908, Sullivan described Millet as a "chorus master" who would bring all of the banking room's colors into harmony. Yet in that same letter Sullivan noted that one of his tasks was to give Millet "delicate initiatives" for decorating the banking room. This statement suggests that Millet was to work in accord with general ideas

The bank as viewed from near the fountain in Central Park

Sullivan used tapestry brick, terra cotta in Teco green, and glass mosaic
to enframe the arched, stained-glass window.

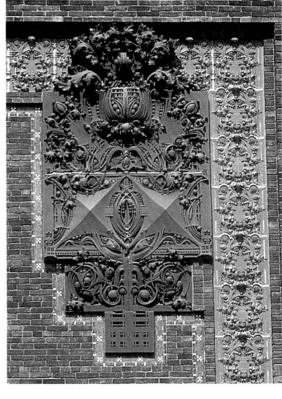

Details of the ornament of the shop and office building show a terra-cotta "B" crest and glazed square (above left) and window pilaster (above center). From the bank, the details include the cartouche (above right) and terra-cotta band (below).

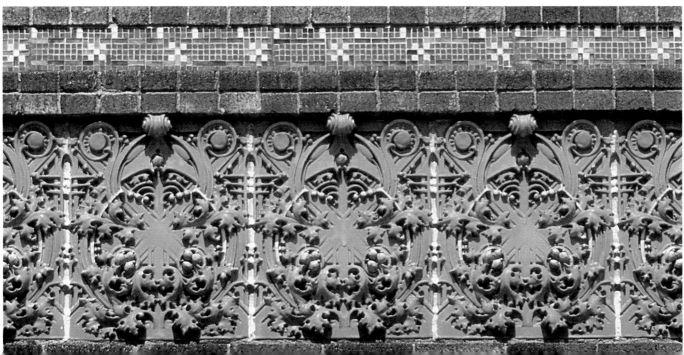

When Sullivan devised the color scheme for the banking room, he had to allow for the filtering effect of the stained glass on sunlight passing through the windows. The pair of pictures on the right shows a stenciled wall and "B" crest photographed by daylight illumination. The pair on the left depicts the ornament as actually seen by visitors to the bank.

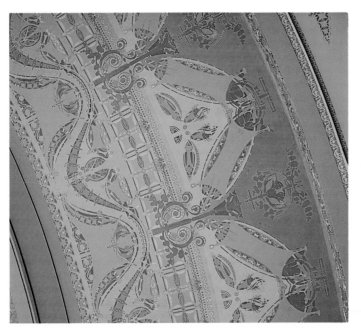

Detail of the base of the arches showing stenciled walls, painted and gilded plasterwork, and Teco green terra cotta

Details of the banking room interior: stained glass (upper left), terra-cotta band over the entryway (upper right), original sign for the president's office (lower left), and entryway light fixtures that mimic the arch and cube of the bank's design (lower right)

The south stained-glass window shows the quality of
light transmitted into the banking room.

The electrolier amid the glory of the banking room's
ornament and Sullivan's color symphony

laid down by Sullivan. Even so, Millet seems to have had considerable leeway in carrying out Sullivan's ideas, just as Elmslie had in designing the ornament. Millet's expertise in color harmony and interior decoration probably was a major factor in the final color palette of the banking room. Moreover, he knew what specialized decorative techniques in plaster, stencil, and glass would be needed to achieve the effects desired by Sullivan.[44]

The stained-glass windows and skylight are perhaps the finest examples of Millet's craftsmanship in the banking room, although the elaborate plaster ornament on the upper walls also demonstrates his skill. It apparently was Elmslie who actually designed the windows and skylight, since they contain the same decorative motifs as other ornament in the bank. However, Millet undoubtedly determined the colors for the stained-glass to ensure that the windows and skylight would harmonize with the rest of the bank's ornament. On the outside of the bank, the only work by Millet is the bright band of glass mosaic that enframes each of the arched windows.[45]

The two large murals beneath the arches on the east and north walls of the banking room are the work of Oskar Gross. Born in Vienna in 1870, Gross studied at the Royal Academy of Fine Arts there and also in Munich and Paris. Although he was trained as a portrait painter, Gross became best known for his murals. His biggest commission along these lines came when he was selected to paint all of the murals for the Austro-Hungarian pavilion at the Vienna World's Fair. Gross immigrated to the United States in about 1903, apparently at the request of Chicago architect and city planner Daniel H. Burnham, who was looking for a good muralist for some of his projects. Exactly how Sullivan came to hire Gross for the bank work is not known. Gross claimed in an interview in 1959, when he was almost ninety years old, that he had never met Sullivan before accepting the Owatonna bank commission. Nor did he ever do any work for Sullivan again.[46]

Gross painted the bank murals on canvas in his Chicago studio, although he undoubtedly made initial sketches during his visit to Owatonna. The mural on the east wall, which depicts a farm scene, is oddly shaped because the top of the vault, as originally built, cut into the area under the east wall arch. In 1958 the mural was further reduced in size when a new opening was cut through the east wall. The bulk of the mural consists of blue sky interspersed with fleecy clouds. But in the lower corner of the mural, to either side of a small balcony under the arch, two harvest scenes are depicted. One scene shows four horses pulling a reaper, while the other shows a farmer carrying refreshments to a group of field hands who are shocking grain.

The other mural in the banking room, located under the arch of the north wall, depicts Holstein cows grazing in a typical Steele County landscape. (The cows were, in all likelihood, drawn from a prize dairy herd on a farm just south of Owatonna owned by Bennett.) In the far background of the mural, barely noticeable, is a creamery. Puffs of smoke can also be seen in the background, but the train that presumably produced them is not pictured.

Neither of the murals is up to the high caliber of the other decorative work in the bank. Even so, they certainly are of professional quality and thus serve an important visual function by bringing a sense of outdoor space, light, and color to the banking room. They reinforce the theme of organic growth Sullivan wanted to emphasize. Moreover, the bucolic scenes depicted in the murals were appropriate in a more direct sort of way, since the bank owed its existence to the wealth generated by the rich farmland around Owatonna.

The cow mural on the north wall of the banking room

The completion of the bank did not end Bennett's relationship with Sullivan and Elmslie. Both men were to be back in Owatonna at various times over the next ten years in connection with projects either commissioned by Bennett or obtained through his influence. Bennett was to be especially successful in securing work for Elmslie and his partner from 1910 to 1920, William Purcell. Yet the bank was in many ways a turning point for all three men, who would afterwards go their separate ways along the curve of the arch. For Sullivan, the bank was the first of several small-town banks that were to be the chief work of his last twenty years and a bittersweet part of his legacy to the American people. His problems — personal, professional, and financial — would soon begin to overwhelm him, and his last years would be spent in poverty and neglect in a world that had passed him by. For Elmslie, the bank was the last great chapter in his career with Sullivan. He would soon go on to a productive partnership with Purcell and in the process design some of the most exquisite buildings ever seen in the Midwest. But he too was to encounter hard times and personal tragedy. In the end his life was to become a curious echo of Sullivan's, following the same sloping path towards obscurity and destitution. For Bennett, the bank was the realization of a dream. He would eventually become its president, a man of wealth and power. But he was to lose everything in one afternoon when the bank, his dream and his monument, became the cause of his undoing.

5

SULLIVAN—THE DESPERATE YEARS

My crisis has, with varying fortunes been steadily approaching during the past 17 years. I have all along intuitively felt that the cause lay in a flaw in my own character which I, alone, could not discover. So I had to pay the price. – Louis Sullivan[1]

THE COMPLETION OF THE BANK brought Sullivan favorable publicity, which he greatly needed, but only a few new commissions, which he needed even more. The October 1908 edition of the *Architectural Record* featured nine photographs of the bank, along with an article written by Millet. The building was also publicized in several bankers' magazines. "Owatonna suddenly found itself famous, and became the Mecca of architectural pilgrimages," architectural critic Montgomery Schuyler wrote in January 1912. "At last report, twenty-five strangers a day were visiting Owatonna expressly to inspect it [the bank]." All of this attention, however, did little in the short run to stave off Sullivan's mounting financial problems. By late 1908 his financial distress became so acute that he was forced to give up his beloved cottage in Ocean Springs because he could no longer afford the payments on the property. The loss of the cottage was a deep hurt, so much so that Sullivan lied about it in *The Autobiography of an Idea*, claiming that the cottage had been "wrecked by a wayward West Indian hurricane."[2]

The new year brought few changes in Sullivan's circumstances. He had only two small jobs in 1909, and he seemed increasingly unable to manage what little money he did have. His mood darkening day by day, he tried to dissolve his desperation in alcohol, to the point that it some-times became obvious to clients that he had been drinking. During this period, Sullivan's friendship with Bennett grew strong and deep. The two men, it appears, exchanged frequent letters, although only a handful have survived. One of Sullivan's most revealing letters to his friend in Owatonna came in June 1909, when Sullivan was nearing another of his periodic crises: "Emotional expression is almost impossible to me nowa-days: otherwise I would talk to you as frankly as you talk to me. Rest assured in any event, that I cherish your friendship beyond the power of any words to express. . . . P.S. It is impossible to discuss my troubles: they seem to be too deep seated."[3]

Sullivan's deep affection for Bennett came through in another letter written two months later:

I am now wondering if I sufficiently expressed to you my appreciation of your wonderful kindness and sense of comradeship. If I did not I wish to do so now. I have often said to Millet, there is only one Carl Bennett. Perhaps you don't realize how true this is.

As to business, I simply don't dare to take a vacation, I have to figure earn-ings and expenses so close.

The Babson House at Riverside [Illinois, designed by Sullivan and Elmslie in 1907] is under roof. The Bradley House at Madison [Wisconsin] is just begun. The drawings and specifications for the Peoples Savings Bank at Cedar Rapids, Iowa [which was not built until 1911] are on the verge of completion. This is all the business, nothing new, and this amount of business does not pay expenses.[4]

As autumn approached, Sullivan's financial situation continued to worsen. He had already been forced to move into smaller quarters in the Auditorium tower, abandoning the great room where he and Adler had once supervised a staff of fifty draftsmen and engineers. Moreover, Sulli-van's penchant for ill-timed displays of temperament soon cost him two jobs. First he quit the Bradley house project in a dispute over money. Shortly thereafter, he walked away from the Cedar Rapids bank project in what Elmslie described as "an arrogant fit of absurd petulance because of their [the bankers'] refusal, until the bids were in, to make an addi-tional payment of his fees." By October Sullivan was so far in debt that he decided on a desperate expedient: he would auction off his most treasured personal possessions in hopes of raising two thousand dollars or more in cash. He described his plan to Bennett in a letter dated October 23:

In addition to my routine work I am engaged now upon a program of selling out at auction all my household effects: books, pictures, bric-a-brac, rugs, furniture, everything, in the last desperate endeavor to raise money.

I have arranged with expert auctioneers here, and the matter will be handled in the best fashion: special catalogues and all that sort of thing.

The sale will take place Nov. 30 and Dec. 1. It will be a "special" and rather "swell" affair. I have about 15 exceptionally fine antique rugs; and extremely good pictures; about 12 pieces of exceptionally fine bric-a-brac. . . .

I suggest that you arrange to come down and attend this sale. You might be able to pick up a few things at satisfactory prices. Although I fancy that for the finer rugs there will be pretty lively bidding as a few of them are of a kind and quality that have not been seen on the general market in 20 years.

I presume this letter will surprise you a bit. But I made up my mind there was no use trying to dispose of my effects piecemeal and that the only way was to make a clean sweep and place the affair in the hands of the experts, and take my chances on the outcome. I feel a certain sense of relief that I have my arrangements finally made.[5]

As it turned out, the auction went poorly for Sullivan. Bennett did not attend the auction, but he learned all the melancholy details in a letter from Elmslie:

The sale went badly for Mr. Sullivan. He expected to realize between 2 and 3 thousand and got just $1,100 net. There was a slaughter on the fine things, with little or no bidding. I am glad you weren't there as he [Sullivan] behaved badly in the auction room I am told, taking a plate away from the auctioneer and dashing it to the floor.

It is a dreadful ending, for such it seems, for a man qualified as he is for great work in days to come. He is only 53 and could do work for 20 years to come. . . .

He is keeping up his drinking and I do not know how much longer he or any man can stand it. Maybe when he is right up against the wall he will quit, but who's to give him work? Who in Chicago will trust him?[6]

Following the auction, Sullivan's fortunes sank to a new low. On December 4, he had to let Elmslie go because there simply was not enough money to pay his salary. Two days later, Sullivan's wife left him for good. "Mr. Sullivan was broken-hearted about having to send his wife away," Mrs. Bennett recalled many years later. "Poor man!" The parting was amicable, however, and Sullivan even gave his wife a thousand dollars (virtually all he had made from the auction) to help her start her long-sought literary career in New York. He later described the situation to Bennett: "She [Margaret Sullivan] is now in New York with the view of attempting a literary career for which she has much native talent, as yet untrained and undisciplined. . . . I made the sacrifice because I believe in the genuineness of her talent, and hope that the seriousness of the situation will arouse in her the necessary persistence and industry. . . . And inasmuch as she has many friends in N.Y. she won't be lonely. . . . So I won't have to worry about her for some time, and I am glad to be left alone to work out my own destiny and start life all over again if I can."[7]

The crush of events did not squeeze the spirit out of Sullivan, but it did force him to do some soul searching. He was helped in this regard by Dr. George Arndt, a physician he had met some years earlier. In December 1909, after the debacle of the auction, Sullivan went to stay with Arndt at his home in Mount Vernon, Ohio. Sullivan described his experiences to Bennett at length:

Insomnia, nervous dyspepsia, poverty, worry and the auction got in their deadly work. Also I had to let Elmslie go. You can imagine what the reaction meant when it speedily came. I was driven before it as a whirlwind drives in to the very verge of insanity or suicide, or nervous collapse. At that very moment who should appear but my dear friend Dr. Geo. Arndt of Mount Vernon, Ohio. . . . He induced me to go home with him, which I did. Upon our arrival in Mount Vernon I was practically all in. After 3 days of intense suffering, mental, moral and physical, I began to mend, and my progress was wonderfully rapid. At the end of 2½ weeks I was practically normal, my courage, strength of nerve, body and brain had returned. . . .

Well, I arrived here [Chicago] Friday last, and here I am practically flat broke and the future, at present, an impenetrable blank. I am living, hand to mouth, on the bounty of a few warm friends who can ill afford the small advances they have made. But their devotion and self-sacrifice warm my heart.

I saved out of the wreck an old master which I am trying to sell to the art institute for $1000.00. . . . I have in addition a Jurgensen watch for which I gave $325.00 and a ruby-spinel worth to buy in a retail store $200.00. . . . These are in substance my assets, and against them I am in a quicksand of petty indebtedness, represented by unpaid bills, rent, etc. My larger indebtedness does not cause me immediate concern. I will not be pressed.

Strange as it may seem to you I feel a powerful sense of relief, now that I have survived the crisis. I am prepared to wipe out the past and face reconstruction in whatever it may take, provided only it furnish an outlet for my long pent-up aggressiveness and productivity. Today I find myself possessed of what many a man would envy me, namely a wonderfully tough and elastic constitution, steady nerves, physical soundness, mental strength and alertness and plenty of courage. My morbidity has entirely disappeared; and the only thing I fear is a possible return of it in the form of mental depression. But I intend to fight this off for all that is in me.

As to program, I have as yet only a vague one. I have a feeling that I want to get out of this town . . . and locate in some other city. . . . But of course the first problem that comes up is the financing of such an adventure. And that's just where I am up against it.

As another asset however, I have a new outlook upon life – I have at last burst the bounds of the prison of self. This is due to my friend Arndt, who, in our heart to heart talks in Mt. Vernon diagnosed me mentally and morally with the same simplicity and precision that he had shown in his physical examination. My crisis has, with varying fortunes, been steadily approaching during the past 17 years. I have all along intuitively felt that the cause lay in a flaw in my own character which I, alone, could not discover. So I had to pay the price. Now comes Arndt and puts his finger deftly on the spot. He says that the simple fundamental trouble that has caused all my unhappiness, bitterness, misery and final break, is none other than my persistent lack of kindly feeling toward my fellow men. He is right – and I intend to change! This is about all I can say at present and I hope you will not have found its perusal altogether disconcerting. By all signs I should have 20 to 30 years of hard work in me yet.

Your own kindness to me I shall never forget. Sorry you were sensitive on the subject of the auction sale. I deeply appreciate your delicacy [Bennett, apparently, did not attend the auction because he felt it would put him in a difficult spot to bid for items being sold by a friend], but just as sincerely wish you might have secured some of the fine things.[8]

Unfortunately, Sullivan's good intentions do not seem to have produced any lasting results. He did, however, manage to patch up his differences with the Cedar Rapids bankers, and the bank was finally built in 1911. Like almost all of the small bank commissions that were the mainstay of Sullivan's late career, the one in Cedar Rapids was obtained as a result of publicity generated by the Owatonna bank. Bennett, who apparently was contacted by the Cedar Rapids bankers in 1909, helped out by giving Sullivan a strong recommendation. The bank Sullivan finally designed in Cedar Rapids is one of his most unusual buildings. It features a two-story lobby with clerestory windows surrounded by a one-story section containing bank offices and service areas. This bank cost far less to build than Bennett's and cannot have brought Sullivan a very large fee.[9]

Despite the ministrations of Dr. Arndt, Sullivan soon slipped back into his old habits. In April 1910, Bennett received word that Sullivan was once again drinking heavily. "I am deeply grieved at Mr. Sullivan's personal conduct," he wrote to William Purcell, "and wish that something might be done to prevent it." But Sullivan continued on his downward slide. He lost his membership in the prestigious Chicago Club because of inability to pay the dues, and his straitened finances also forced him to move his residence to a less than fashionable hotel on the south side of Chicago. Still, Sullivan did manage to obtain one commission, in November 1910, for a church in Cedar Rapids. Bennett, who was in Chicago at the time for a dairy show, reported that Sullivan appeared to have sobered up: "It happened that during my stay in Chicago he received his commission to build the Cedar Rapids church. I could not help but feel glad that he received this commission. As far as I could judge he was perfectly 'straight.' Both Millet and his draftsman informed me that he had not been drinking at all for some time. Doubtless this had become a necessity."[10]

By this time Sullivan still employed one draftsman, a talented young man named Parker Berry who apparently had been hired shortly before Elmslie left. With Berry's help, Sullivan completed plans for the church complex by the spring of 1911. The design was an unusual one, calling for a semicircular church structure connected to a rectangular school and social building. Bennett kept apprised of the work, reporting to Purcell: "If he [Sullivan] were a little more pliable from a businessman's point of view he would doubtless get more work and I wish very much that I could help him to get this work—at least in sufficient amount to afford him a living. He writes me that he has nothing doing just now. He is awaiting a decision from the church committee at Cedar Rapids, and the project in Clinton, Ia. [for a four-story commercial building] is not yet ready."[11]

Sullivan's first set of plans for the church was rejected in June 1911 as being too expensive, and his second set of plans met a similar fate. In March 1912 Sullivan finally quit the project in a huff. Meanwhile, Bennett continued to correspond with Sullivan, offering him encouragement: "There is nothing else for you to do than to try your best to get sufficient work to keep things going," he wrote. "And I fancy that your present predicament is no worse than you have successfully met in the past." The next day, Bennett told Purcell in a letter: "I am corresponding constantly with Louis. Financial matters are again giving him great concern. I wish that he were a business manager like you are and then I would consider his troubles in this respect as ended."[12]

Earlier in the year, Bennett had decided to help out Sullivan in the most direct way possible by offering him another commission. This time, the commission was for a new house in Owatonna for Bennett and his growing family. The house was to be located on a huge L-shaped lot on Main Street adjoining Pillsbury Academy, where Bennett had attended high school. The main body of the L was a four-hundred-foot-long strip of property between the academy on the south and four small houses fronting Main Street on the north. This long strip connected with a smaller lot fronting Main Street to the west of the four houses. Bennett intended to build his new house at the crook of the L. The lot along Main Street directly east of this property contained a small two-story house that Bennett and his wife had lived in for several years after their marriage. Bennett's plan was to move back into this house and from there superintend the construction of his new residence.[13]

Sullivan and his two draftsmen (Berry had been joined by a young newcomer named Homer Sailor) began working on the house plans early in 1911. As was sometimes the case with Sullivan, the design soon became more elaborate than the client wanted or needed. Bennett, however,

In 1912 Sullivan drafted house plans for the Bennett family.

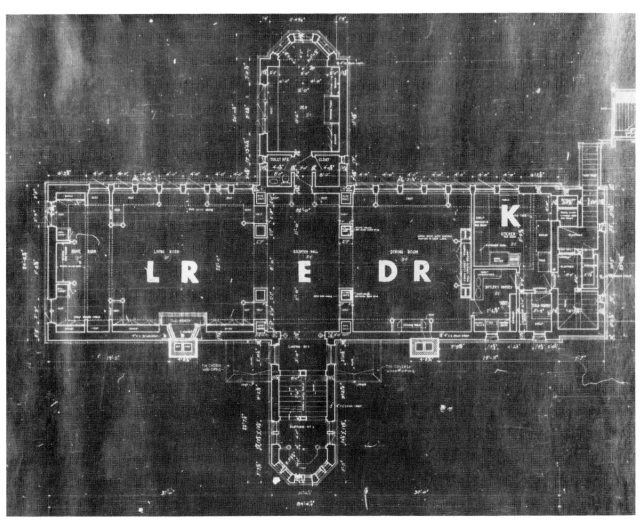

tried to keep costs from getting out of hand. "We are at work on the house plans endeavoring to reduce the size and total expenses," he wrote to Purcell in November 1911. None of Bennett's correspondence to Sullivan during this period survives, but a letter from Sullivan to Bennett in December 1911 makes it clear that Bennett was intimately involved in the smallest details of planning the house. The letter also shows how highly Sullivan regarded his client from Owatonna. Sullivan wrote:

Yours 5th [a letter from Bennett on December 5] duly received; contents carefully noted and incorporated in the drawing as required. Have but one question: wouldn't it be better to keep the closet door (in the entrance vestibule) at the back line of former seat? This will preserve the immediate view of ascending stairs, and the amplitude of the vestibule, as intended. The small amount of closet-space gained by your notation (door flush with foot of stairs) is not, in my judgment, worth such sacrifices.

You are the only client I have ever had whose vision has penetrated the true nature of my work. I want to thank you for that word "Finality" [a reference to an earlier letter in which Bennett had described Sullivan's buildings as having an "air of finality"]. It's true. But I had never thought of it except in paraphrase. I can see its value as a "talking point." Your plan to delay building [the new house] until you get your lumber as you want it, at the price you want, and air-season it, is far-sighted and sound. . . .

I haven't been able to concentrate on your work, of late, as I could wish to, for reasons you will understand. But shortly I hope to do so as it is now about ready for "fine tuning." I needn't assure a man of your faith that, when I am through with it, the thing will "sing."

By the end of 1911, Sullivan was still working on the house plans, although Bennett reported that he had received "pretty complete pencil sketches" of the house in early November.[14]

Meanwhile, Sullivan continued his efforts to climb out of debt, with the usual lack of success. Bennett, it appears, even went over Sullivan's financial records at one point in hopes of getting him straightened out. This is suggested in a letter from Sullivan to Bennett dated December 6, 1911:

I have your [letter of November] 25th and bank statement [apparently returned by Bennett after examining it]. I know just how you feel; but you don't know the stress of life in the big city. It is *impossible* for me further to reduce expenses unless I quit the game – which I have no intention of doing as long as I have any teeth left.

Just how I'll get out of my present fix I don't know, but I am doing now some pretty heavy thinking. Have been in tight places before. Things do sometimes drop from the sky. . . .

You are mistaken when you assume that two can live cheaper double than single: at least in my case. Mrs. Sullivan has been away just 2 years today. I have made and am making every sacrifice for her. I want her to get on her own feet. I have no word of reproach. Her parents made a spoiled child of her and I continue their work.[15]

In early February 1912 Bennett went to Chicago to discuss the house plans, which by then were almost completed. Later, Bennett reported to Elmslie in a letter that he had found Sullivan in bad shape once again:

I am sorry to say that Louis did not seem to be in very good physical condition. He was suffering with a very bad cold and also seemed to have eczema. As you stated to me previously at that time he seemed mentally distracted. He was preparing an article [for *Collier's* magazine] . . . and was much more interested in getting that out of his mind than he was in plans or work for making a little money. I went [to Chicago] at his request to go over and decide some details concerning the house plans. I was astonished to notice that he had forgotten some of the details which he had already designed. Altogether to me his condition seemed one to occasion some alarm. But you know him better than I do and possibly this is one of his moods.[16]

It was not until August 1912 that Bennett finally received completed blueprints for his house.

Sullivan did most of the work on the house himself, rather than turning it over to his draftsmen, and the result was one of the most striking designs of his career. His design called for a huge three-story house with a cruciform plan. The main axis of the house, eighty-five feet long and twenty-five feet wide, was to run parallel to Main Street. The house's north side, facing the street, was to be extremely severe and monumental, with only a few small windows breaking up the fortress-like appearance of the walls. The south elevation, which was to overlook the Pillsbury campus, featured a continuous band of stained-glass windows on each floor. Sullivan's design also called for small wings, with octagonal ends, to project from the north and south sides of the house. The north wing was to contain the main staircase, while the south wing had a den on the main floor. The house was to be faced with Roman brick on the bottom, vertical redwood siding in the middle, and plaster on the top—a combination of materials Sullivan had used only once before. Except for the stained glass, there was to be very little exterior ornament other than prominent motifs in sawn wood near the top of the house's two chimneys.[17]

Inside, particularly on the main floor, the design was equally monumental. The plan for this floor featured a fifteen by twenty-two-foot reception hall flanked on the west by a large dining room connected to the kitchen and on the east by an even larger living room. Opening out from the living room was a music room, which was to have large windows facing east across a terrace toward the garden Bennett intended to build on the long part of his L-shaped lot. The music and living rooms, the entrance hall, and the dining room were to be separated only by two sets of twin piers, so that together the four rooms would form one huge space, seventy feet long and twenty-two feet wide. The plans called for no north-facing windows in any of these rooms, thereby ensuring complete privacy from the street as well as protection from the prevailing winter winds. The rooms were all to be paneled in redwood and were to contain many built-in bookcases, seats, cabinets, and other furnishings. Sullivan also set aside wall space for murals above the fireplaces in the living and dining rooms. The top floor of the house was to have five bedrooms, all facing south, while the ground floor was to contain servants' quarters and a playroom, among other things.[18]

Sullivan's design, with its careful symmetry and axial planning, reflected his Beaux-Arts training and his insistent formalism. It also

The south exposure of the Sullivan-designed house consisted of rows of windows. In winter the sun's warmth would be welcome, and in summer the view toward Pillsbury Academy campus would be lovely.

showed how far removed he was from Wright, whose Prairie houses of
this period involved far more complex arrangements of space than
Sullivan was willing to attempt. Yet the plan of the Bennett house was
in some ways strikingly advanced, especially in its use of a virtual wall
of south-facing windows, which would have saved energy by providing
a great deal of passive solar heating in winter. Perhaps the house's major
failing was its decidedly undomestic appearance, as Purcell once noted:
"It [Sullivan's design] seemed to be wholly lacking in any feeling for the
Bennetts as a living family. . . . It was much more in the nature of a
Club House that would be suitable on a city lot where one could only
look abroad upon adjoining buildings. Mr. Sullivan simply had no concept whatever of American family life."[19]

Yet the fact remains that both Bennett and his wife seem to have liked
the design. Mrs. Bennett later wrote:

Mr. Bennett and I merely indicated to Mr. Sullivan the arrangement and numbers of bedrooms and baths and the number and size of rooms on the living
room floor; Mr. Sullivan then drew the first sketches for our study and, as I
remember it, we approved of everything he had planned, and suggested no
changes. . . .

Mr. Sullivan's conception of our home was that it should be like a flower
opening its petals toward the sun so he made the south side of the house mostly
windows, and the north wall had *no* windows as I remember it. . . .

Its reasons, aside from the artistic notion, were (1) the climate—much sunshine and very cold north winds—and protection from the public gaze (it was
the street side); (2) *much space* on the south and [a] very interesting view of [the]
Pillsbury Campus and of its activities.

But his main idea was that he wanted this residence to be like a flower opening toward the sun in a location where there was so much space that there was
nothing in the way to prevent the sun from shedding its kindly rays on the
"flower" as it opened to receive the sun's blessing.

We thought this a very beautiful conception indeed and were in love with
all its implications. . . . It was a bitter disappointment that we were never able
to build and occupy that house.[20]

As it turned out, the house would have cost more than Bennett was
willing or able to pay at the time. In the fall of 1912 he decided to delay
the project, apparently hoping that a way could be found at some later
date to reduce construction costs. By the next autumn, however, he was
once again ready to move ahead with his building plans, and he and his
family moved into the small house they owned adjacent to the site. During the same period, Bennett commissioned Sullivan and a Minneapolis
landscape architect to prepare a plot plan of the property. The plan, how-

ever, must have been either unsatisfactory to Bennett or slow in coming, because in 1914 he hired Purcell and Elmslie to prepare another landscape design. Purcell and Elmslie's plan, dated November 3, 1914, included a garage of their design, but still showed the outlines of Sullivan's house. Bennett was considering whether to build the house, which would have cost an estimated $20,000 in 1914, when World War I broke out. He decided not to build during the war years, even though some landscaping of the property had been done by 1914. This work, according to Mrs. Bennett, included the construction of a pond filled with goldfish and water lilies as well as the planting of trees and shrubs. One consequence of the war was a sharp increase in construction costs. When the war ended in 1918, Bennett found that the house designed by Sullivan would have cost $40,000 to build. That was more than Bennett could afford, and he reluctantly abandoned the project for good. "How I wish we could have built it," Mrs. Bennett said many years later, "for ourselves yes! but also as a monument to Sullivan!"[21]

Even though Bennett never built his dream house, he undoubtedly paid Sullivan a fee for the design. Sullivan desperately needed the money because he had few commissions during this period. Through most of 1913 he had only two projects going: the building in Clinton, Iowa, which housed a dry-goods store; and a tiny one-story bank building in Algona, Iowa. Later that year, however, Sullivan secured his third significant bank commission, this time for the Merchant's National Bank in Grinnell, Iowa. The Grinnell bankers hired Sullivan after making a visit to Owatonna to meet with Bennett and tour his bank. The bank in Grinnell turned out to be one of Sullivan's best, a pristine brick box featuring a huge burst of terra-cotta ornament above the main entrance. This ornament – in the form of superimposed circles, squares, and diamonds – surrounds a large circular window, an effect that has caused the bank to be likened to a treasure chest with an elaborately decorated keyhole. The interior of the bank is crisp and elegant but not nearly so ornate as the banking room in Owatonna.[22]

The Grinnell bank was completed in 1914, another sparse year for Sullivan. He obtained commissions for two minuscule banks – one in Newark, Ohio, and the other in West Lafayette, Indiana. Neither of these projects brought much money into his depleted coffers. Sullivan did receive some pleasant news that year, however, when he learned that his wife had finally managed to publish her first novel, an epic romance entitled *Goddess of the Dawn.* Unfortunately, the book failed to set the reading public aglow and quickly sank into literary oblivion.[23]

It was also in late 1914 that Sullivan had a reunion with Wright, whom he had seen only once since their bitter parting in 1893. If Elmslie is to be believed, Sullivan held a low opinion of Wright's character, but there is no question that Sullivan recognized Wright's genius and was proud of his former draftsman's achievements. The reunion occurred when Wright attended a lecture given by Sullivan in Chicago. Wright, it is said, wept when he greeted the man whom he was fond of calling, in somewhat faulty German, "der lieber meister" (beloved master). Visiting Sullivan later, Wright found him sitting on a desk littered with papers and photographs of some of his small banks. Sullivan, Wright wrote, did not look well, although "his eyes burned as brightly as ever. The old gleam of humor would come in them and go. But his carriage was not the same: The body was disintegrating."[24]

After completing the Grinnell bank, Sullivan went through another long period with virtually no work. Then, in late 1916, he received a chance for a second large commission in Owatonna after voters approved a $150,000 bond issue to build a new high school. In December, the Owatonna school board voted to seek plans for the building. The president of the school board at this time was none other than Guy Bennett, Carl's brother. Guy shared his brother's enthusiasm for Sullivan's architecture and lobbied hard to win Sullivan the commission. All told, twenty architects submitted plans to the board, but Sullivan clearly had the inside track because of Guy Bennett's efforts on his behalf. The Bennetts also displayed a color drawing of Sullivan's proposed high school in the bank lobby in hopes of securing public favor for his design. This drawing apparently has been lost, and no other drawing of the school building is known to exist. A member of the school board said many years later, however, that Sullivan's design called for a two-story circular building, faced in brick, with at least some ornamentation, presumably in terra cotta. There was apparently to be a power plant at the core of the building and few if any windows facing the street.[25]

In early April 1917 Sullivan himself, along with Parker Berry, traveled to Owatonna to discuss their proposal with the school board. The board at this time apparently favored Sullivan's plan by a four to three margin, mainly as a result of Guy Bennett's exertions. But Sullivan's pride and arrogance soon torpedoed whatever chance he may have had to win the commission. He became embroiled in a heated dispute with a board member over some insignificant point, and the job was lost. "I remember distinctly the morning when Mr. Sullivan and Mr. Berry returned from their trip to sell this job that Mr. Berry was very much disappointed that it had developed into an argument between one of the members of the school board and Mr. Sullivan about something that was entirely irrelevant to the school project," one of Sullivan's draftsmen recalled. The board finally awarded the commission to the Chicago firm of Jacobson and Round, one of whose members – Nelson Jacobson – was a native of Owatonna. Sullivan, as far as can be determined, never visited Owatonna again.[26]

Sullivan managed to obtain one significant commission in 1917, for the People's Savings and Loan Association Bank in the small farming community of Sidney, Ohio. Like all of his best banks, this is a brick box brought to vibrant life through ornament and color. Among other elements, the bank features a beautiful marble base and a big terra-cotta and glass-mosaic arch over the main door. Millet created the stained-glass windows and mosaic work – apparently the last time the two old friends worked together. There was little other work in 1917, however, and all three of Sullivan's draftsmen quit by the end of the year, leaving him alone and virtually penniless.[27]

The Peoples' Savings Bank in Sidney, Ohio, designed by Sullivan

For Sullivan, 1918 was to be, as he later described it, "that nightmare year." The first jarring blow came on February 18, when he was forced to leave his offices in the Auditorium tower because of inability to pay the rent. Sullivan had occupied the tower for almost thirty years, and his unceremonious eviction must have hurt him deeply. He moved to cheaper quarters on the building's second floor, which offered a less than inspiring view of the Wabash Street elevated tracks. During this time, Sullivan corresponded frequently with Wright, who sent condolences and, occasionally, money. Sullivan's desperation was apparent in a letter to Wright on April 1: "I am not ill, Frank, and have not been recently. I simply have to 'lay to,' every once in a while, from sheer exhaustion due to too much corroding anxiety, and repair my strength as best I can. My worry is of course primarily a money worry, but it is truly awful to one of my nature. With the future blank I am surely living in hell. To think I should come to this at 61."[28]

Sullivan's money troubles continued to mount through April and May of 1918. On May 18 he was told either to pay his month's rent of fifty dollars or face eviction. He immediately dashed off a letter to Wright, asking for money: "I hate to write in a panicky tone but I can't help it. It is hell!" Wright apparently sent twenty-five dollars, while Sullivan struggled to come up with the rest of his rent payment. On May 21 the owners of the building locked Sullivan out of his office until he could pay the rent, which he finally managed to do a few days later with the help of another friend. But worry about future rent payments, along with the metallic squealing of the elevated trains outside his window, finally drove Sullivan from the Auditorium Building for good on May 31. "My stuff went to warehouse yesterday and I turned over my office key," Sullivan told Wright in a letter on June 1. "This gives me a sense of relief—and I am foot-loose and ready to jump at whatever my offer: U.S. East-California-Japan-Timbuctoo—anywhere. My health is excellent and I am not 'downhearted' yet."[29]

Sullivan's next job, however, did not come from any exotic locale. Instead, he managed to obtain one final commission for a bank, this time in Columbus, Wisconsin, a small community near Madison. For the Farmers' and Merchants' Union Bank, Sullivan produced another beautiful little building with fine brick and terra-cotta work and an arched window above the entrance. The bank, completed in 1919, also features an unusual side elevation, with five arched windows set above an inwardly slanting wall that gives the building a vaguely Egyptian feeling.[30]

After leaving the Auditorium Building, Sullivan rented a small office on the near south side of Chicago, but he spent most of his time at the Cliff Dwellers Club in the Loop. Although he had long since been unable to pay his dues, the club officers had come to his rescue by making him an honorary lifetime member. At the suggestion of a friend, he began work in the summer of 1918 on a revised version of the *Kindergarten Chats,* which he hoped to have published in book form. He was living now off the largesse of his friends. Wright, Winslow, and Gates, as well as several other friends in the Chicago architectural community, regularly "loaned" him money in amounts ranging from five to one hundred dollars. He also raised money by selling off shares of his Auditorium Association stock. Sullivan had received 250 shares of the stock, issued at one hundred dollars a share, as part of his fee for designing the building. Because the complex had never been a financial success, he was forced to sell the stock for as little as fifteen dollars a share.[31]

Sullivan's situation failed to improve much in 1919. He managed to obtain one small job for remodeling a bank in Manistique, Michigan. "It [the remodeling] doesn't run heavily into money," he reported to Wright, "but will keep the wolf away for a couple of months." There was very little for him to do most of the time, however. Gradually, he became a kind of shadow, haunting the rooms of the Cliff Dwellers Club, his only haven amid a growing tide of misfortune. Elmslie would sometimes see him there, "a sad and pathetic smile on that masterful face." Sullivan took some consolation from the fact that he had finished his revised version of the *Kindergarten Chats,* but he had trouble finding a publisher. "I am uncertain as to when the work will appear," he wrote Wright in January. "However I can wait six months or a year until publishers get over being crazy, as they certainly are now." As it turned out, he would not live to see the revised *Kindergaten Chats* in print, because there was simply no market for his brand of heavy-handed prose.[32]

Although his career for all practical purposes was finished, Sullivan kept up a brave front, frequently informing friends of "prospects" for work that had come his way – "prospects" that seldom materialized. Late in 1919, for example, Sullivan was asked to study the possibility of designing a chapel for St. John's Military Academy in Delafield, Wisconsin. In a letter to Wright, who was then in Tokyo working on his Imperial Hotel, Sullivan reported that the possible chapel project came about as a result of his work in Owatonna: "It seems that the commandant of cadets [at the academy] . . . was in Owatonna, Minn., and saw my bank there. It impressed him, if you please, as having an ecclesiastical character: and I am wondering if there is any basis for that impression." The commandant was not the first visitor to the bank to be struck by its religious aura, but despite his recommendation, Sullivan did not get the job in Delafield. Nor was he able to nail down a possible library job in DeKalb, Illinois, apparently because he was not satisfied with the fee.[33]

Sullivan was no more successful finding work in 1920, and reported in November that his only recent job had been designing the pedestal for a statue of the governor of Illinois. During this time, Sullivan continued to live a hand-to-mouth existence, never knowing where the next dollar might come from. By August 1921, he found himself flat broke and so once again had to go begging to friends. On August 19, he sent an urgent cable to Wright in Tokyo, asking for money. "I have been hung up by the thumbs for weeks," he told Wright in a letter sent the same day, "and the nervous strain has become unbearable – hence this cable, and my hope that you will be able to respond." Four days later, Sullivan sent a desperately blunt letter to Wright: "If you have any money to spare, now is the urgent time to let me have some. As I do not know how you are fixed, I cannot specify any sum; I can merely say that I am in a very serious situation: indeed it is now a sheer matter of food and shelter. So many of my friends are out of town on vacations that the situation has become very peculiar – I seem to have lost my way."[34]

Yet Sullivan somehow scraped the money together to go on. A few months later, in the autumn of 1921, he received what was to be his last commission. It was for the facade of a small music store on Chicago's north side. He used his favorite material, terra cotta, to create an elevation overflowing with ornamental motifs. Perhaps he realized this store would be his last chance and so tried to compress all he knew into its tiny facade.[35]

Although Sullivan was now through as a practicing architect, he kept busy with his writing. He believed that his greatest contribution to posterity would be as a teacher and writer, and he hoped that from the seedbed of his ideas a new American architecture would sprout and grow strong. But as he struggled in his last years to put his ideas into book form, the battle was already lost, for by the 1920s Beaux-Arts eclecticism reigned supreme in Chicago and elsewhere across America.[36]

Still, Sullivan hung on, filling the long days with writing and reading or simply idling about the Cliff Dwellers Club. Early in 1922 friends urged him to write two books: one would be an autobiography, the other a book of drawings illustrating his philosophy of ornament. Sullivan, always anxious to spread his architectural gospel, seized on both ideas and set to work at once. The two books that resulted were *The Autobiography of an Idea,* which first appeared in monthly installments in an architectural magazine beginning in June 1922, and *A System of Architectural Ornament According with a Philosophy of Man's Powers,* finished in June 1923 but not published until 1924. The *Autobiography* is a curious book, as revealing for what it omits as for what it includes, since it contains nothing about Sullivan's life after 1893. What it does provide

are many fascinating details of his early life, all rendered in Sullivan's most rhapsodic style. *A System of Architectural Ornament* consists of twenty plates that form a kind of primer in the art of ornament. The best of the drawings show Sullivan's extraordinary talent for transforming simple geometric forms into graceful ornamental motifs that seem almost to come alive on the page.

When Sullivan started work on the two books in 1922, his financial condition remained desperate. He managed to maintain his small office on the south side of Chicago until late that year, when he ran out of money to pay the rent. Gates then stepped in and provided him with a small office, rent free, at American Terra Cotta. Sullivan apparently was able to obtain a few small jobs in the form of architectural piecework during this period. His last commission, received from a hardware company, is said to have been an ornamental design for a tin platform used under pot-bellied stoves. The job paid two hundred dollars. Yet Sullivan remained so short of money that he apparently resorted to panhandling acquaintances on the street. "I saw him once – the big man – touching me for a quarter on Michigan Boulevard," Oskar Gross recalled. Virtually all of Sullivan's personal possessions disappeared along with his money, and about all he had to his name were his drafting instruments, a sheaf of personal drawings, some clothes (Wright bought him a new suit at one point), and a few small personal items, such as a picture of his mother.[37]

In August 1923 Sullivan suffered a severe personal blow when an elderly paramour who had been looking after him for several years died. The woman, a milliner by trade, had been devoted to Sullivan, and her death left him alone and facing a bleak future. On September 3, he wrote to Wright: "This is my birthday: 67 long years of experience, which after all may amount to little. I am beginning to feel that I have received a mortal wound, although perhaps it is too early to say. We shall see. Never before have I felt how sordid are the faces one sees upon the street." Yet he continued to seek work, reporting to Wright that he was pursuing a bank project in Macon, Georgia. The project, of course, never materialized.[38]

Toward the end of 1923, Sullivan's health began to deteriorate rapidly. His heart, swollen to twice the normal size, was beating fiercely in his chest, and chronic neuritis was gradually making his right arm and hand useless. By March 1924 Sullivan's heart condition left him so exhausted that he could no longer undertake the short cab ride from his apartment to the Cliff Dwellers Club. He was living in a nine-dollar-a-week room at the Warner Hotel south of the Loop, and there was no one to take care of him except the hotel's proprietor, who was a faithful friend but who had plenty of other business to attend to. As Sullivan's condition

Plate 16 from Louis Sullivan's *A System of Architectural Ornament* (1924)

continued to worsen, he grew increasingly difficult to deal with. He sometimes could be heard pounding furiously on the table if he did not get his daily dose of coffee, which was all he seemed to live on. His condition finally deteriorated to the point that his friends decided to hire a nurse to care for him in his apartment.[39]

By April 1924, it was obvious to everyone, including Sullivan, that the end was near. He could hear now "the constant, solvent song of death," as he had once called it, but there were still a few things he hoped to accomplish before becoming part of the melody. Most of all, he wanted to see his two books in print. The *Autobiography* and *System of Architectural Ornament* were soon to appear, and the publishers were instructed to do everything possible to speed up their work. The result was that Sullivan, in early April, was able to see first copies of both of his books, and this event gave him great joy. Among his visitors during these last days was Wright, to whom Sullivan gave the sheaf of drawings that was his most prized possession. Much later, Wright recalled his final hours with Sullivan:

In town a few days later, I went to see him again.

He seemed better. There – at last – the first bound copy of the "Autobiography"! The book had just come in and was lying on the table by his bed. He wanted to get up. I helped him, put my overcoat round his shoulders, as he sat on the bed with his feet covered up on the floor. He looked over at the book.

'There it is, Frank.'

I was sitting by him, my arm around him to keep him warm and to steady him. I could feel every vertebra in his backbone as I rubbed my hand up and down his spine to comfort him; and I could feel his enlarged heart pounding.[40]

Three days later, on April 14, 1924, Sullivan slipped into a coma and died. He was buried the next day at Graceland Cemetery, within sight of the exquisite tomb he had designed more than thirty years earlier for Elisha Getty. Elmslie, Kristian Schneider, and Wright were among the pallbearers, and there was a brief service at graveside, before Sullivan was placed next to his father and mother in the plot that was one of his few earthly possessions when he died. "Well, we buried the greatest architect of our generation today," Elmslie wrote to a friend, and so they had.[41]

There is a moving passage in the *Kindergarten Chats* that does much to explain Sullivan's great achievements as an artist while also suggesting the cause of his painful failings as a man. Sullivan wrote:

When you accumulate, accumulate abundantly, absorb totalities, not fragments. Grasp the largeness of things, not the petty isolated aspects. Lay hold upon the warm significance of realities, not the mere cold currency passing from hand to hand. Seize upon the drift, the color, the intensity, the what-you-may-call-it of the moving, teeming life about you, not merely upon its broken facts of definition, and follow, follow, follow every path, every trail that leads toward emotional and spiritual riches—paths hidden alike to the heedless and the over-sure—and then, when you give, give of your abundance: And this it is to live.

If you receive not, you cannot give. And to receive of life you must be awake to it. Shut the heart and you close the open door of sympathy upon yourself, and in the doing exclude the light of the world.[42]

As an artist, Sullivan followed this advice, for he sought in his best buildings to express the "largeness of things" through a wedding of structure and ornament that he saw as a reflection of the larger unity of nature itself. Moreover, he brought to everything he did an intensity and passion that few architects have ever matched. Yet he was unable in his personal life to find the "emotional and spiritual riches" that characterize his designs. He pursued his vision of a new American architecture with such single-mindedness and truculent certainty that he became in time a lonely and isolated figure. Sullivan was thus in many ways a victim of his own search for artistic truth, for "in the doing" he frequently lost sight of "the light of the world" as reflected in his fellow human beings.[43]

The ironies that marked Sullivan's life continued after his death. He had always dreamed of laying the groundwork for an authentic American architecture, free from foreign influence. Yet his work had its greatest impact on a group of European architects who, in the 1920s and 1930s, often invoked his name but never really understood the poetry of his buildings. These architects, who created the elegant but frequently sterile International Style, hailed Sullivan as the prophet of modern architecture. They mouthed his motto—form follows function—and they expressed deep admiration for his great skyscrapers. But they ignored, or even scoffed at, his ornament. In fact, in the same year that the Owatonna bank was completed, one of the founders of the International Style, Adolf Loos, wrote an article entitled "Ornament and Crime" in which he denounced ornament as a form of perversion. Cities all over the world are now deadened by featureless boxes of glass and steel that are part of the legacy of the International Style.[44]

Although Sullivan undoubtedly would have condemned this sort of architecture, he is nonetheless often depicted as the first "modern" American architect. He certainly was modern in his efforts to express the structural forms of buildings and to design from the inside out in accord with functional needs. Yet much of the enduring appeal of his buildings lies in their old-fashioned qualities: lavish ornamentation, rich colors, and fine craftsmanship. In several respects, he was the most brilliant practitioner of the theories espoused at the École des Beaux-Arts. Many of his better buildings feature simple shapes, axial floor plans, carefully integrated ornament, and close attention to proportions and detailing—all attributes of the more neoclassic structures usually associated with the Beaux-Arts style. It was perhaps with this in mind that Solon Beman, a prominent architect in the Chicago School, remarked that "if Sullivan would turn his thought in that direction, he could become the greatest classic architect of his time." All things considered, it is thus probably fairer to say that Sullivan was one of the last great nineteenth-century architects than to depict him as the first master of twentieth-century building design.[45]

It is difficult to assign Sullivan's work to any convenient niche in the architectural pantheon, although many historians have tried. He is often associated with the so-called Chicago School, a group of architects who perfected the metal-frame skyscraper in the 1890s. Sullivan certainly must be accounted a member of the school, since he knew its other members and shared many of their ideas. Yet some of Sullivan's large commercial buildings, such as the Wainwright and Guaranty, are so striking in their color and ornamentation that the rather standardized skyscrapers turned out by a number of other Chicago School architects seem pale in comparison. Furthermore, no other member of the Chicago School produced anything quite like Sullivan's small-town banks.[46]

Sullivan has also been grouped with the Prairie School architects, mainly because of his banks and a few houses that were probably designed chiefly by Elmslie. There can be no doubt that Sullivan, with his emphasis on organic architecture, provided much of the school's intellectual foundation. Sullivan's influence on the school, however, was not a direct one, since his ideas were largely filtered through Wright. Moreover, it was Wright, not Sullivan, who established the main features of the school's style. Thus, whereas Wright sought in his Prairie houses to "destroy the box" by creating new vistas of space, Sullivan—especially in his little banks—worked to glorify the box through the use of ornament. Given these divergent approaches, it is not surprising that Wright once dismissed the Owatonna bank as a "high wall with a hole in it."[47]

In the final analysis, attempts to confine Sullivan to any particular school or style seem futile, perhaps because he was one of those creative figures—Wright was another—who were always a bit out of the mainstream. Nowhere is Sullivan's originality as a designer more evident than in his little banks. The best of these banks—in Owatonna, Grinnell, Sidney, and Columbus – are among the most fascinating works of his career. Forced by tragic circumstances to work in miniature, Sullivan poured a lifetime of learning and dreaming into these buildings in the hope that they might somehow point the way to a new age in American architecture. But the new age, as Sullivan envisioned it, never arrived. As a result, his banks remain magnificent oddities – brilliant, inventive, and utterly individualistic, just like the man who made them. Rich in color and life and flowing with ornament that was the delight of Sullivan's soul, they form perhaps the most poignant body of work in American architecture, with all the tantalizing beauty of a dream that failed.[48]

6

ELMSLIE AND BENNETT—
TRIUMPHS AND TRAGEDIES

I wish I could understand things a bit, read a line of the obscure page, and know where she is. I want her so, to tell me she has forgiven me my failure and smile her heavenly smile. — *George Elmslie*[1]

Why is it that when we are young we don't go to the place where we know that we ought to go? — *Carl Bennett*[2]

WHEN GEORGE ELMSLIE finally left Sullivan in December 1909, he was ready to begin the most creative and, for a short while, the happiest period of his life. The break with Sullivan, although hardly unexpected, had nonetheless been a traumatic episode for Elmslie. He had thought of leaving Sullivan years before, but he had never been able to bring himself to do it. Elmslie was still uncertain about his plans as late as November, when he wrote: "The time is not ripe for me to break with L. H. S. That depends largely on the flow of events and my own livelihood." But less than a month later, following the disastrous auction, Elmslie had been given his walking papers. "It has been a dreadful time and has cost me almost the last ounce of mental and physical endurance," he wrote two days after being fired. "The wrench is terrible, so many years. And now Mr. Sullivan is unfit for any commercial enterprise and appears on his last legs."[3]

Elmslie had no worries about finding another job. William Purcell had for some time been trying to persuade Elmslie to join him in

Minneapolis, where Purcell had his own architectural firm in partnership with an engineer named George Feick. Purcell realized that Elmslie, who had few equals as a draftsman, would be an invaluable addition to the firm. Moreover, Purcell shared Elmslie's devotion to the ideal of an organic and original American architecture. In early 1910, Elmslie agreed to move to Minneapolis, and so the firm of Purcell, Feick, and Elmslie was born. During the next decade, Purcell and Elmslie (Feick was never a real force in the firm and left in 1913) produced a series of elegant banks, offices, and houses, mainly in the Midwest. Much of their work is in Minnesota, and it represents perhaps the finest body of architecture ever produced in the state. Like all of the Prairie School architects, Purcell and Elmslie drew much of their stylistic inspiration from Wright, while their artistic philosophy was largely derived from Sullivan.

Feick, Purcell, and Elmslie (from left to right) in their office in Minneapolis

Yet they gradually developed their own distinct style, especially in their residential designs.⁴

In Purcell, Elmslie found just the sort of partner he needed. Although he was no match for Elmslie at the drafting board, Purcell was a capable designer. More importantly, he was adept at keeping Elmslie's designs under control, since Elmslie – by his own admission – tended toward artistic overindulgence. The son of a wealthy Chicago business executive, Purcell was born in 1880 in Wilmette, Illinois. The family moved to the western Chicago suburb of Oak Park in 1893, the same year that Wright set up his home and studio there. Purcell, however, spent many of his summers at his grandparents' cabin in northern Wisconsin and there developed the love of nature that was common to all of the Prairie School architects.⁵

After studying architecture at Cornell University, Purcell returned to Chicago, where he met Elmslie at a social gathering in 1903. The two men quickly became friends. Elmslie convinced Sullivan to hire Purcell as a draftsman later that year, but Purcell left in December when the work ran out. In 1907, Purcell set up his architectural firm in Minneapolis with Feick, a friend from college days. Elmslie had corresponded with Purcell for several years before leaving Sullivan, and in the process Purcell became Elmslie's only true confidant. "You are the only man on earth I can talk about them [his problems] to, so I generously conspire to send all my troubles to you," Elmslie wrote in a typical letter dating from 1909. There were to be many more such letters during the two men's lifelong, if at times very strained, friendship.⁶

During his first year in partnership with Purcell, Elmslie was wrapped up in more than his work. His attention was also directed toward a young woman named Bonnie Marie Hunter, with whom he had fallen in love. He had met her in 1908 in Chicago, where she lived with her parents, who were active in the local Scottish community. She was twenty-seven at that time, an attractive, dark-haired woman – not exactly beautiful. She had a vivacious spirit that Elmslie, who tended toward melancholia, found very appealing. She was the daughter of a well-to-do insurance broker and had attended Wellesley College, where she apparently developed an interest in art and architecture. In wooing his beloved, Elmslie was the very epitome of a bashful suitor. The details of his halting courtship are sparse, but a letter to Purcell in July 1908 provides insight into Elmslie's frame of mind:

I simply cannot somehow consider myself as a factor in *her* fair thoughts. . . .
I think she is very fine and appeals [to] me wonderfully. I never saw anyone that

appealed so much. But that is not love. Whether *that* flower is going to bloom I do not know. Time will write it all out some day. I do hesitate to bother her with my presence. I am *so* much of an antiquity and with so much behind me that was ill-fated and spelled catastrophe from the first, and never could have produced peace and happiness. I did not know a moment's happiness for many years, and the flame burned low, for many clear cut and now quite definite reasons, which would take me a week to tell you. I should regret much if she knows aught of my past as it would surely make her sympathetic and that must not be – not in that direction. I need sympathy enough, but not manufactured out of a miserable past.[7]

Having delivered himself of this testament to the power of positive thinking, Elmslie nonetheless forged ahead with his courtship, which waxed and waned through 1909. In August, he wrote to Purcell: "The day is coming when she will be to me and I to her everything or nothing." During this time, the uncertain status of Elmslie's love life, along with increasing anxiety over his job situation, took a fierce toll on his always delicate constitution. In September, Elmslie reported that he was "on the verge of physical collapse." But once he had finally left Sullivan for good, Elmslie quickly recovered, and in 1910 he at last won his Bonnie. They were married in Chicago on September 14, in the same church and by the same minister who had married Sullivan eleven years before. "She was . . . [a] charming, distinguished woman," Purcell recalled many years later. "George got a real jewel there." Sullivan, however, was less than enthralled by Elmslie's prospects for connubial bliss. "George, do you mean to tell me you are going to get married," he said. "Don't. It cost me $100,000, my God."[8]

After their marriage, the Elmslies moved to Minneapolis, where they were to spend the next two years. These were exceptionally happy times for Elmslie. He still was not making much money (his top pay as Purcell's partner was about forty dollars a week), but he was busy doing the work he loved, and he had finally found someone with whom he could share his life and his dreams. Between 1910 and 1912, Purcell and Elmslie received more than twenty commissions, most of them for houses. The firm also designed a number of small banks during this period, including the Merchants Bank in Winona, Minnesota, dating from 1912.[9]

Elmslie once claimed that Bennett preferred the Winona bank to his own. While this seems doubtful, there is no question that the Winona bank is a superb building. It is an elegant little structure in Roman brick, terra cotta, and stained glass, more Wrightian in its subtle geometrics than the Owatonna bank and with a straightforward and very functional interior far ahead of its time. The bank's exterior also contains some of Elmslie's most lyrical ornament. The Merchants Bank does not quite have the monumental power of the Owatonna bank, in part perhaps because its setting is less impressive, but it is nonetheless a work of the first rank.[10]

Elmslie was full of energy and enthusiasm during these years, and with Bonnie at his side, he also seemed to find the peace of mind that had always eluded him. Then, in late August 1912 Bonnie was admitted to a Chicago hospital for surgery. Nine days later, barely a week before what would have been her second wedding anniversary, she was dead at age thirty-one. According to her death certificate, she died of a blood clot in the lungs after undergoing an appendectomy. But Purcell, in an interview many years later, said that she died following an unnecessary operation that was botched by the surgeon. One of Elmslie's sisters, Edith, offered yet another version of what happened, saying that Bonnie had undergone surgery so that she could have children. If true, this would

George and Bonnie Elmslie in about 1911

help to explain the powerful feelings of guilt that are apparent in many of Elmslie's letters after his wife's death.[11]

One thing is certain: Bonnie's death was a shattering blow to Elmslie. Suddenly alone once again as he had been for so much of his life, Elmslie was tormented day and night by her memory. Bennett sent his condolences, while Purcell tried to keep Elmslie busy, in the hope that work might serve as an anodyne. By late January 1913, Purcell reported to Bennett that Elmslie seemed to be recovering, yet Elmslie's own letters make it clear that he never really did. Bonnie's death punched an irreparable hole in the fragile fabric of Elmslie's spirit, and within a few years

Merchants National Bank, Winona

his energy and his creative powers began to ebb away. "It is so difficult, this all alone business," Elmslie wrote from Chicago in January 1913. He was staying then with several of his sisters and had decided to work out of Chicago, even though Purcell wanted him to return to Minneapolis. Yet despite his growing loneliness, Elmslie refused to budge.[12]

With its partners four hundred miles apart, the firm of Purcell and Elmslie struggled to keep going. Moreover, Elmslie continued to be consumed by grief, complaining at one point that he had lost his "green interest in life." The firm was very busy at this time, and Purcell wrote in April that some jobs might be lost unless Elmslie could turn out more work. By September, however, Elmslie was little better: "Am not managing well these days and so am not responsive to the things most needed to be done. Forgive. . . . If I can get a grasp I'll use it all I . . . possibly can." A week later, as Purcell was working long hours struggling to clear a backlog of work in the office, he received this letter from his still grieving partner in Chicago: "Oh, these days of the depth I fancy they will never come to an end. I had bodily strength last year and a clear mind when the day [of his wife's death] came and the recurrence has simply taxed me beyond all reason. Ye Gods, the cost of it all and the darkness and the finality and the total eclipse. I feel savage and strange at times and have the impulse of a thief. Walking along the margin of the lake at eventide sometimes helps and I just talk right out loud, asking so many questions. Sometimes *quietness* comes. Sometimes terror."[13]

Elmslie clearly was a man who had begun to lose his way, but he

The Hoyt house in Red Wing is a Purcell and Elmslie creation.

somehow managed to keep on working. The firm stayed busy through 1913 designing banks and residences, including a magnificent little house for Purcell's first wife near Lake of the Isles in Minneapolis. By 1914, however, commissions began to decline, putting the firm in jeopardy. The two partners soon began to bicker over money and other matters. Purcell had minimal skills as a businessman, while Elmslie had none at all, and some rather testy letters flew back and forth between Minneapolis and Chicago as the partners considered what to do. Their partner-

For the Edna Purcell house in Minneapolis, Purcell and Elmslie designed all of the interior decoration and furnishings. This view is of the writing nook.

ship had never been a financial success, and it had been necessary for Purcell to pour a great deal of his father's money into the firm to keep it afloat. But Elmslie, who could be very contrary at times, seemed completely unable to understand the firm's precarious financial situation. For his part, Purcell could be egocentric and often seemed insensitive to his partner's plight in Chicago. The result was that the partnership began to come apart in about 1916. Elmslie, meanwhile, was still haunted by his wife's death. At one point, he wrote to Purcell: "I wish I could understand things a bit, read a line of the obscure page, and know where she is. I want her so, to tell me she has forgiven me my failure and smile her heavenly smile. I could go tonight with rejoicing to see that smile."[14]

It was in 1915–16 that Elmslie designed his last great building, the Woodbury County Courthouse in Sioux City, Iowa. The commission actually went to William L. Steele, but he felt unable to undertake so large a project by himself and called in Elmslie, whom he had met while working as a draftsman for Sullivan. Although Steele supervised the project, he let Elmslie handle virtually all of the actual planning and designing of the courthouse, which cost $850,000 and caused considerable controversy in Sioux City because of its radical design. Covering a quarter of a city block, the courthouse is by far the largest civic structure ever built by a Prairie School architect. Its outstanding feature is an interior court full of lavish, gigantically scaled ornament in terra cotta. The courthouse, completed in 1918, was Elmslie's ultimate exercise in the art of ornament, for never again was he given an opportunity to let his imagination roam so freely or on so large a scale.[15]

By 1918, the firm of Purcell and Elmslie was for all practical purposes defunct, although the partnership was not formally dissolved until four years later. Purcell left Minneapolis in 1918 to work for an advertising firm in Philadelphia. Suffering from poor health, he later moved to Portland, Oregon. Elmslie, meanwhile, still held out hope that the partnership could be salvaged. In mid-October he wrote a long, aggrieved letter to Purcell, who had complained earlier about Elmslie's financial ignorance. "The big creative job was to dream a big business and make it come true, the doing of it secondary," Elmslie wrote. "It didn't come true but it must come true. You and I have done work warranting more business. It isn't all my fault that we haven't. . . . WE MUST MAKE IT."[16]

Elmslie went on in his letter to describe his contribution to the firm, but he also admitted that he had made a serious mistake by refusing to rejoin Purcell in Minneapolis after 1912: "I have given us some of the most notable buildings in the country. I am disregarding your share for the moment because I had the history of the Owatonna bank behind me before I came up [to Minneapolis]. So that I was capable of organic think-

Woodbury County Courthouse, Sioux City, Iowa

ing at the beginning and you were not until later. . . . It always was and is disastrous for me to work alone away from the main inspiration and source. I will be candid and frank and say you are both and that the office [in Minneapolis] was my place." He concluded by telling Purcell: "It's all been for you. I have given you my work and my life."[17]

The partnership could not be revived, however. Responding to Elmslie's letter, Purcell wrote that the firm had run out of both money and creative energy. "In the same sentence in which you again build a future that you again believe to be real," Purcell wrote, "you tell me as you have almost weekly for the past two years that you are now old and that your period of best work is past." Elmslie's continuing mental anguish, which apparently caused him to be hospitalized several times in the years after his wife's death, also played a major role in the demise of the partnership. "He [Elmslie] was really going to pieces as far back as 1918," Purcell wrote many years later. "That's one of the reasons I quit — a blessing I did." Without a partner to seek out business aggressively, Elmslie was lost, and by 1920 he found himself in a situation very similar to Sullivan's. He was alone, in Chicago, with little work and less money, facing a dismal future.[18]

For Carl Bennett, the years between 1908 and 1920 were, for the most part, prosperous and happy ones. His family grew with the births of two more daughters in 1910 and 1913, giving him four in all. His bank also grew, rebounding nicely from a brief business depression in 1907–08. Over the next twelve years, the bank's assets nearly tripled, largely as a result of continuing farm prosperity. Bennett was involved in other business interests as well. He started a company that manufactured butter churns, although this enterprise was never very successful, and he also owned a small investment firm with his brother.[19]

There was one other interest to which he devoted a great deal of his time and energy, even though he was never paid a cent for his work. For during this period, Bennett functioned almost like a third partner in the firm of Purcell and Elmslie. He was the firm's point man, scouting out new commissions and in general promoting what he referred to as "the cause of the new architecture." Bennett also served as a sort of informal adviser to the firm, since Purcell and Elmslie would sometimes ask him to critique floor plans of their commercial buildings. The architects sought Bennett's advice on personal matters as well. Thus, when Elmslie was debating whether to leave Sullivan, he turned to Bennett for counsel. "I went over the Sullivan situation with Mr. Bennett by letter the other day and will let you hear his views," Elmslie wrote to Purcell in November 1909. Elmslie later reported that he had received "two good letters" from Bennett in reply.[20]

Bennett's efforts on behalf of Purcell and Elmslie put him in a delicate position, since he also felt that he "ought to be loyal to Sullivan." Bennett gave aid to Sullivan whenever possible, as the history of his own house project and the Grinnell bank make clear. Yet Bennett knew all too well that Sullivan could not always be counted on to act responsibly, which may be why he found far more commissions for Purcell and Elmslie than for Sullivan. Furthermore, Bennett took pains to ensure that Sullivan would not find out about some of his lobbying on behalf of Purcell and Elmslie. For example, when Bennett helped the two architects obtain the Winona bank commission in 1912, he wrote to them that he intended "to make no mention of this matter to Mr. Sullivan."[21]

Exactly how many of Purcell and Elmslie's commissions were obtained through Bennett's efforts is difficult to determine. The evidence suggests, however, that Bennett helped to bring at least ten commissions to the firm. Bennett's assistance sometimes consisted of no more than sending out information about his bank in response to written inquiries. In other cases, he would go a step further by offering tours of his bank to other bankers who were considering a new building. After Bennett had given one of his patented tours to a banker from Grand Meadow, Minnesota, in early 1910, Purcell wrote: "Our securing the work [for the Exchange State Bank in Grand Meadow] was due in no small way to the consideration which you extended [to the banker] when he visited Owatonna at our suggestion." That Bennett used these tours to make a strong pitch for "the new architecture" is clear from a letter he wrote to Purcell in 1911 describing an upcoming visit by some bankers from Mankato, Minnesota: "I will take pains," he wrote, "to spend some time with them to drive home some of the ideas in our bank building."[22]

In addition to helping Purcell and Elmslie obtain several bank jobs, Bennett found two house commissions for them in Owatonna. The first of these was a practical bungalow, built in 1912 for Charles I. Buxton, a friend of Bennett's and a member of the bank's board of directors. A year later, Purcell and Elmslie designed a house for Dr. James Adair, another of Bennett's acquaintances.[23]

Purcell and Elmslie designed one other house in Owatonna, and that was for Bennett himself. The two architects became involved in the project as early as 1914, when Bennett was still undecided about the house designed by Sullivan. Purcell and Elmslie did not submit their final house plan until 1920, however, because Bennett had been unable to build during the war years. Sullivan's house, besides being too expensive, had perhaps been too stiff and formal to suit Bennett's taste. By contrast, the residence designed by Purcell and Elmslie for the family was rambling and picturesque. It was a two-story, five-bedroom house with a high gabled roof and small wings jutting out here and there — a sort of Queen Anne house done in the Prairie School idiom. There was even to be a pointed Gothic arch — an unheard of touch in a Prairie house — between the living room and a small alcove. Purcell later wrote: "Our house was full of light and sunshine, broad and low, intimately connected with the garden and outdoors and a beautiful and satisfying scheme in every way. Bennett liked it, was ready to build it, but perhaps had a premonition of the gathering economic storm, for he delayed making a start from year to year." As it turned out, the house was never built, probably for the same reason that Sullivan's design had to be shelved: World War I drove prices up so high that Bennett simply could not afford his dream home.[24]

Farm commodities shared in the price surge brought on by the war, which greatly increased the demand for food abroad. The government told farmers it was their patriotic duty to plant every available acre, but demand was so great that prices continued to rise despite record production. As crop prices rose, so did the price of farmland, which in some areas of the Midwest more than quadrupled between 1910 and 1920. During this time, many farmers borrowed heavily to expand their land holdings.[25] Bennett's bank, as one of the largest in southern Minnesota, did a booming business in farm loans, not only in the state but in the Dakotas and Montana as well.

In the meantime, Bennett kept busy with his many interests. He

Purcell and Elmslie called for brick, wood, plaster, and terra cotta in their plans for the Bennett house.

SOUTH ELEVATION

played the organ occasionally at church and led a music club that performed sacred cantatas and other choral works. Dairy shows and other expositions frequently drew him to Chicago, where he usually stopped in to visit with Sullivan. Bennett would also drop by Elmslie's small office for a chat, often giving him leads on possible commissions. In addition, Bennett continued to be in constant correspondence with Purcell and Elmslie, whom he occasionally commissioned to design stationery and furnishings for the bank.[26]

About the only sad note in Bennett's life during this period occurred in February 1916 when his father, L. L. Bennett, died of pneumonia at age seventy-six. Carl, who had actually run the bank for many years, now became president in name as well as in fact. As the decade of the 1920s approached, Bennett's future seemed cloudless. At age fifty, he was president of a bank with well over $2 million in assets, and he had numerous other business interests that promised to make him even wealthier in the years ahead.[27]

Yet it was about 1920 that the course of Bennett's life began to change in response to forces over which he had little control. The years of prosperity on the American farm were soon to dissolve into years of disaster in which Carl Bennett would become one of the casualties.

Beneath the frantic glitter of the 1920s, the nation's farm economy was slowly rotting away. The boom in prices for farmland and farm products touched off by World War I turned into an unprecedented bust after the

Elmslie executed several small commissions for Bennett, including designing the bank's stationery.

war ended. When government price supports for wheat, corn, and other crops were lifted in May 1920, prices plunged. Wheat, which had sold for as much as $3.54 a bushel in Minneapolis during the war years, fell to $1.00 a bushel by 1923. Corn plummeted from $2.27 to $.37 a bushel during the same period. Overall, net farm income dropped from just over $10 billion in 1919 to $4.1 billion by 1921. Meanwhile, farmers who had mortgaged themselves to the hilt to buy land during the war found themselves facing crushing debt loads at a time when their income was falling rapidly. In Steele County, as elsewhere in the farm belt, land values fell along with crop prices. The two thousand farms in the county depreciated in value by an average of $4,300 between 1920 and 1926.[28]

The crisis in agriculture spelled trouble for rural banks, which had helped finance the land boom of the war years and were holding a tremendous number of farm mortgages. By the early 1920s, large numbers of farmers, caught in the squeeze of high mortgage costs and low crop prices, began defaulting on these loans. As more and more defaults occurred, many rural banks found themselves pressed for cash to meet depositor demand. Moreover, as the price of farmland continued to sink, the banks could find no one interested in buying their mortgages. The result was that in small towns across the country, banks began to fail in record numbers. Some of these failures involved small banks that had been founded with more hope than capital under the lax banking rules that prevailed during the early years of the century. But even large, established banks such as Bennett's were feeling the pressure. Between 1914 and 1920 there had been fewer than three hundred bank failures in the United States; between 1921 and 1926, that number jumped to more than twenty-two hundred. Minnesota was not immune to this trend. During the period from 1920 to 1926 about 235 banks failed in Minnesota, almost all of them in rural areas.[29]

In 1911 Sullivan had written to Bennett: "Your bold but cautious methods will some day make you a rich man." But during the war years and after, Bennett did not always exercise caution in his financial affairs. In fact, both Carl and Guy Bennett seem to have been caught up in the speculative spirit of the 1920s, judging from the number of investment schemes they were involved in during the decade. Among other things, they were doing test drilling for iron ore in northern Minnesota on some property they had financed, at least in part, through legally questionable means. In this case, a district court judge later ruled that Guy had improperly used more than twenty thousand dollars in trust money that was supposed to have been invested in first-class mortgages. The court found that Guy instead funneled some of the money through the bank's janitor, who was used as a dummy, so that it could be invested in iron ore land owned by Carl. Later, the Bennetts defaulted on their own mortgage on the property, foreclosed on it, and then had the bank buy it back. The original investor knew of none of these dealings. The court found these activities violated the trust agreement and ordered all of the trust money to be repaid.[30]

Besides their banking interests, Carl and Guy Bennett were also active in the stock market through an investment firm known as L. L. Bennett and Sons. Court records from numerous lawsuits later filed against the brothers indicate that they sometimes placed clients' money in highly speculative investments. Moreover, in some cases they apparently disguised their losses by making dividend payments out of bank funds. There were also allegations in another lawsuit that Carl backdated a stock certificate in an effort to recoup the losses of a client whose money Bennett had invested in an automobile manufacturing firm that went bankrupt.[31]

These risky and ill-advised investments may well have been an attempt on the Bennetts' part to raise some quick cash in hopes of helping their faltering bank. By the early 1920s, Carl must have realized that his bank, the oldest and once the largest in Steele County, was in very serious difficulty. Published bank statements from this time pointed to the heart of the trouble: too many of the bank's assets were tied up in mortgages and other loans to farmers, many of whom were unable to meet monthly payments because of depressed crop prices. Whereas in 1907 less than 15 percent of the bank's assets were in loans, by the mid 1920s that figure jumped to 50 percent. Yet Bennett apparently was reluctant to foreclose on his farm customers, even though the bank was in mounting jeopardy. As the bank's portfolio of bad loans grew, its deposits shrank, dropping from $2.3 million in 1920 to about $1.4 million in 1926.[32]

The Bennetts kept up appearances, although by 1926 the situation was becoming critical. The bank's advertising campaign during this period tried to strike a note of confidence. A typical advertisement in January 1926 carried the headline, "Farmers on Top Again," and cited figures purporting to show that the farm depression was finally coming to an end. At the annual meeting of the bank's board of directors that month, Carl painted an optimistic picture:

We made good progress during the past year and conditions for this year are very satisfactory, the outlook for 1926 being especially good. The purchasing power of the farmer has been restored, we have passed thru [sic] the cycle of five bad years and now seem due for five good years. The best authorities agree that the farming business is in for at least five continuous years of prosperity, which means better conditions in Steele county.

There is practically no demand for short time loans, deposits are on the increase and rates of interest are bound to decline as a result. The thing which has distinguished the banking business during the past year has been the carrying of large cash reserves and readily salable securities.[33]

But he was whistling in the dark. The bank's quarterly statements, published in the local newspapers, showed its increasingly unsound condition. By this time, about two-thirds of the bank's assets were tied up in loans or in real estate, including the bank building itself. As a result, the bank had few assets readily convertible to cash in the event of trouble. And trouble quickly came. Sometime in the spring of 1926 there was apparently a run on the bank. A quarterly statement from this period shows that its deposits payable on demand dropped by more than one hundred thousand dollars or close to 15 percent between mid-April and mid-July. Later that summer, farmers in North and South Dakota defaulted on several large loans, further weakening the bank's financial position.[34]

Meanwhile, there were other events in Owatonna that may have affected the bank's stability. In August the Ku Klux Klan, then a significant force in Minnesota, held its annual state "konklave" in Owatonna. More than five hundred robed Klansmen marched through the town on the night of August 8, the crimson glow of railroad fuses lighting their way along streets jammed with curious onlookers. In later years, Lydia Bennett linked this event to the bank's troubles, suggesting that false rumors about the Bennetts being involved in the Klan may have caused Catholics to take their money out of the bank. "It was such a strange thing, wasn't it, to have a thing like that be the cause of closing a bank," she told an interviewer. Yet the bank's financial troubles were so deep-seated that the Klan activities cannot have been more than a minor factor in its growing insolvency.[35]

On September 2, the bank ran its usual two-column advertisement in the Owatonna *People's Press*. Headlined "An Asset of Good Fortune," the advertisement said: "That man is best prepared for Opportunity and for Success who has built for himself over a period of years, the friendship of a strong, helpful bank. . . . Such a friendship might prove to be a 'priceless asset' to you some day. Let's get better acquainted." There was not much time left for getting acquainted, however. On September 7, Carl and Guy Bennett, along with the bank's board of directors, drove to Minneapolis for a meeting with federal examiners. Lydia Bennett had prepared a large picnic lunch for her husband that morning, but he left it behind in his rush to get to Minneapolis. As it turned out, a missed lunch was to be the least of his worries that day. The news from the examiners was grim. In going over the bank's ledger sheets, they quickly diagnosed the bank's fundamental problem, which was an acute shortage of cash caused by depositor withdrawals, defaulted loans, and too many assets "frozen" in farm mortgages and real estate. One of the examiners told Bennett: "I have been after you for eighteen months to get up your [cash] reserve. Either get it up immediately or I'll close your bank tomorrow morning."[36]

All told, the bank needed to raise three hundred thousand dollars at once. The Bennetts, as majority stockholders, agreed to throw their personal funds into the bank – stocks, bonds, cash, everything they had – in an attempt to save it. But it was not nearly enough. As the meeting dragged on into the evening, the Bennetts realized that their situation was hopeless. At ten o'clock, Carl Bennett convened what was to be the last meeting of the board of directors of the National Farmers' Bank. By a unanimous vote, the board decided to suspend business, effective immediately. The bank, fifty-three years old, was one of the largest to go under in Minnesota during the 1920s, and its failure left Carl Bennett a ruined man.[37]

The next day a crowd quickly gathered in front of the bank as word spread through town about what had happened. The bank was locked, and the only explanation was provided by a handwritten note, affixed to the door, that said: "Bank closed, by order of the Board of Directors. The National Bank examiner has taken full charge." The closing of the bank caught most of its more than three thousand depositors by surprise. It was the first bank failure in Owatonna in fifty-five years, and it was a severe blow to a community where thrift was regarded as one of the supreme virtues.[38]

Almost at once, rumors began circulating. There was one story that the Bennetts or other bank employees had looted the safe-deposit boxes before the bank was closed. There was also a suggestion that embezzlement by the bank's officers had caused it to fail. These rumors became so widespread that the government-appointed receiver of the bank, Herbert E. Skinner, finally felt constrained to lay them to rest in an interview with the *Journal-Chronicle*. Skinner pointed out that it would require two keys, one held by the depositor and one by the bank, to open any safe-deposit box. As for the embezzlement theory, Skinner said there was simply no evidence of dishonesty on the part of any of the bank's officers. Moreover, a federal bank examiner was later quoted as saying that the failure "was the cleanest in his experience."[39]

For Bennett, there was nothing to do but to weather the storm and hope that, somehow, he could begin to reassemble the shattered remains of his life. The bank's failure had affected, in one way or another, almost everyone in town, and there was much bitterness in its wake. Bennett's cultural aspirations, along with his patrician lifestyle, had made him enemies in Owatonna, and there were those who felt that he had received a well-deserved comeuppance. But there were also some old friends, such as Buxton, who stood beside Bennett and consistently supported him in the long and draining ordeal that was to follow.[40]

The ignominy of presiding over a failed bank was brought home to Bennett in many ways. Only a day after the bank closed, the Owatonna library board was forced to pass an emergency resolution to borrow one thousand dollars to make up for funds frozen in the bank. Bennett was then a member of the board, as he had been for twenty-five years, and it must have hurt him deeply to see the library system put in financial jeopardy by the failure of his own bank. He must have felt embarrassment, too, over the hundreds of Owatonna school children whose small savings accounts were threatened by the bank's failure. The Owatonna school board, perhaps fearing an outbreak of youthful improvidence, soon announced that the town's other two banks would make good the children's losses. "Members of the board are agreed," the *Journal-Chronicle* reported, "that there shall be no loss to the children and consequent blow to the schools' efforts to build up habits of thrift among the younger generation."[41]

Although a large percentage of the bank's listed assets were later found to be dubious or worthless, attempts were made to reorganize it during the fall of 1926. On September 25, about sixteen hundred of the bank's depositors met to discuss the situation. It appears to have been a surprisingly cool-headed gathering. The *Journal-Chronicle* reported that "only a very few [depositors] were inclined to somewhat hysterical outbreaks regarding the bank and its officers and affairs." At the meeting, a committee of seven local businessmen and civic leaders was named to investigate the possibility of reorganization. On October 30, depositors held another meeting and voted unanimously to reorganize the bank through the sale of $150,000 worth of new stock, but the efforts to reopen the bank eventually petered out. There was bickering among the depositors, and the money needed to put the bank on sound footing simply could not be raised.[42]

After the bank failed, Guy Bennett was hired by Buxton, who was the president of a large insurance company in Owatonna. Carl stayed on at the bank, helping to preside over the dissolution of his life's work. The bank's safe-deposit vault remained open to customers, and Bennett worked in that department while also assisting Skinner in the task of liquidating the bank's assets. His daughter Arabella recalled that she never heard her father complain, despite all that had happened. "Father was so stoic and brave," she said. "I don't think he ever felt sorry for himself."[43]

Adding to his woes was a flood of lawsuits. More than twenty suits were filed against Carl or Guy or both in the years following the bank's failure. Some of the suits alleged that the Bennetts had improperly invested money on behalf of clients; others simply sought payment of debts owed by the Bennetts. But few, if any, of the numerous judgments obtained against them were ever satisfied because both brothers quickly went bankrupt. They filed for bankruptcy in federal court in December 1926 and were declared bankrupt in September 1927.[44]

By 1927 Carl Bennett was hopelessly insolvent. His salary of six thousand dollars a year as bank president was gone, and virtually everything he owned was tied up in the bank receivership. Under the bankruptcy laws, he was allowed to keep his small house on Main Street. But since he no longer had any use for the big lot next door on which he had planned to build his new house, he donated the property to Pillsbury Academy.[45]

Bennett's problems continued to mount in 1928, when he suffered a nervous breakdown under the strain of events. One event that must have been especially painful was the sale of his beloved bank building at auction, which took place in nearby Waseca, Minnesota, on April 30. Both the bank and its adjoining building were put up for sale. The high bidders were Carrie, Mark, and Donald Alexander, members of a prominent Owatonna family that already owned a good deal of property in town. The purchase price was sixty-three thousand dollars, about half of what it had cost to construct the buildings. Several months later, the Alexanders began negotiations to sell the bank building to the Security State Bank of Owatonna, which for many years had done business in rented quarters across the street from Bennett's bank. The deal was completed in March 1929. The purchase price finally agreed on was thirty-five thousand dollars, a bargain by any standard.[46]

Meanwhile, Bennett's attorneys had managed to fend off most of his creditors, but there was one large lawsuit that still hung over his head. The suit had been brought by an elderly Owatonna man, E. C. Moulton, for whom Bennett and his bank had invested a sum of seventy thousand dollars since 1922. The investments had all turned sour, and Moulton wanted his money back. He eventually agreed, however, to accept a cash settlement of nineteen thousand dollars. Of this amount, sixty-five hundred dollars was to come from Bennett himself. Bennett was able to raise about half the amount by selling his home. To scrape together the

THE CURVE OF THE ARCH/144

remaining money, Bennett's wife and brother decided to appeal directly to friends. Among those who were asked to help was William Purcell, who in March 1929 received a long letter from Mrs. Bennett. The letter, which Bennett may not have been aware of, provides the only detailed account of his personal and financial problems in the years immediately following the bank failure. The letter began with a description of the Moulton suit and the trouble it was causing Bennett:

Because of the love and loyalty to Mr. Bennett which you have shown on so many occasions and in so many ways, I have the boldness to write to you now to ask you to help him in this, his greatest hour of need. You are doubtless well aware of the trail of troubles always resulting from the closing of a bank – our bank liquidation has proven no exception to this rule. All have been successfully overcome now, except one – the case of an old man who refuses either to be pacified or to be reasonable.

Through a technicality, he has finally succeeded in bringing suit against the bank and Mr. Bennett to recover some $80000 [actually $70,000, according to court records] in cash he claims to have placed in their hands from time to time. His claims are absurd, but it is one of those cases where a technicality has power to turn the tide the wrong way. So Mr. Bennett's lawyers have been using every effort in their power to bring about a cash settlement. The bank Receiver has consented to give $12500, taking Mr. Bennett's personal note (to be paid on monthly installments) for $1250 of this amount; we are to sell our home and turn in the equity of $3500 (there is a mortgage on it for $3500); there still remains $3000 to be raised to meet the demands of the old man. There is no way to raise this except by an appeal to friends.

Mr. Bennett's brother has very kindly undertaken with my assistance, to raise this amount by this means. It occurred to us that because of your happy associations with Mr. Bennett in the past, because you have always been congenial spirits in your love and appreciation of beauty in all its aspects, because you have always been devoted friends, you might wish to help him in his present extremity by contributing a sum to assist in the raising of the $3000 or by loaning him some amount on his personal note with the understanding that if he should succeed in getting back financially he would pay this note as fast as he was able.[47]

After making her appeal, Mrs. Bennett went on to describe her husband's emotional problems and his efforts to begin a new career, at age sixty, as a stockbroker in New York:

Unfortunately, Mr. Bennett had a nervous break-down last spring due to the terrible strain and to his sensitiveness of nature, so that we placed the mortgage for $3500 on our home to enable him to go to a Sanitarium for treatment. He remained there a month, not long enough but as long as he dared financially, then went to New York to study stock manipulations at first hand. He had always been a close student of stocks and bonds and hoped to get into this kind of work in some way to eventually recoup his finances. He was too much exhausted to do much for a time, but finally went to work to learn the game where it was being played to the limit. By August he felt prepared to attempt speculation on a margin and started in with the $1800 he now had left. He has succeeded so astonishingly that he has been able to support himself in New York and yet keep intact his $1800. His lawyers insist that this must be kept as an "emergency fund" until he can find a position which will enable him to support himself and family.[48]

The decision to go to New York must have been an agonizing one for Bennett. For one thing, his wife had been seriously ill with heart trouble for several years and was for the most part confined to bed. "I was not yet able to be downstairs when Mr. Bennett left [for New York]," she told Purcell in her letter, "but we all insisted that he must go." Bennett's move was made easier by the fact that his daughter Arabella had gone to New York a month earlier and was then working at the Saks Fifth Avenue store. Later, another of Bennett's daughters, Sylvia, also joined him in New York.

In the meantime, Mrs. Bennett and the couple's youngest daughter, Lydia, remained in Owatonna. Mrs. Bennett reported in her letter to Purcell that she had managed to "keep things going" by collecting old loans owed to her husband. "So you see," she wrote, "not one of us has been lacking in courage or initiative and we have lived to the utmost for the sake of each other. We should have been able to maintain our independence and get established soon in New York together had not this most distressing suit suddenly loomed on the horizon. . . . Mr. Purcell, we do not want you to do anything which will bring you any hardship but we shall deeply appreciate any cooperation which you can give us in our supreme effort in Mr. Bennett's behalf. . . . A man of Mr. Bennett's proud spirit would never ask help for himself, but his brother and I are willing to do even this for one we love."

Two weeks later Purcell replied that he was strapped for cash himself as a result of some poor real estate investments and could not help out. But other friends were able to provide some financial assistance. Even Elmslie, who seldom had any money to spare, chipped in two hundred dollars at one point. In fact, Mrs. Bennett's appeals on behalf of her husband were so successful that the three thousand dollars needed to settle the Moulton suit was raised by April 1, 1929, when the settlement was approved by a district court judge.[49]

Yet Bennett never really recovered financially from the bank failure. Court records show, for instance, that he managed to repay only $25.00 on the $1,250.00 loan he had secured from the bank's receiver in connection with the Moulton suit. Eventually, the receiver was forced to sue Bennett in a futile effort to collect the balance owed on the loan. Meanwhile, Bennett continued to speculate in the stock market but without any long-term success. He apparently was wiped out several months before the Great Crash occurred because he returned to Minnesota in the summer of 1929 to look for work. He finally obtained a job in Northfield at Carleton College, on whose board of trustees he had once sat. Despite all that had happened, Bennett maintained a mantle of optimism. In August he wrote to Purcell describing his situation:

I remained in New York City until about the middle of June when I left there and joined hands with Carleton College on the basis of a very kind and helpful proposal made to me by Dr. Cowling, the President of the College.

I disliked to leave New York very much. But I was without any cash capital with which to work and since it was a question of employment and work with some one anyway, I decided that it was more desirable to work with friends than with strangers. . . . My work is not definite[ly]-outlined as yet. But it will be in the nature of financial and probably connected with the treasurers office in some manner. Thus far I am enjoying my life and work very much. My family are here with me and we shall live in a small and very old house right next to the home of the president of the college.

I miss being in business. A salary is a fixed amount and is never enough. I thank you very much for your helpful suggestion to Mr. Price [a friend of Purcell's] and I wish I might have been in New York at the time of his return. Investment Securities is my line and I am well posted therein. I could do research work or sell securities. . . .

I am feeling well and have put my former troubles out of my mind and am looking forward to the future with hope and confidence.

I really long for a life in New York. Why is it that when we are young we don't go to the place where we know that we ought to go?[50]

The wistful final paragraph of Bennett's letter was undoubtedly a reference to his decision as a young man to return to Owatonna to work in his father's bank, rather than to seek the career in music that had been his true desire. Bennett stayed in Northfield for several months, until a new tragedy struck. In November his oldest daughter Beatrice died of peritonitis at age twenty-four. Bennett returned to Owatonna to bury her in the family plot, and it may well have been the last time that he ever visited the town where he had spent almost all of his life.[51]

Bennett remained in Northfield until early 1930 when he moved to Minneapolis to work as the assistant manager of a small candy company. About a year later, however, Carleton College rehired him. The college owned several apartment buildings in Minneapolis, and Bennett was to manage them. He was well into his sixties by this time, and the work was something of a strain, since it involved operating the buildings' boilers and doing other maintenance chores. He was earning enough money to get by, but because there were still more than a dozen court judgments pending against him, his financial situation remained precarious.

About 1935, Bennett had to give up his job because of poor health. When his family began noticing signs of senility, he was taken to a doctor. The diagnosis was congenital hardening of the arteries, and the family was told that the condition would only get worse. Bennett suffered from increasing mental confusion and once wandered off all day on a streetcar, causing the family much worry. By the following year, he was in need of constant care. The family did not have the money to pay for care in a private home, and so the painful decision was made to commit him to the state hospital in Hastings, Minnesota. There, among red brick buildings he sometimes mistook for those at Harvard, he spent the last years of his life.[52]

He was a patient at Hastings on March 8, 1939, when the books of the National Farmers' Bank were closed for good, after the receiver had paid out approximately sixty cents on the dollar to the bank's former depositors. He was at Hastings when his farm south of Owatonna was sold to pay off debts. And he was at Hastings in 1940 when Security Bank officials decided to "modernize" their famous little building and in the process destroyed some of its finest features. It is unlikely that Bennett comprehended any of these events, and that was perhaps the only redeeming feature of the illness which finally took his life. He lingered on at the hospital until August 29, 1941, when he died at age seventy-two.

There was a five-paragraph obituary the next day on the back page of the Owatonna *Daily People's Press.* The headline identified him simply as a "former local resident." Bennett was buried a few days later beside his parents and his oldest daughter in a hillside cemetery overlooking Maple Creek in Owatonna, just a mile from the building that is his monument. His gravestone is very plain, for he was, as Oskar Gross remembered, "a man that wanted simplicity." It was left to George Elmslie to offer some final thoughts on this remarkable small-town banker whose vision had made possible the creation of a magnificent work of art. Elmslie wrote to Mrs. Bennett:

That was sad news that your Arabella conveyed to me 10 days ago. . . .
Doubtless in view of his illness it is all for the best. Carl was a man of the real
old school and I was very fond of him. His memory will linger with me all my
remaining days. Upright, generous to a fault as well as being a very able man.
There were few like him. The world is poorer for his absence from the things
he could do so well. My sisters join me in sympathy for you in the loss of your
Carl.[53]

Elmslie had experienced his own share of tribulations after his partnership with Purcell ended in 1922. His whole life had been an attempt to
climb out of poverty, but he never really made it. The breakup with
Purcell forced Elmslie to try to make a living on his own, a task for which
he was ill suited. He had little business sense and lacked the aggressive
temperament needed to compete for and win commissions. Still, a few
jobs came his way, even though – as Purcell observed – "the fire had gone
out of his soul." During the 1920s, Elmslie's commissions included a
savings and loan building in Topeka, Kansas; a home, a chapel, a small
bank, and a gas company building in Illinois; and several buildings for
Yankton College in South Dakota. All of these works show traces of
Elmslie's great skill as a designer, but they also bear witness to how much
he missed the guiding hand of Sullivan and, later, Purcell.[54]

Elmslie's deficiencies as a solo designer are apparent in the six-story
Capitol Building and Loan Association Building in Topeka. This building – the largest of Elmslie's independent career – is surely one of the
oddest creations of the Prairie School. The lower two stories are reminiscent of Purcell and Elmslie's small banks, while the four floors above
with their continuous columns and recessed, heavily ornamented spandrels seem to come from one of Sullivan's skyscrapers. This unusual
combination is then topped with a steep gable roof, perhaps harkening
back to some of Sullivan's early commercial designs or even to the gable-
roofed houses Purcell was so fond of. All told, it is a building of fascinating parts that do not quite come together, which is the problem Elmslie always had when he worked alone.[55]

Unable to support himself with the few commissions he had during
the 1920s, Elmslie began to rely increasingly on periodic checks from
Purcell. Elmslie also depended on his sister Edith, who worked for *Interiors* magazine and helped support two sisters in addition to her brother.
The onset of the depression in 1929 further reduced their circumstances
as new construction virtually came to a halt. Elmslie, in fact, managed
just three commissions in the 1930s: an additional building at Yankton
College and high schools in Indiana and Illinois designed in association

Elmslie during the latter part of his career

with architect William S. Hutton. Elmslie apparently did some other work as an anonymous designer, but it brought in only a small amount of money.[56]

During these years, Elmslie became the official keeper of the Sullivan legend, an assignment he seems to have approached with mixed feelings. He had been named the executor of Sullivan's estate and was thus in a position to preserve some of Sullivan's most valuable papers, including his meticulously maintained diary. Instead, Elmslie threw out the diary, as well as other Sullivan papers, in what seems to have been an act of both love and revenge. Elmslie sincerely believed, as his letters make clear, that the often unpleasant aspects of Sullivan's personal life should not become fair game for historians. An intensely private man himself, Elmslie felt Sullivan was entitled to the same privacy, even after death. Complaining of Wright's account in his *Autobiography* of Sullivan's last days, Elmslie wrote: "How delicate, and as an act of grace, it would have been to have dropped a veil over those last days and kept them from the curious public gaze." Later, in another letter to Purcell, Elmslie commented: "Let him [Sullivan] be expressed as he was and not as expressed in lapses of later years." In this same letter, Elmslie explained why he had torn up so many documents: "I did not, believe me, do anything impatiently. . . . There was a welter in the office and I was sick at heart to a depth you cannot know about the end of things for me."[57]

At the same time, it seems likely that Elmslie, who felt he never received proper credit for his work with Sullivan, may have destroyed the diary as a way of striking back at the man in whose shadow he had labored for so long. Purcell described Elmslie as being "emotionally torn" by his loyalty to Sullivan on the one hand and his deep-seated resentment on the other. That resentment, according to Purcell, stemmed from the fact that Sullivan had never made Elmslie his partner. Elmslie seldom expressed his negative feelings toward Sullivan, but every so often in his letters to Purcell he would vent his frustrations. "I have thought so much about Sullivan, all of my life practically, and gave so much of it *to him* that I am sick and tired about the whole business," he wrote in one letter, and that may well have been the way he was feeling when he discarded Sullivan's diary. Elmslie's ambivalence also surfaced in his rather half-hearted efforts at designing a suitable tombstone for Sullivan. He had been asked by a special committee of architects to design the memorial, but he dallied with the assignment for so long that another architect had to be called in to do the work.[58]

In addition to his other troubles, Elmslie had to contend with the activities of Wright, who manipulated historical fact and architectural space with equal aplomb. Wright's *Autobiography* appeared in 1932, and in it he depicted himself as Sullivan's most beloved pupil while ignoring or belittling just about everyone else who had ever worked for Sullivan, including Elmslie. For the most part, Elmslie kept quiet about all of this, as was his way. He did, however, express his anger periodically in letters to Purcell and others. Comparing Sullivan and Wright, Elmslie wrote that "the one [Sullivan] walked in the sun like a man, the other preferred devious ways." In another letter, Elmslie called Wright "an unprincipled egoist, a liar and a cheat." Wright was also an architect of extraordinary genius, as Elmslie—to his enduring credit—was always the first to admit.[59]

Elmslie's patience finally ran out in 1936 when Wright wrote a mean-spirited review of Hugh Morrison's biography of Sullivan, which had been published the year before. Among other things, Wright suggested that Elmslie's work was part of the "backwash" of Sullivan's career. This gratuitous observation prompted Elmslie to compose a long letter to Wright in which he defended, with beautifully controlled anger, both his own work and that of Sullivan. The letter concluded: "You, of course, *are* a great genius, and no one knows this better than I. But I do bespeak entrance into your mind of the still, small voice of truth, of fair play, dignity, and high honor, and the exit of your strange claims of omniscience when you come to write on a great Master [Sullivan] and an infinitely greater man than yourself."[60]

Meanwhile, Elmslie in 1935 obtained his last commission of any significance when he and Hutton designed a high school in Hammond, Illinois. Elmslie was by then sixty-four years old, a tired and melancholy old man, and a very poor one, too. "I am totally cleaned out and in debt now," he had written to a friend some months before, and his financial situation continued to deteriorate through the 1930s. Purcell reported in April 1938 that Elmslie and his sisters "are in desperate need of money," and that seems to have been true for the rest of Elmslie's life. In 1939, Elmslie was nearly evicted from his small office in Chicago because of failure to pay the rent, and about his only regular income came from the checks sent monthly by Purcell. "Our budget is such that we have to pare corners off everything," he wrote Purcell in 1939. "My personal expenses for several years include 21 cents for lunch and 10 cents for two cigars which I somehow need to smoke."[61]

During these years, Elmslie increasingly became a man living in the past. In 1939, he wrote to Purcell: "Memories are beautiful and definite entities and I thank God for them, as they are all I possess." As Elmslie moved into his seventies, there was one memory in particular that continued to haunt him, for he still mourned his wife, dead for more than thirty years. "How happy we two were. How happy, and no fear, infinite hope," he wrote to Purcell in 1943. Three years later, her memory still burned in his mind. "Lord of life! How I miss my sweet, now more than ever," he wrote. "What a life it would have been, with ease and peace in our old age."[62]

As he surveyed the architectural scene in his old age, Elmslie found little to please him. "How futile seems most of the new work at home and abroad," he wrote. "There seems so little of an animating spirit behind it. It is so dry; so composed; so set. . . . It needs a resurgence of the spirit of the real pioneer, the lyric poet, the romanticist, the clairvoyant – Sullivan – to animate it, to give it vertebrate life." But the International Style, with its sleek but cold glass boxes, was soon to sweep all before it, leaving Elmslie as a lonely voice from a vanished era.[63]

In 1946, however, Elmslie did receive at least one piece of cheering news when the American Institute of Architects awarded a long-overdue gold medal to Sullivan. Elmslie was invited to receive the posthumous award but was too ill to travel to the ceremonies in Miami Beach. Instead, he sent some written comments in which he extolled Sullivan's achievements. Yet it is doubtful that many of those who listened to Elmslie's comments that night knew what he had done long ago when he – far more than Wright – was "the pencil in the Master's hand." Not long after the ceremonies, Elmslie learned that the Owatonna bank, one of the great achievements of his collaboration with Sullivan, had been brutally remodeled. Elmslie was especially grieved to hear that the tellers' wickets – possibly the most beautiful creations ever to flow from his pencil – had been removed from the banking room and sold for scrap. "It seems to be the order of the day to throw away the precious things to prepare for the new. So passes [sic] the grilles," he wrote to Purcell. "It sickens me."[64]

In his final years, the great hope of Elmslie's life was that he might be able to return to his homeland for one last visit, "to dream in the shadows of my ancient hills." He wrote: "Ah me, I'd like to see it all once more, and hear the curlews calling on the windswept moors. 'Hame, Hame, Hame, I fain would be where the oak and the ash and the bonnie birchen tree are a growin green the north countrie. Hame, dearie, hame.' A young Scot with a fine tenor used to sing that to us in Chicago years ago." But Elmslie never made it home. Crippled with arthritis and suffering from heart disease, he hung on into his eighties, long enough at least to learn that his work had not been entirely forgotten. The Walker Art Center in Minneapolis was planning an exhibit of Purcell and Elmslie's work in 1953, but Elmslie did not live to see it. He died in Chicago on April 23, 1952, at age eighty-one and was buried three days later in Graceland Cemetery, beside his lost Bonnie.[65]

7

A TRUE AND LASTING WORK OF ART

I have often likened your [Sullivan's] work to that of the great musicians or poets, and have thought of ourselves as though we possessed exclusively . . . one of the symphonies of Beethoven. This feeling is what led me to write that there is an air of finality to all your works. This is absolutely true. — Carl Bennett[1]

THE "AIR OF FINALITY" that Bennett associated with his bank turned out to be very short-lived. For when Bennett lost his building, the structure was deprived of an owner who would never have allowed it to be ill used. By contrast, the owners who took over in 1929 appear to have been largely ignorant of the building's special qualities. They did not really understand what they had gained, nor did they appreciate how much they could lose by tampering with Sullivan and Elmslie's creation. The result was that within eleven years of becoming the Security State Bank, the building was grievously damaged by remodeling. Some changes in the banking room were inevitable, given the growth of the bank through the years. But the work done by the Security Bank in 1940 was so extensive, so utterly inept, and so out of keeping with the character of the building that it destroyed forever the opportunity of future generations to experience the banking room as Sullivan and Elmslie had designed it. Their original concept survives only in a few black-and-white photographs that serve as graphic reminders of what was lost.[2]

The president of the Security State Bank during this period was Paul Evans, who had been involved in banking in Owatonna since 1904. Like

Bennett, Evans came from an old Yankee family. His father, Norman Evans, was a New York native who migrated to Minnesota in 1878 and operated general stores in several small communities before establishing a business in Owatonna in 1890. The elder Evans began his banking career in 1898 when he purchased a bank in the nearby town of Dodge Center. A few years later Paul, his oldest son, joined him in the business. In 1907 the two men bought a controlling interest in the Security State Bank of Owatonna. It was then the smallest bank in town, with assets of only three hundred thousand dollars. Under the Evanses' management, the bank grew steadily and had assets of more than $2 million by the early 1920s. Norman Evans remained president of the bank until his death in 1922. Paul, who had been the bank's cashier for many years, then became president.[3]

Paul Evans's life in many ways resembled Carl Bennett's. Both men were born into the upper class in Owatonna, both graduated from Pillsbury Academy, and both became presidents of family-owned banks. Both men also did the sorts of things expected of pillars of the business community. Like Bennett, Evans was a Republican in his politics, active in civic affairs (he served on the Owatonna school board from 1916 to 1924), and a member of all the appropriate organizations, including the Masons and the Owatonna Commercial Club. Unfortunately, Evans's many virtues apparently did not include an appreciation of the unique qualities of Sullivan and Elmslie's bank building.[4]

The availability of Bennett's bank building after 1926 must have struck Evans as a piece of heaven-sent good fortune, for at that very time, he was searching for a new home for his bank. Since its founding, the Security Bank had been located in rented quarters in the Kelley Block, a three-story building across Cedar Street from Bennett's bank. By the mid-1920s, however, the Security Bank's quarters had become so cramped that Evans began looking for more space. His initial idea was to purchase the entire Kelley Block, and in 1926 he made an offer of eighty thousand dollars for the building. But the owner held out for a higher price, so Evans then considered building a new bank, which he estimated would cost at least sixty-five thousand dollars.[5]

Any idea Evans had of erecting a new bank quickly disappeared once Bennett's building came on the market. Here was a first-class bank building located at the most desirable business corner in town and available at an unbelievably low price. In a memorandum written in 1926, Evans had estimated the value of the National Farmers' Bank building at $125,000. Yet he was able to purchase it three years later for just thirty-five thousand dollars. Evans must have been, as the old phrase goes, laughing all the way to the bank. Yet a windfall can sometimes have unfortunate consequences, and the bargain-basement price for which the building was obtained may help explain why it was treated so shabbily by Evans in the years to come.[6]

The first remodeling of the bank was done in 1929 before the new owners moved in. This work involved relatively minor alterations in the arrangement of the banking room in order to meet the Security Bank's specific needs. One of the changes entailed a restructuring of the bank's vault, located along the east wall. As originally built, the vault was divided into two sections—one for money and the other for bookkeeping items. The Security Bank, however, had the partition removed so that the entire vault could be used for money, and bookkeeping items were moved to the basement. At the same time, a new door was created on the north side of the vault. Both old doors were then bricked in. In addition, the interior of the vault was lined with new steel plating as a security measure. The result was a larger, stronger money vault; however, this work had the unfortunate effect of removing an important visual element—the money vault door—from the banking room.

As part of the 1929 remodeling, several of the rooms arranged around the bank lobby were assigned new uses. The women's room along the north wall became the trust department. Various service departments were placed in what had been the bank officers' area along the south wall, and a spiral staircase was constructed to link these departments to the new bookkeeping vault in the basement. Another change involved the tellers' wicket located between the women's room and the savings department. The Security Bank had this wicket moved to the right side of the tellers' enclosure in front of the money vault, thereby creating an extra teller's window in the banking room.

While these changes affected the functional use of the banking room, they had little impact on its appearance. All of Sullivan and Elmslie's original fixtures and furnishings remained intact, as did the basic floor plan of the room. When the remodeling work was completed in early September, the Security Bank officially opened for business in its new quarters. For the next decade there were no significant alterations in the banking room. Then, much of the beautiful interior on which Sullivan and Elmslie had lavished so much care was destroyed in the name of "modernization."[7]

On March 22, 1940, the Owatonna *Daily People's Press* reported that work had begun on remodeling the banking room of the Security Bank and Trust Company: "Several corners will be eliminated . . . and added working space will be made available as a result of the change, with greater convenience to be effected for both employees and patrons of the bank. A design of marble and walnut will predominate in the new glass cages, an increased number of which will appear both in the savings and tellers departments. Streamlined effects will be noted in the modern designs."[8]

This work was undertaken in an effort to create more space in the banking room. When Bennett built the bank, he had only about eight employees. By 1940, however, the Security Bank probably employed at least twice that number. To enlarge its working space, the bank decided to remove virtually all of the brick enclosures that defined the perimeter of the bank lobby; only those along the west wall, to either side of the front entrance, remained intact. The enclosures, as originally designed, were capped with a band of green terra-cotta blocks. These blocks were simply discarded, although some of them were discovered sixteen years later piled on the back lot of the Owatonna building contractor who did the 1940 remodeling. In its ruthless quest for modernization, the bank also tossed out a number of ornamental light fixtures that had originally been positioned around the banking room. Nor were Elmslie's magnificent tellers' wickets spared. They were removed and sold to an Owatonna scrap dealer, who in turn apparently disposed of them to collectors around the country. To replace the brick enclosures, the bank installed low marble-and-walnut tellers' counters, of the sort found in a thousand other banks. The bank then used wooden pilasters to cover the scars left by the removal of the enclosures.[9]

None of this work was done by an architect. Instead, the bank simply hired a contractor and a bank fixtures firm and let them prepare plans for the remodeling. From a purely aesthetic point of view, the remodeling was a disaster. The nondescript fixtures installed at floor level clashed with the lush ornament of the banking room's upper walls, destroying the decorative scheme so carefully worked out by Sullivan, Elmslie, and Millet. The loss of the brick tellers' enclosure in front of the vault also left the lobby without a focal point. About the only survivor of this wholesale destruction was Elmslie's bronze and terra-cotta clock, which was left to occupy a rather forlorn perch atop the vault.[10]

These ill-conceived "improvements" not only failed to meet the bank's functional needs, but also created new problems – particularly with lighting – that had to be dealt with in another remodeling just fifteen years later. When the brick enclosures were ripped out, so too were the wall lights Sullivan and Elmslie had designed to illuminate work areas for tellers and other bank employees. It eventually dawned on Security Bank officials that they would have to find some new way of providing ade-

The clock wall was stripped of the brick tellers' enclosures, the terra-cotta ornament, and the magnificent wickets in 1940. Fluorescent lighting was then installed over the tellers' counters, and wooden pilasters were used to cover the scars left by removal of the brick enclosures.

quate lighting. Their solution was to install fluorescent lights on steel channels mounted over the tellers' counters and other work areas. These bright lights destroyed the softly glowing ambience of the banking room. Moreover, the fluorescent glare made it difficult for bank visitors to see and appreciate the ornament of the upper walls.

The irony of the 1940 remodeling is that it was a classic case of being penny-wise and pound-foolish. The bank left no corners uncut in its effort to remodel as cheaply as possible, and it is doubtful that more than

ten thousand dollars was spent on the project. In the process, the bank discarded fixtures and ornament that, by conservative estimate, would later be worth more than five hundred thousand dollars.

In January 1955 a new president took charge of the bank. Clifford C. Sommer went to Owatonna from Minneapolis, where he had been a vice-president of Midland National Bank. By his own admission, Sommer knew little about Sullivan or Elmslie or their famous bank building, but he was soon to receive an education. Sommer, however, knew banking very well, and when he walked into the Owatonna bank for the first time,

Visitors found it difficult to see and appreciate the bank's ornament because of the glare from the fluorescent lights.

he realized at once that something would have to be done. The problem so readily apparent to Sommer was an acute shortage of space. The original Sullivan and Elmslie cube contained about forty-six hundred square feet. By Sommer's calculation, that was approximately half the amount of floor space needed by a bank of the Security's size. About thirty employees were jammed into the bank, trying to do business in a structure that had been designed for less than a third of that number. Sommer felt that some of the crunch could be alleviated by reorganizing the banking room. But there was only so much space that could be created in this way, and it soon became clear to him that the bank would either have to burst the bounds of the original cube or find somewhere else to do business.[11]

There were two possible ways to expand – north or east. Going north would entail acquiring one or more of the nondescript commercial buildings along Cedar Street next to the bank. Going east would mean expanding into the two-story shop and office structure that had been built along with the bank. Early in 1955 A. Moorman and Company, a Minneapolis firm specializing in the design and renovation of bank buildings, was hired to begin studying possible expansion of the Owatonna bank. The company was then the architect for Northwest Bancorporation, which as the Owatonna bank's parent institution had to approve any expansion plans.[12]

The first plan prepared by Marlow Ihling of the Moorman firm in July 1955 was for a northward expansion. The proposal called for an opening to be punched through the north wall of the banking room beneath the large cow mural. Two adjacent buildings, which the bank hoped to rent or buy, could thus be connected to the banking room and provide space for the bank's bookkeeping and accounting departments on the ground floor. The arrangement of the banking room itself was also to be changed. Ihling's plan called for additional tellers' windows to be placed along the east wall in front of the vault, while the officers' work area was to be expanded along the south wall. These ideas were not entirely satisfactory to bank officials, however, so Ihling prepared a revised plan in September. This second proposal differed from the first mainly in that it called for demolishing the second building north of the bank to make room for a parking lot and drive-up tellers' windows. As it turned out, neither of Ihling's schemes received much consideration because the bank was unable to acquire or lease the two buildings at an acceptable price.[13]

With no opportunity to expand to the north, Sommer began examining a possible eastward expansion into the shop and office building, which had been owned since 1928 by the Alexander family of Owatonna.

The western part of this building, immediately adjacent to the bank, contained a shop on the ground floor with offices above. The eastern section, separated from the shop by an alley, housed the offices and printing plant of the *Owatonna Journal-Chronicle*. From the bank's point of view, an expansion into all or part of this building offered a number of advantages, even though expanding to the north might have been less costly. For one thing, the shop and office building had been designed to complement the bank. The building to the north, by contrast, was an undistinguished structure that would have been difficult to relate to the bank in a visually coherent way. Moreover, the shop and office building was of better quality construction than the building north of the bank. During 1955, Sommer began negotiating with the Alexanders to obtain all or part of the shop and office building. A deal eventually was struck by which the bank was able to lease the western part of the building for twenty years, with an option to buy the entire structure at the end of that period.[14]

Ihling, meanwhile, had been busy preparing a preliminary design for the eastward expansion. Completed in October 1955, his proposal became the basis for an extensive remodeling and renovation of the bank that began the next year. Ihling's plan called for a complete rearrangement of the banking room, beginning with the vault, which would be moved from the east wall and relocated in a toilet and storeroom area next to the northeast corner of the cube. Tellers' counters were to be installed in the area formerly occupied by the vault and along the south wall, which had been the bank officers' work area. The officers were then to be moved to an area along the north wall under the cow mural. In addition, the president's office was to be relocated from the southwest corner of the cube to the old farmers' exchange room north of the main entrance. The bank's bookkeeping, accounting, insurance, and installment loan offices, which had been located along the north wall of the banking room, were to be transferred into the newly leased building next door. Customer access to these departments was to be made easier by creating a second entrance to the bank on the south side at its juncture with the shop and office building. The part of this building leased by the bank was also to undergo extensive remodeling under Ihling's plan.[15]

Early in 1956, the bank's board of directors and the Northwest Bancorporation approved Ihling's plans. He was then authorized to prepare working drawings, which he completed in October. The bank set November 13 as the date for opening bids, but when the bank's plans were made public in late October, they caused something of a furor in architectural circles.

The year 1956 was the centennial of Sullivan's birth, and an exhibit of his work organized by the Art Institute of Chicago was touring the country. With Sullivan's achievements drawing considerable attention in Minnesota and elsewhere, the plans for remodeling one of his most famous buildings received close scrutiny. There were several aspects of Ihling's plan that critics found objectionable. To solve the lighting problems created by the 1940 remodeling, Ihling proposed to install a low ceiling around the perimeter of the banking room. Critics feared that the ceiling would make it difficult for visitors to see the rich ornament on the upper walls. Ihling's plan also drew fire because it made no provision for Elmslie's great clock, which would lose its place in the banking room once the vault was removed from the east wall. Stanton Catlin, a former curator of the Minneapolis Institute of Arts, offered another criticism, complaining that Ihling's plan would "introduce commercialistic elements" into the bank. Catlin, however, did not explain how a building devoted to the use and storage of money could avoid commercialism. The controversy over the remodeling plans eventually found its way into the newspapers, with an article appearing November 2 on the editorial page of the *Minneapolis Tribune.*[16]

One group especially concerned about the fate of the bank was the Minnesota Society of Architects, which on October 29 adopted a resolution requesting that a "Sullivan-school" architect be hired to assist in the remodeling. The society then formed a committee of architects and art historians to discuss the remodeling plans with Sommer. The committee met with Sommer in early November in a session that turned out to be fruitful for both sides. "I have nothing but high praise for the committee," Sommer said many years later. "They may have saved me from a serious mistake." For their part, committee members were pleased to discover that Sommer was more than willing to listen to their ideas.[17]

During the meeting, a number of architects were suggested as being qualified to advise on the remodeling, but all of them were eliminated from the running for one reason or another. "Well, who should we get?" Sommer asked at one point. "Frank Lloyd Wright?" The committee, however, was not interested in calling on Wright, then well into his eighties and as temperamental as ever. "We don't think you could get along with him," a committee member told Sommer. After a lengthy discussion, the committee finally recommended a suitable candidate for the remodeling job: Harwell Hamilton Harris, an architect practicing in Fort Worth, Texas.

Harris, then fifty-three, was a California native who had studied sculpture before turning to architecture. In the late 1920s, he had worked under Richard Neutra, an Austrian-born architect known for his International Style houses in southern California. Harris was employed in Neutra's Los Angeles office until 1932, when he set out on his own.

During the next twenty years, Harris produced a series of highly regarded houses, mainly in California. He was particularly fond of Wright's work but developed his own style in keeping with the informal quality of most California houses. Like Neutra and Wright, Harris showed himself especially adept at working with wood, a material he used liberally in many of his best designs. Perhaps Harris's most famous work before 1955 was the Havens House, a large two-story residence built in 1941 in Berkeley on a site overlooking San Francisco Bay. The house features an upward-soaring roof line and seems almost ready to take flight from its hillside setting. Harris had done little in the way of commercial design before coming to Owatonna, but he was familiar with the bank, having driven several hundred miles out of his way to see it while traveling through the Midwest in 1954.[18]

Following his meeting with the architects' committee, Sommer telephoned Harris and agreed to meet him in Chicago later that day. The two men spent the next three days together, including a weekend in Owatonna. "We would sit in the bank for hour after hour, talking and thinking," Sommer recalled. The result of these intense discussions was that Harris agreed to study the bank's remodeling plans and recommend changes where necessary. Harris then returned to Fort Worth to begin work. In the meantime, bid opening for the project was delayed until November 30 to give Harris time to review Ihling's plans.[19]

For Harris, the commission was unusual in that the basic plan of the remodeling effort had already been approved, thus limiting his options. He was able to make a number of recommendations, however, that greatly improved the quality of the remodeling by helping to preserve the spirit of the building. His first recommendation, a particularly fine one, was to retain Elmslie's clock in its original position. This could be done, Harris determined, by creating a balcony over the area that would be vacated by the vault's removal from the east wall. Sommer agreed with Harris's proposal, and the balcony was built using original bricks and terra cotta that were salvaged when the vault was relocated. The balcony, which is still in use, not only provides a setting for the clock but also serves as an excellent vantage point from which visitors can view the banking room.[20]

As remodeling work began after bids were opened on November 30, Harris made a number of other changes in Ihling's plan. Most importantly, Harris rejected the idea of constructing a low ceiling around the perimeter of the banking room. Instead, he created wooden canopies to hold the lighting needed above the tellers' counters and other work areas. These canopies, or trellises as Harris called them, were largely open on top so as not to obscure the view of the upper walls from the bank floor.

The clock wall after the 1958 remodeling had a new tellers' counter designed by Harwell Harris. Two of Harris's lighting trellises are visible (lower left).

In addition, Harris made drawings for a new tellers' counter to fit under the balcony and redesigned the lobby side of all the other new tellers' counters that were to be installed as part of Ihling's plan. For the counters, Harris specified a facing of quarter-sawn white oak, the same wood that had been used throughout the bank originally. He also tried to improve the acoustics of the banking room by placing sound-absorbent tiles on the top panels of the lighting trellises. Finally, he took charge of designing a bank directors' room to be built in the rear of the leased portion of the shop and office building.[21]

Ihling, a meat-and-potatoes architect not given to excessive concern over the artistry of his creations, was obviously upset by Harris's sudden entrance into the picture. Ihling's numerous letters to Sommer during the more than year-long remodeling process were unfailingly polite but seldom had anything complimentary to say about Harris's proposals. The lighting trellises designed by Harris did not meet with Ihling's approval, nor was he fond of Harris's plans for the directors' room. Ihling's correspondence from this period suggests that he was not especially sympathetic toward the bank building or toward Harris's efforts to preserve the original atmosphere of the banking room in the remodeling. In one letter, for example, Ihling referred to the banking room as being "ponderous," and he constantly emphasized the need to modernize it.[22]

Harris, meanwhile, was clearly exasperated by Ihling's behavior. In particular, Harris found that Ihling was extremely slow in sending along his drawings, which Harris needed before he could make any revisions in the remodeling plan. The man in the middle during these disputes was Sommer, who acted as the final arbiter on all design questions. In virtually every case, Sommer decided in Harris's favor. "By engaging Harwell Harris we acquired absolute acceptance of what he did," Sommer later said.[23]

As the remodeling work progressed through 1957, Sommer came to rely on Harris for advice on a multitude of details — a parallel, perhaps, to Bennett's experience with Sullivan and Elmslie. Before installing a wastebasket in his office, Sommer checked with Harris to make sure it was suitable. Even the color of the telephones to be installed in the bank was submitted to Harris for his consideration. (He specified black.) It was also probably Harris who vetoed the idea of a time-and-temperature sign on the corner of the bank. Special wiring was installed to accommodate a sign, but the idea never went further than that.

The remodeling project included extensive renovation of much of the ornament and art in the banking room. This work, done in January 1958, was entrusted to Louis M. DeNardo of St. Paul. His father, Louis A. DeNardo, was a native of Florence, Italy, where he had received his art

As part of the 1958 remodeling, stencils, plasterwork, and murals were cleaned and repaired. Louis De Nardo's crew used scaffolding to reach most of the artwork.

training. He immigrated to St. Paul around the turn of the century and established a decorating studio that specialized in church restoration. By 1958 the studio employed seven artisans in addition to the DeNardos.[24]

The younger DeNardo and his assistants spent fifteen days in the banking room, cleaning and restoring the two big murals and repairing much of the ornament on the upper walls. The murals were in especially

poor condition. DeNardo and his workmen took the murals down, cleaned them with shaving cream (which removes dirt without affecting the colors), and then repainted them as needed. The mural on the east wall was badly faded and had to be almost completely repainted. In addition, DeNardo made new molds to repair broken plaster ornament on the upper walls. He also restored the stencilwork that had almost disappeared with age. All told, DeNardo had to mix and match forty-nine colors of paint in order to restore the art and ornament to their original appearance.

Among the pieces of ornament restored by DeNardo were the eight large "B" crests in the upper corners of the banking room. The "B"s, of course, stood for the Bennett family, whose involvement in the bank was by 1958 only a memory. But as the remodeling neared completion, Sommer one day received an unexpected visitor. Winifred Bennett, Guy Bennett's widow, came to the bank to see once again the place where her husband had worked for so many years. She told Sommer she had not set foot in the bank since its failure in 1926. Later, her son Leonard, for a long time a teacher in Owatonna, also stopped in to view the work in progress, and for him, too, it was the first visit to the bank in a number of years.[25]

The remodeling and restoration work was finally completed in the spring of 1958. It had been a time-consuming and expensive project. Ihling's initial cost estimate for the project was $172,000, but the final figure was closer to $250,000 because of the changes and additions made by Harris with Sommer's approval. In June, a two-week-long series of events marked the rededication of the bank. Ivy Baker Priest, then the treasurer of the United States, attended the ceremonies, as did architects from around the country. But the ceremonies also attracted thousands of ordinary people. In fact, it almost seemed as though all of Owatonna came to an open house at the bank on the weekend of June 7–8. An estimated ten thousand persons toured the bank that weekend, and some brought with them memories that reached back fifty years. The elderly owner of the Wisconsin quarry that had provided the sandstone for the bank was there, and he must have been pleased to see how beautiful his stone still looked. Another old man recalled how, in 1908, he had helped to unload the great electroliers when they arrived by railroad flatcar from Chicago.[26]

The rededication ceremonies came to a close on June 12 when the Minnesota chapter of the American Institute of Architects held a special meeting in Owatonna. The speaker for the occasion was James M. Fitch, a distinguished architectural historian from Columbia University. Fitch commented briefly on Carl Bennett's role in the history of the bank, but most of his speech dealt with Sullivan. Nor did Elmslie receive much mention; it would be several more years before most scholars began to appreciate his contributions to the design of the bank.[27]

The scant mention of Carl Bennett during the rededication ceremonies was a great disappointment to his widow, Lydia, who later wrote: "Some way should be found to let the world know who was responsible for the building of the beautiful bank in Owatonna. Last year the present banking firm there celebrated the 100th [*sic*] anniversary of Sullivan's birth. . . . Many articles were published by them in papers but not one mentioned the name of Carl Bennett and his brother and father as the reason for the building's existence until a protest was made by friends of the Bennetts. Then mention was finally made of the Bennett's [*sic*] part but in a very niggardly fashion." Mrs. Bennett, nearly eighty years old and in poor health, still hoped to have a plaque placed in the bank to commemorate the Bennett family. But it was not until 1981, sixteen years after her death, that a plaque with Carl Bennett's name on it was finally installed near the bank president's office.[28]

The work done in 1957–58 received widespread publicity and drew loud hurrahs from the architectural establishment. The *Architectural Forum,* in a six-page article entitled "Making a Monument Work," hailed the remodeling, as did the *New York Times, Time* magazine, and other publications. The remodeling was unusually farsighted for its era because of the effort made to preserve as much of the original spirit of the bank as possible. The 1950s were a time when old buildings were far more likely to be razed than renovated, and the work on the bank must be accounted as a major achievement in a decade otherwise undistinguished for the quality of its architecture. Sommer, Harris, and officials of the Northwest Bancorporation all received well-deserved praise for their efforts.[29]

Still, it is possible to find fault with the work done in 1957–58. "This, to me, is the most powerful Sullivan building," Harris once said in describing the bank. Yet many of his tellers' counters, light trellises, and other fixtures seem a bit too delicate for the robust space originally conceived by Sullivan and Elmslie. This shortcoming was especially noticeable in the wood-faced tellers' counter (now removed) that Harris designed to fit under the balcony. The counter, with its rather spindly grilles to either side, appeared to be overwhelmed by the mass of the brickwork above. A more substantial counter, perhaps in brick, might have provided a visually stronger base for the balcony. All things considered, Harris's fixtures seem more reminiscent of Wright than of Sullivan, particularly in the geometric ornament atop the trellises. Harris also insisted on staining all of his woodwork a very light color. His choice helped to brighten the banking room but was not in keeping with its original appearance. The Craftsman furniture specified by Sullivan and Elmslie had a much darker, greenish stain that fit in very nicely with the over-all color scheme of the lobby.[30]

Although it is possible to quarrel with some of the details of the 1957–58 remodeling, it also can be fairly said that the work was necessary to ensure the building's survival as a bank. Had the bank been unable to reorganize and expand outward from the original cube, it may well have had to find other quarters, leaving the bank building to an uncertain fate.

Sommer served as president of the bank through 1971, and during his tenure there were few additional changes in the bank building. In 1964, however, the bank built a drive-up facility across Broadway Street just to the east of Central Park. Harris was called on to design this facility, and he produced a very unobtrusive brick composition that relates nicely to the bank without trying to compete with it. After Sommer left, one major change for the worse was made in the banking room. Because an increasing number of the bank's customers conducted their business at the drive-up facility, the officers decided in the early 1970s that fewer tellers' counters were needed in the banking room. As a result, the counter constructed under the balcony in 1957 was removed. This alteration left a gaping void at the focal point of the banking room, although it did create more space for the bank's growing staff.[31]

Two other changes of note occurred during this time. The first involved the stained-glass skylight, which had been cleaned in 1957–58 and then illuminated from above with fluorescent lights. The lights were necessary because the skylight had been boarded over for many years after developing a leak. In the early 1970s, the bank repaired the leak and removed the boards and fluorescent lights, thereby allowing natural light once again to filter through Millet's stained glass. The name of the bank also changed during this time. It became the Northwestern Bank of Owatonna in 1971 following reorganization under a national bank charter.[32]

By the mid-1970s, as the bank's business continued to grow, space again became a problem. The number of bank employees had doubled from about thirty to sixty over a twenty-year period, and the extra space gained in the 1957–58 remodeling was no longer sufficient. So, for a second time, the bank began studying the idea of expanding to the north. In 1975, Val Michelson and Associates, a St. Paul architectural firm, was hired to study the problem. A year later, the firm came up with a proposal for an addition north of the bank on Cedar Street. The addition was

The tellers' counter beneath the clock wall was removed in the early 1970s.

to feature a two-story glass facade, recessed slightly at the top and an-chored on its north side by a wall of brick similar to that of the bank building. But the addition was never built, in part because the bank—as had been the case in 1957–58—was unable to obtain the property to the north at an acceptable price.[33]

The bank then decided to concentrate on expanding to the east and in 1976 was able to acquire the remainder of the shop and office building on Broadway. Thus, for the first time since 1928, the entire bank and office complex as originally built was owned by the bank itself. As it turned out, the bank's space shortage was alleviated by other means as

Natural light once again filtered through the stained-glass skylight after the leak was fixed and the fluorescent lights removed.

The banking room in 1975

well. In 1980 a change in state law made it possible for the bank to open a branch office on the south side of Owatonna, thus further reducing customer traffic in the banking room. The result was that by 1980 bank president Kenneth E. Wilcox, with the support of the Northwest Bancorporation, was able to begin considering plans to eliminate excess tellers' space in the banking room. And this opportunity in turn meant that it would be possible to restore parts of the banking room to something approaching their original appearance.[34]

David Bowers, an architect with the Michelson firm, was put in charge of the restoration and renovation work. His plan, carried out in 1982–83, resulted in the construction of a brick tellers' enclosure under the east-wall balcony and the restoration of the president's office. The new enclosure consists of a central teller's window with wings jutting out

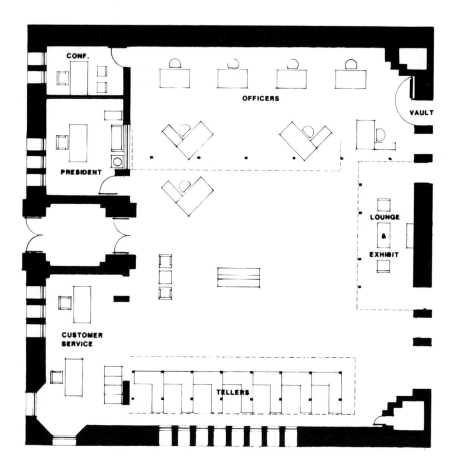

The floor plan of 1975

to either side. It was not possible to reintroduce the prow shape of Sullivan and Elmslie's original enclosure because it would have intruded too far into the lobby to suit the bank's needs. Nor was it possible to duplicate exactly the brickwork, although Bowers managed to find a small company in Kansas that was able to produce burgundy-colored bricks which almost match the originals. The new enclosure is capped by green terra-cotta blocks rescued from the bank's basement, where they had been sitting since 1940. Some of the blocks had to be recut, a tricky proposition since terra-cotta masons are no longer to be found. Bowers also was able to resurrect some black Belgian marble from the bank's basement to use for tellers' counters in the new enclosure. All of the original counters in the bank were made of this marble, which is no longer available because the quarries from which it came have long since closed.

The floor plan of 1982, as well as that of 1975, shows the use of public and office space.

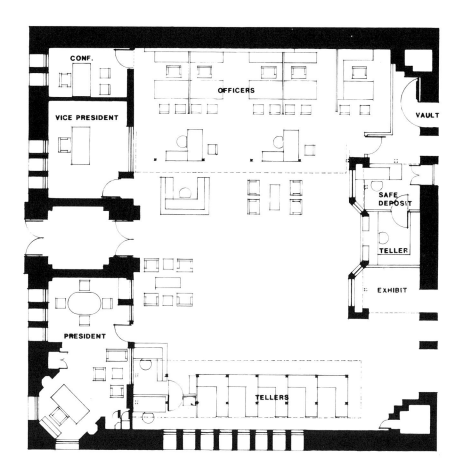

The original enclosure also contained four of Elmslie's famous wickets. It was not possible to make copies of these, but glass etched in the pattern of the wickets was used for two windows in the new enclosure. All told, the enclosure designed by Bowers provides a convincing base for the balcony and clock, and it also gives a strong sense of how this part of the banking room originally appeared.[35]

Restoring the president's office entailed re-creating a space that had been substantially altered during the 1957–58 remodeling. At that time the president's office was moved from its original position in the southwest corner of the cube to the northwest corner. The old office area, beautifully paneled in oak, was then opened up to accommodate more tellers' counters. By 1982 there was no longer any need for these counters, making it possible to restore the space to its original use. A major feature of the restoration was the installation of new quarter-sawn white oak paneling where needed, with the wood stained to match the original. Several other features of the original office, such as built-in bookcases with stained-glass windows, were also restored. In addition, Bowers created a small ceiling cove above the president's desk to make more room for an original cast-iron light fixture found in the bank basement.

The 1982–83 remodeling also included installation of carpeting and new furniture, which is in a squarish style that suggests the original Craftsman pieces. "Our goal was to introduce some of the materials from the original [banking room] . . . and yet to make it as functional as possible," Wilcox said. That goal was achieved on both counts. The banking room continues to work well for its intended purposes, yet it is now closer to its original appearance than at any time since 1940.[36]

"Each building stands as a social act," Sullivan once wrote. "In such act we read that which cannot escape our analysis, for it is indelibly fixed in the building, namely, the nature of the thoughts of the individual and the people whose image the building is or was." Despite many changes through the years, the bank still reveals much about Sullivan, Elmslie, and Bennett. Their vitality, their idealism, their love of beauty, and their passion for doing things right are all evident in the bank.[37]

Perhaps more than anything else, the building speaks to the powerful religious impulses that drove Sullivan and Elmslie. It is said that first-time visitors to Owatonna sometimes mistake the bank for a church, and in many respects that is exactly what the building is. "I regard spiritual or psychic facts as the only permanent and reliable facts — the only solid ground," Sullivan once said. He also wrote that "behind every form we see there is a vital something or other which we do not see, yet which makes itself visible to us in that form." Sullivan and Elmslie always sought to express that "vital something" by capturing the timeless flow of nature and then releasing it through the power of their art. This feeling is especially evident in the bank's almost infinitely varied ornament, which is Sullivan and Elmslie's ultimate paean to nature. For both men, architecture was truly a sacred calling, no matter to what secular uses their buildings might be put.[38]

It is doubtful that Bennett shared this mystic vision; his religious beliefs were more orthodox than those of Sullivan and Elmslie. Yet he did

A new brick tellers' enclosure was installed in front of the clock wall in 1982. The enclosure is topped with decorative terra cotta and features glass windows etched with the pattern of Elmslie's cast-iron wickets.

share their idealism and their love of beauty, and like them he understood that architecture is both a practical and a spiritual exercise. "A great architect does his best work for a great client," Harwell Harris once remarked, and Bennett must surely be adjudged as the most sympathetic and understanding client Sullivan and Elmslie ever had. The bank came about because of Bennett's desire for "a true and lasting work of art," and it is a measure of his wisdom and sound judgment that he was able to obtain exactly what he wanted.[39]

Bennett's youngest daughter, Lydia, remembered how as a child she would go to the bank with her father, walking through the low vestibule and then into the great space of the banking room, with its rich and mysterious light. "I always thought of it as a holy place," she said, and that feeling undoubtedly is shared by many of the visitors who every year journey to Owatonna to see her father's dream.[40]

REFERENCE NOTES

The papers of George Grant Elmslie and William Gray Purcell are part of the collections of the Northwest Architectural Archives at the University of Minnesota. These papers are a rich source for twentieth-century American architecture, in part because they apparently were not culled before being donated. During their twelve-year partnership, the two men for the most part maintained separate offices (Elmslie in Chicago and Purcell in Minneapolis), forcing them to carry on a business dialogue by letter instead of conversing face-to-face as most business partners would do. Much of this correspondence survives, and it includes memos, notes on envelopes, fragments of letters, and other similar miscellaneous material. Thus the very nature of the collection makes citation of individual items difficult, and some can only be called untitled, undated manuscripts. The Northwest Architectural Archives has organized the Purcell and Elmslie Papers, constructed finding aids, and plans to publish a comprehensive guide to the papers to enable researchers to make maximum use of this valuable collection.

Introduction

1. Louis H. Sullivan, *Kindergarten Chats and Other Writings,* ed. Isabella Athey (New York: George Wittenborn, 1947; New York: Dover, 1979), 24.

2. Carl K. Bennett, "A Bank Built for Farmers," *The Craftsman* 15 (November 1908): 176–85.

3. Hendrik P. Berlage (1856–1934), generally regarded as the founder of modern Dutch architecture, said the bank "cannot, as far as I am aware, be matched by anything similar on the European continent"; quoted in Leonard K. Eaton, *American Architecture Comes of Age: European Reaction to H. H. Richardson and Louis Sullivan* (Cambridge, Mass.: MIT Press, 1972), 217. Berlage visited the United States in 1911 and met Sullivan in Chicago. As part of his tour, Berlage intended to travel to Owatonna to see the bank. Bennett, in fact, made plans to entertain the Dutch architect during his visit. But Berlage became homesick while in Chicago and left for the Netherlands without ever visiting Owatonna. See William G. Purcell to Carl K. Bennett, December 6, 1911, William G. Purcell and George G. Elmslie Papers, Northwest Architectural Archives (hereafter cited as NAA), University of Minnesota, Minneapolis. (All correspondence and manuscript material cited below, unless otherwise noted, is from this collection.) For Hitchcock's concern about plans to remodel the bank, see Henry-Russell Hitchcock to Security [later Norwest] Bank of Owatonna, [?] [?], 1956, Norwest Bank of Owatonna. The bank's status as an architectural masterpiece was recognized in August 1981 when it was among sixteen buildings selected for

a series of "Architecture USA" postage stamps issued by the United States Postal Service. The eighteen-cent stamp shows the bank's front elevation, under which is written "Louis Sullivan, 1856–1924, Bank, Owatonna, Minn."

4. Sullivan, "What Is Architecture: A Study in the American People of Today," in *Kindergarten Chats,* 234.

5. Bennett to Purcell and Elmslie, April 7, 1911.

Chapter 1: *A Banker's Dream*

1. Bennett, "Bank Built for Farmers," 176.

2. *Owatonna Journal-Chronicle,* March 15, 1907, p. 1, 3, 6.

3. A statement published in the *Journal-Chronicle,* February 1, 1907, p. 12, listed the bank's assets at $787,220. Much of the information about Owatonna in this chapter is taken from Edgar B. Wesley, *Owatonna: The Social Development of a Minnesota Community* (Minneapolis: University of Minnesota Press, 1938).

4. Owatonna's name is derived from the Dakota Indian word "ouitunya," meaning straight. The river that runs through town apparently was given that name by the Dakota because it runs in a generally straight northward course. See Wesley, *Owatonna,* 11.

5. The old courthouse still stands and provides a nice counterpoint to the bank on the other side of the park.

6. Wesley, *Owatonna,* 50, 76, 77, 126–55.

7. Bennett to Purcell, August 2, 1910. In his letter, Bennett said the bank and its adjoining shop and office building cost $110,000, not including architects' fees. It is not known how much Sullivan was paid for his work, but his fee and other miscellaneous expenses probably pushed the total cost of the project to about $125,000.

8. Wesley, *Owatonna,* 124, 142.

9. *American Contractor,* a Chicago building magazine, reported on October 16, 1906, that Sullivan was working on plans for a bank and office building in Owatonna that would cost $100,000. This indicates that Bennett and the bank's board of directors knew full well how expensive their new building was going to be.

10. For a discussion of the clients attracted by "progressive" architects during this period, see Leonard K. Eaton, *Two Chicago Architects and Their Clients: Frank Lloyd Wright and Howard Van Doren Shaw* (Cambridge, Mass.: MIT Press, 1969).

11. According to an application for membership in the Sons of the American Revolution prepared by Carl Bennett in 1906, his great-great-great-grandfather was Isaac Cody, who fought at the battle of Saratoga in 1777, often regarded as the turning point of the Revolutionary War. Bennett's application says Cody was in the thick of the action and "stood so near that he heard all that was said when [the British commander] Gen. [John] Burgoyne surrendered his sword to [the American commander] Gen. [Horatio] Gates." Bennett's application, which led to his acceptance as a member, is in Sons of the American Revolution Papers, Division of Archives and Manuscripts, Minnesota Historical Society (hereafter cited as DAM-MHS), St. Paul. The comments of Lydia N. Bennett on her father-in-law's work as a doctor were made to Harwell H. Harris during rededication ceremonies at the bank in 1958. See Harris, "Design Dimensions," *North Carolina Architect,* September 1966, p. 16.

12. Franklyn Curtiss-Wedge, *History of Rice and Steele Counties, Minnesota* (Chicago: H. C. Cooper, Jr., and Co., 1910), 739–41.

13. Lydia Bennett Freeman, interview with author, August 21, 1982. Mrs. Freeman is Carl Bennett's youngest daughter. Mrs. Leonard (Marjorie) Bennett, interview with author, March 19, 1983. Marjorie Bennett is the widow of Guy Bennett's son.

14. Carl Kottke, interview with author, March 19, 1983. Kottke, ninety-one years old at the time of the interview, operated a jewelry store in Owatonna just a few doors away from the bank for more than sixty years. He is the source for the anecdote about Carl Bennett and his wife riding their horses through town.

15. David P. Bowers, "The National Farmers' Bank of Owatonna: A Documentation Project for the Northwestern Bank of Owatonna, Minnesota," 1976, unpaginated, unpublished report, copy in Norwest Bank of Owatonna. Bowers, a St. Paul architect, prepared this report at the request of the bank, which then made a limited number of copies. Much of the information in this chapter about the Bennett family is drawn from the work of Bowers, who kindly

made his research notes available to the author as well.

16. Bowers, "National Farmers' Bank."

17. Mrs. Carl (Lydia Norwood) Bennett, tape-recorded interview with Richard Nickel, May 23, 1958, tape in the possession of the Richard Nickel Committee (hereafter cited as RNC), Chicago. Mrs. Bennett died in 1965 at age eighty-four. Nickel was a scholar and photographer who spent more than fifteen years getting material for what was to have been the definitive study of Sullivan's life and work. But Nickel was killed in a tragic accident in 1972 during the demolition of the Chicago Stock Exchange, designed by Sullivan in 1894. Nickel died when part of the building collapsed on him as he was photographing the interior.

18. Bowers, "National Farmers' Bank"; Wesley, Owatonna, 114.

19. Bowers, "National Farmers' Bank"; Wesley, Owatonna, 146; Mrs. Freeman, interview.

20. Arabella Bennett Winston, interview with author, June 24, 1983. Mrs. Winston is Carl Bennett's third-born and elder surviving daughter.

21. Mrs. Freeman, interview; Mrs. Winston, interview.

22. Bowers, "National Farmers' Bank."

23. Bennett, "Bank Built for Farmers," 176, 183.

24. Bankers Magazine 76 (June 1908): 986. L. L. Bennett provided a similar description of the bank in an untitled article in Chicago Banker, May 30, 1908, p. 28.

25. Sullivan, "What Is Architecture," in Kindergarten Chats, 234–35.

26. Mrs. Carl Bennett, interview with Richard Nickel; Carl K. Bennett and James W. Ford, report to the Owatonna Public Library Board, September 7, 1898, Owatonna Public Library.

27. For a description of the Quincy library, see William H. Jordy, American Buildings and Their Architects, vol. 3, Progressive and Academic Ideals at the Turn of the Century (Garden City, N.Y.: Doubleday, 1972), 323–24.

28. Here and three paragraphs below, Bennett and Ford, report to the Owatonna library board.

29. There were at least twenty buildings designed by Adler and Sullivan in or near downtown Chicago at the turn of the century. By the 1980s, however, the only major Adler and Sullivan structure still standing in downtown Chicago was the Auditorium Building. The Carson Pirie Scott Store and the Gage Building, both designed by Sullivan after his partnership with Adler broke up, also remained in the Loop.

30. For a good description of the Transportation Building, along with several photographs, see Stanley Appelbaum, The Chicago World's Fair of 1893: A Photographic Record (New York: Dover, 1980), 53–54, 58–59.

31. Sullivan's knack for making accurate cost estimates is illustrated in an anecdote told by the president of a bank in Sidney, Ohio, designed by Sullivan in 1917. The president said Sullivan came to Sidney, spent two days studying the site, then drew a rapid sketch of the new bank and provided a cost estimate. The estimate turned out to be within one thousand dollars of the final cost of the building. The anecdote is related in Hugh Morrison, Louis Sullivan: Prophet of Modern Architecture (New York: W. W. Norton and Co., 1935, Norton Library reprint, 1962), 180.

32. Alan K. Lathrop, "The Prairie School Bank: Patron and Architect," in Prairie School Architecture in Minnesota, Iowa, Wisconsin (St. Paul: Minnesota Museum of Art, 1982), 55; Bennett, "Bank Built for Farmers," 176.

33. The newspaper advertisements appeared almost weekly in both of Owatonna's newspapers during the period that the bank was under construction.

34. As early as 1892, Sullivan had designed a banking room to be incorporated into an office building in St. Louis, but the project was never built.

35. Sullivan's first visit to Owatonna had to have been sometime before October 20, 1906, when the American Contractor article appeared announcing that Sullivan was at work on the bank.

Chapter 2: The Man from Chicago

1. Elmslie to Lewis Mumford, April 20, 1931.

2. Biographical details of Sullivan's life come primarily from Morrison, Louis Sullivan,

and from Willard Connely, *Louis Sullivan: The Shaping of American Architecture* (New York: Horizon Press, 1960).

3. Connely, *Louis Sullivan,* 243–45.

4. Connely, *Louis Sullivan,* 279 (first quotation); Sullivan, *Kindergarten Chats,* 44 (second quotation).

5. Elmslie to Purcell, August [?], 1944; Sullivan to Bennett, January 4, 1910, letter in the possession of Mrs. Freeman, San Diego, Calif. For published versions of this and other letters in Mrs. Freeman's possession, see Robert R. Warn, "Bennett and Sullivan, Client and Creator," *Prairie School Review* 10 (Third Quarter 1973): 5–15. See also Morrison, *Louis Sullivan,* 179.

6. Oskar Gross, tape-recorded interview with Richard Nickel, December 10, 1959, RNC.

7. Sullivan, "The Young Man in Architecture," in *Kindergarten Chats,* 214.

8. Sullivan, *Kindergarten Chats,* 110, 77; Sullivan, "What Is Architecture," in *Kindergarten Chats,* 238.

9. Sullivan, *Kindergarten Chats,* 164, 139; Elmslie to Lewis Mumford, May 29, 1931, copy in NAA.

10. For a discussion of some of the practical problems with Sullivan's houses, see Narciso G. Menocal, *Architecture as Nature: The Transcendentalist Idea of Louis Sullivan* (Madison, Wis.: University of Wisconsin Press, 1981), 102–27.

11. Sullivan, "Emotional Architecture as Compared with Intellectual: A Study in Subjective and Objective," in *Kindergarten Chats,* 195.

12. Louis H. Sullivan, *The Autobiography of an Idea* (1922; New York: American Institute of Architects, 1924; reprint, New York: Dover, 1956), 118–19.

13. Sullivan, *Autobiography,* 187.

14. For more on Furness's influence on Sullivan, see James F. O'Gorman, *The Architecture of Frank Furness* (Philadelphia: Philadelphia Museum of Art, 1973), 32–37.

15. Sullivan, *Autobiography,* 190–96.

16. David Lowe, *Lost Chicago* (Boston: Houghton Mifflin, 1978), 97; Sullivan, *Autobiography,* 200–13 (quotations, 200, 202).

17. Sullivan, *Autobiography,* 219–33.

18. Sullivan, *Autobiography,* 240.

19. Richard Chafee, "The Teaching of Architecture at the Ecole des Beaux-Arts," in *The Architecture of the Ecole des Beaux-Arts,* ed. Arthur Drexler (New York: Museum of Modern Art, 1977), 83–85.

20. Connely, *Louis Sullivan,* 79–85.

21. Sullivan, *Autobiography,* 252–57 (quotation, 252).

22. Sullivan wrote that he became a full partner with Adler in 1881; *Autobiography,* 257. But Menocal, after examining Chicago builders' directories from that period, concluded that the partnership actually began in 1883; *Architecture,* 43. See also Connely, *Louis Sullivan,* 93–94.

23. Frank Lloyd Wright, *Genius and the Mobocracy* (New York: Duell, Sloan and Pearce, 1949), 43, 45. Wright's memoirs must be used cautiously, since fact and opinion were often one and the same to him; however, he provides a good deal of information about Sullivan's personality and style that is not available elsewhere. There is a biographical sketch of Adler in Morrison, *Louis Sullivan,* 283–93.

24. Sullivan, *Autobiography,* 256, 288.

25. For a detailed description of Chicago building during this period, see Carl W. Condit, *The Chicago School of Architecture: A History of Commercial and Public Building in the Chicago Area, 1875–1925* (Chicago: University of Chicago Press, 1964). See also Jordy, *Progressive and Academic Ideals,* 1–82.

26. Condit, *Chicago.*

27. For more on Victorian architecture, see John Burchard and Albert Bush-Brown, *The Architecture of America: A Social and Cultural History* (Boston: Little, Brown and Co., 1961), and James M. Fitch, *American Building: The Historical Forces That Shaped It* (Boston: Houghton Mifflin, 1966).

28. Morrison, *Louis Sullivan,* 55–79.

29. For a detailed analysis of Richardson's work, see Henry-Russell Hitchcock, *The Architecture of H. H. Richardson and His Times,* rev. ed. (Hamden, Conn.: Archon Books, 1961).

30. For the influence of Richardson's store on Sullivan, see Morrison, *Louis Sullivan,* 87–88; Jordy, *Progressive and Academic Ideals,* 28–38; Sullivan, *Kindergarten Chats,* 28–31. The details about the Auditorium Building are taken from Daniel H. Pearlman, *The Auditorium Building: Its History and Architectural Significance* (Chicago: Roosevelt University, 1976), 18.

31. Morrison, *Louis Sullivan,* 99, 104–8.

32. Morrison, *Louis Sullivan,* 87–88, 99–104. Although the Auditorium was, in many

respects, a highly advanced building for its day, it was also somewhat old fashioned in that its exterior walls were of load-bearing masonry. This created a problem in balancing the weight of the tower and the lower parts of the building, a problem Adler did not quite solve. The result was that the building settled as much as eighteen inches in some parts, causing Adler great concern. Wright, in fact, suggested that Adler's death at the relatively young age of fifty-six was caused by his worry over the settling problem; Wright, *An Autobiography*, rev. ed. (New York: Horizon, 1977), 288.

33. Wright, *Genius*, 43; Wright, *Autobiography*, 118.

34. Wright, *Autobiography*, 131. Despite the high quality of its design, the Auditorium Building was never a financial success. In the case of the hotel, part of the problem was plumbing, or lack of it. According to Tim Samuelson, a historian with the Commission on Chicago Historical and Architectural Landmarks, the Auditorium Hotel did not have bathrooms with most guest rooms. Instead, there were central toilets on each floor as was the usual arrangement for hotels at that time. Shortly after the Auditorium Hotel opened, several big hotels were built along Michigan Avenue that did provide a bathroom with each room. Lacking this amenity, the Auditorium Hotel was unable to attract the wealthy clientele it had been intended to serve. The Chicago Auditorium Association, which had issued stock to build the complex, went bankrupt in 1930. Plans were then made to demolish the building, but those plans eventually were abandoned because it simply would have been too expensive to raze the massive structure. In 1946 the building was purchased by Roosevelt University, which now occupies all of it except the theater. See also Pearlman, *Auditorium*, 8–24.

35. Connely, *Louis Sullivan*, 123.

36. Connely, *Louis Sullivan*, 128, 242.

37. For discussions of Sullivan's philosophy, see Sherman Paul, *Louis Sullivan: An Architect in American Thought* (Englewood Cliffs, N.J.: Prentice-Hall, 1962); Jordy, *Progressive and Academic Ideals*, 100–20, 164–79; Menocal, *Architecture*, 3–16, 78–101, 146–52.

38. Wright, *Genius*, 56.

39. Sullivan, "Essay on Inspiration," in Menocal, *Architecture*, 163–66; Sullivan, *Autobiography*, 272.

40. Sullivan, "Essay on Inspiration," in *Architecture*, 166.

41. Sullivan, *Kindergarten Chats*, 43, 45; Sullivan, "What is the Just Subordination, in Architectural Design, of Details to Mass?" in *Kindergarten Chats*, 185.

42. Sullivan, *Kindergarten Chats*, 64; Sullivan, "Natural Thinking: A Study in Democracy," in *The Testament of Stone: Themes of Idealism and Indignation from the Writings of Louis Sullivan*, ed. Maurice English (Evanston, Ill.: Northwestern University Press, 1963), 108; Sullivan, *Autobiography*, 279; Sullivan, "Natural Thinking," in *Testament*, 109.

43. Jordy, *Progressive and Academic Ideals*, 164–79.

44. Sullivan, *Kindergarten Chats*, 140–41.

45. Connely, *Louis Sullivan*, 124–25, 248–49; Sullivan, *Autobiography*, 297.

46. Sullivan, "The Tall Office Building Artistically Considered," in *Kindergarten Chats*, 206. The Wainwright Building is discussed in Morrison, *Louis Sullivan*, 144–50. Ellis Wainwright was something of a freebooter and fled the country in 1902 after being indicted in St. Louis on bribery charges in connection with his efforts to secure a streetcar franchise. See Connely, *Louis Sullivan*, 229.

47. For more on the history of the tall office building, see Condit, *Chicago*; Jordy, *Progressive and Academic Ideals*; Winston Weisman, "A New View of Skyscraper History," in *The Rise of an American Architecture*, ed. Edgar Kaufmann, Jr. (New York: Praeger, 1970), 113–60.

48. Jordy, *Progressive and Academic Ideals*, 41–51.

49. Sigfried Giedion, *Space, Time and Architecture*, 5th ed. (Cambridge, Mass.: Harvard University Press, 1967), 184–208, 249–55; Condit, *Chicago*, 6–7.

50. Jordy, *Progressive and Academic Ideals*, 6–8.

51. Condit, *Chicago*, 21. See also *Dictionary of American Biography*, s.v. "Otis, Elisha G."

52. Weisman, "A New View," in *Rise of American Architecture*, 119. See also Sarah B. Landau, "Arcaded Buildings of the New York School, c. 1870–1890," in *In Search of Modern Architecture: A Tribute to Henry-Russell Hitchcock*, ed. Helen Searing (Cambridge, Mass.: MIT Press, 1982), 136–64.

53. Wright, *Genius*, 79.

54. Sullivan, "The Tall Office Building," in *Kindergarten Chats*, 206.

55. Morrison, *Louis Sullivan*, 121–22, 124–26, 162–65; Connely, *Louis Sullivan*, 144–49.

56. Connely, *Louis Sullivan*, 160.

57. Wright, *Autobiography*, 132–33.

58. For Wright's role in the early history of the Prairie School, see H. Allen Brooks, *The Prairie School: Frank Lloyd Wright and His Midwest Contemporaries* (Toronto: University of Toronto Press, 1972; New York: Norton, 1976), 14–44. See also by the same author, *Frank Lloyd Wright and the Prairie School* (New York: George Braziller, 1984).

59. Appelbaum, *Chicago World's Fair*, 7–52. See also J[oseph] C. Furnas, *The Americans: A Social History of the United States, 1587–1914* (New York: G. P. Putnam's Sons, 1969), 761–68.

60. Appelbaum, *Chicago World's Fair*, 53–54, 58–59; Morrison, *Louis Sullivan*, 182–87; Connely, *Louis Sullivan*, 132–42, 146–47, 153–55.

61. Connely, *Louis Sullivan*, 159–60; *The Education of Henry Adams: An Autobiography* (Boston: Houghton Mifflin, 1918), 339, 340.

62. Jordy, *Progressive and Academic Ideals*, 70–80.

63. Sullivan, *Autobiography*, 322, 325. Every state had an exhibit building at the fair. These were done in a bewildering array of styles, ranging from American Colonial to French Gothic to Spanish Mission. Minnesota's contribution to the confusion was an Italian Renaissance villa.

See Appelbaum, *Chicago World's Fair*, 83–92; Morrison, *Louis Sullivan*, 185.

64. Here and below, Connely, *Louis Sullivan*, 164, 197–201; Morrison, *Louis Sullivan*, 174–81.

65. Morrison, *Louis Sullivan*, 172–74; Wright, *Genius*, 70. The Guaranty Building was restored in 1983 after years of neglect. See Thomas J. Dolan, "Something to Make Us Proud," *Buffalo News*, December 11, 1983, magazine section, p. 10.

66. Wright, *Genius*, 70; Morrison, *Louis Sullivan*, 283–92.

67. Menocal, *Architecture*, 66–68.

68. Connely, *Louis Sullivan*, 156–57, 161, 198, 203–4.

69. Connely, *Louis Sullivan*, 235. For a detailed account of the construction of the Schlesinger and Mayer Store, see Menocal, *Architecture*, 168–78. A Chicago-style window consists of a large plate-glass window with a smaller double-hung window to each side. This type of window arrangement was common in office buildings constructed in Chicago during Sullivan's time.

70. Connely, *Louis Sullivan*, 210–13; Wright, *Genius*, 40.

71. Connely, *Louis Sullivan*, 244.

72. Connely, *Louis Sullivan*, 216–17, 237, 239; Morrison, *Louis Sullivan*, 201–2, 236–37; Menocal, *Architecture*, 96. An edited version of *Democracy: A Man Search* was finally published in 1961.

73. The draftsman was William L. Steele. His comment can be found in Morrison, *Louis Sullivan*, 179.

Chapter 3: *Design and Construction*

1. Bennett, "Bank Built for Farmers," 176.

2. There was also a large wooden bandstand in the center of the park in 1906. It was later torn down. The fountain, however, remains.

3. George G. Elmslie, "The Chicago School: Its Inheritance and Bequest," *Journal of the American Institute of Architects* 37 (July 1952): 36.

4. The author is indebted to David Bowers for pointing out that Central Park was originally oval shaped.

5. Louis H. Sullivan, *Democracy: A Man Search*, ed. Elaine Hedges (Detroit: Wayne State University Press, 1961), 338; Mrs. Freeman, interview.

6. Mrs. Bennett, interview with Nickel.

7. Connely, *Louis Sullivan*, 248; Mrs. Bennett, interview with Nickel.

8. Mrs. Bennett to Nickel, February 19, 1957, RNC.

9. Gross, interview with Nickel; Mrs. Bennett, interview with Nickel.

10. Sullivan, *Kindergarten Chats,* 37. The cost of the bank building and its adjoining structure amounted to more than one-seventh of the bank's total assets in 1907, which were listed that year as being just under $800,000; *Journal-Chronicle,* February 1, 1907, p. 12.

11. Brooks, *Prairie School,* 134.

12. The Felsenthal Store is described in Morrison, *Louis Sullivan,* 202.

13. Ellis's design is discussed and illustrated in Brooks, *Prairie School,* 133, 135. For more on Ellis, an interesting character in his own right, see Roger G. Kennedy, "The Long Shadow of Harvey Ellis," *Minnesota History* 40 (Fall 1966): 97–108.

14. Brooks, *Prairie School,* 135–36.

15. David Gebhard, "Letter to the Editor," *Prairie School Review* 4 (Third Quarter 1967): 34.

16. The Getty Tomb is discussed in Morrison, *Louis Sullivan,* 128–29. The bank's resemblance to a mausoleum was noted by Kenneth W. Severens, "The Reunion of Louis Sullivan and Frank Lloyd Wright," *Prairie School Review* 12 (Third Quarter 1975): 13.

17. *American Contractor,* October 20, 1906, p. 15.

18. Elmslie to Bennett, December 7, 1909, Mrs. Freeman. The surviving drawings of the bank's ornament are in the Avery Architectural Library at Columbia University. They are discussed by Paul E. Sprague, "The National Farmer's [*sic*] Bank, Owatonna, Minnesota," *Prairie School Review* 4 (Second Quarter 1967): 5–21.

19. Elmslie to Purcell, April 18, 1939, October 15, 1940.

20. Elmslie to Purcell, August 14, 1942, October 8, 1946.

21. Elmslie to Purcell, May 2, 1939.

22. Elmslie to Purcell, September 4, 1944; Elmslie to Wright, October 30, 1932.

23. Wright, *Autobiography,* 119.

24. Purcell's comment is in David Gebhard, "William Gray Purcell and George Grant Elmslie and the Early Progressive Movement in American Architecture from 1900 to 1920" (Ph.D. diss., University of Minnesota, 1957), 74.

25. Elmslie to Purcell, September 4, 1944.

26. Elmslie to Purcell, April 13, 1939; Elmslie, "Autobiographical Sketch," undated manuscript [1940s?].

27. Elmslie, "Autobiographical Sketch"; Gebhard, "Purcell and Elmslie," 72.

28. Elmslie to Purcell, July 17, 1938. For somewhat differing views on the role played by Elmslie in Sullivan's later designs, see David Gebhard, "Louis Sullivan and George Grant Elmslie," *Journal of the Society of Architectural Historians* 19 (May 1960): 62–68, and Sprague, "National Farmer's Bank," 5–21.

29. Mrs. Bennett to Nickel, February 19, 1957, RNC.

30. For further evidence of Sullivan's important role in designing the bank, see Sullivan to American Terra Cotta and Ceramic Company, May 21, August 30, September 27, 1907. These letters—which ask for shop drawings, diagrams, and other information about terra-cotta pieces intended for the bank—suggest that Sullivan was very much involved in the ongoing design work for the bank project.

31. Bowers, "National Farmers' Bank." The author has relied heavily on Bowers's work for many details relating to the design and construction of the bank and adjoining building. Original blueprints of the bank and adjoining building are in the possession of the Norwest Bank of Owatonna.

32. Elmslie, untitled, undated manuscript.

33. Here and three paragraphs below, Bowers, "National Farmers' Bank."

34. *Journal-Chronicle,* March 15, 1907, p. 3, March 22, 1907, p. 1; *Daily People's Press* (Owatonna), March 15, 1907, p. 10, April 19, 1907, p. 1. The *Journal-Chronicle* misspelled Sullivan's first name as "Lewis."

35. Here and two paragraphs below, Bowers, "National Farmers' Bank."

36. Detailed information about the girders was supplied by Bowers. In determining the size and placement of the girders, Sullivan undoubtedly consulted with Louis Ritter, a Chicago structural engineer who worked on many of Sullivan's buildings.

37. *Journal-Chronicle,* September 20, 1907, p. 3, October 4, 1907, p. 3.

38. *Journal-Chronicle,* April 17, 1908, p. 3.

39. Gross, interview with Nickel.

40. *Journal-Chronicle,* July 17, 1908, p. 1.

Chapter 4: *The Final and Logical Flowering*

1. Sullivan to Bennett, April 1, 1908, Mrs. Freeman.

2. Although the bank had little direct impact on design in this country, it did have some influence on Dutch architecture from about 1910 to 1930, mainly because Berlage and other avant-garde Dutch architects greatly admired Sullivan's work. See Eaton, *American Architecture,* 231–32.

3. Here and two paragraphs below, Bennett, "Bank Built for Farmers," 176–85. Bennett's article, which probably was prepared with the help of Sullivan and Elmslie, still remains the most complete description of the banking room as it originally appeared.

4. Most of Sullivan's later banks also featured a vault that was clearly visible through the front entrance.

5. One of the most detailed discussions of the bank's ornament is Paul E. Sprague, "The Architectural Ornament of Louis Sullivan and His Chief Draftsmen" (Ph.D. diss., Princeton University, 1968).

6. Sullivan, *Kindergarten Chats,* 41; Wright, *Genius,* 55.

7. Sullivan, "Ornament in Architecture," in *Kindergarten Chats,* 187, 189.

8. Sullivan, "Ornament," in *Kindergarten Chats,* 189; Elmslie, quoted in Gebhard, "Purcell and Elmslie," 263.

9. Elmslie to Purcell, January 4, 1947; W. G. Purcell and G. G. Elmslie, "The Statics and Dynamics of Architecture," in *Prairie School Architecture: Studies from "The Western Architect",* ed. H. Allen Brooks (Toronto: University of Toronto Press, 1975; New York: Van Nostrand, 1983), 69.

10. One of the better discussions of Sullivan's ornament is in Jordy, *Progressive and Academic Ideals,* 118–64.

11. For the argument that Sullivan's ornament should be classified as Art Nouveau, see Diane C. Johnson, *American Art Nouveau* (New York: Harry N. Abrams, 1979), 134, 137, 159, 162.

12. Elmslie, "Sullivan Ornamentation," *Journal of the American Institute of Architects* 6 (October 1946): 155–58. There has been a great deal written on the sources of Sullivan's ornament and there is some disagreement among scholars as to which sources were more important. For varying views, see Sprague, "Architectural Ornament of Louis Sullivan"; Menocal, *Architecture;* Vincent Scully, "Sullivan's Architectural Ornament," *Perspecta* 5 (1959): 73–80; Theodore Turak, "French and English Sources of Sullivan's Ornament and Doctrine," *Prairie School Review* 11 (Fourth Quarter 1974): 5–30.

13. Elmslie to Purcell, October 15, 1940, July 31, 1943. Elmslie, a perfectionist, was not entirely happy with his own work on the bank. In an untitled manuscript [1939?] he wrote: "I wish I had the doing of this bank again – junky in some spots." Elmslie did not say which spots he thought were "junky."

14. Sullivan, "Ornament," in *Kindergarten Chats,* 188. Elmslie himself provided evidence, perhaps inadvertently, that Sullivan had the final say as to placement of ornament in and on the bank. In an untitled and undated manuscript, Elmslie wrote: "I was for omitting these [terra-cotta cartouches] in the [upper] corners [of the bank's exterior] but he [Sullivan] thought my idea was fine and wouldn't let me. Ho hum! Who was right?"

15. Louis H. Sullivan, *A System of Architectural Ornament According with a Philosophy of Man's Powers* (1924; reprint, New York: Eakins Press, 1967), 6.

16. The bank's interior and exterior ornament was cataloged by Bowers in 1976 as part of his documentation project.

17. For an interesting discussion of Sullivan and Elmslie's use of ornament in the bank, see Philip Larson, "Ornament as Symbol," in *Prairie School Architecture in Minnesota, Iowa, Wisconsin,* 68–74.

18. Sullivan once told Elmslie, "All we need George [to create ornament] are the square, the circle and the hexagon"; Elmslie to Purcell, July 17, 1938.

19. Elmslie to Purcell, September 18, 1941, July 9, 1947. On the fate of the wickets, see Chapter 7, note 9, below.

20. Sullivan to Bennett, April 1, 1908, Mrs. Freeman.

21. The Schiller Theater, McVicker's Theater, and Stock Exchange are gone; however, the Stock Exchange's trading room, with its gorgeous stencil work, was reconstructed and can be seen in the Art Institute of Chicago. See

John Vinci, *The Art Institute of Chicago: The Stock Exchange Trading Room* (Chicago: The Art Institute of Chicago, 1977).

22. The anecdote about the green mortar is related by Purcell in an untitled, undated document.

23. Bennett, "Bank Built for Farmers," 176.

24. Sullivan, "Artistic Brick," *Prairie School Review* 4 (Second Quarter 1967): 24–26.

25. Jordy, *Progressive and Academic Ideals*, 128.

26. Sharon S. Darling, *Chicago Ceramics and Glass: An Illustrated History from 1871 to 1933* (Chicago: Chicago Historical Society, 1979), 54–58.

27. Bennett, "Bank Built for Farmers," 176.

28. Morrison, *Louis Sullivan*, 209. The windows were designed to be practical as well as beautiful. To guard against the extremes of Minnesota's climate, the windows consist of two layers: plate glass on the outside and stained glass on the inside, with a hermetically sealed air space in between.

29. Although Sullivan relied on Chicago craftsmen to produce his and Elmslie's ornament, most of the actual construction of the bank was done by workmen from the Owatonna area; see National Farmers' Bank, dedication pamphlet, 1908, copy in Norwest Bank of Owatonna.

30. Darling, *Chicago Ceramics*, 170–72.

31. The author is grateful to Tim Samuelson, whose research unearthed the fact that Schneider had his own firm at the time he made the models for the bank's terra cotta.

32. Darling, *Chicago Ceramics*, 54–70, 169–79.

33. Most of the details relating to the manufacture of terra cotta were provided to the author by Tim Samuelson.

34. Wright, *Genius*, 58, 61; Elmslie to Purcell, October 15, 1940.

35. Here and below, information provided by Samuelson.

36. Larry Berghs, interview with author, September 6, 1984. Berghs said his father William G. Berghs, a mason in Owatonna for many years, installed the terra cotta on the bank.

37. Here and below, Eaton, *Two Chicago Architects*, 67–73.

38. Elmslie to Purcell, October 19, 1940.

39. David Hanks, "Louis J. Millet and The Art Institute of Chicago," *Bulletin of the Art Institute of Chicago* 67 (March-April 1973): 13–19; Darling, *Chicago Ceramics*, 104–8.

40. Hanks, "Louis J. Millet," 13–14.

41. Hanks, "Louis J. Millet," 14–17.

42. Darling, *Chicago Ceramics*, 105.

43. Hanks, "Louis J. Millet," 17.

44. Sullivan to Bennett, April 1, 1908, Mrs. Freeman.

45. Millet described his and Sullivan's work on the bank in "The National Farmers' Bank of Owatonna, Minn.," *Architectural Record* 24 (October 1908): 249–54.

46. Gross, interview with Nickel.

Chapter 5: *Sullivan — The Desperate Years*

1. Sullivan to Bennett, January 4, 1910, Mrs. Freeman.

2. Millet, "National Farmers' Bank," 249–54; *Bankers Magazine* 76 (June 1908): 986; *Chicago Banker*, May 30, 1908, p. 28; Montgomery Schuyler, "The People's Savings Bank of Cedar Rapids, Iowa," *Architectural Record* 31 (January 1912): 46; Sullivan, *Autobiography*, 297. Another factor in Sullivan's loss of the cottage was that in about 1904 his brother, Albert, left his job as assistant second vice-president of the Illinois Central Railroad. Sullivan was thus no longer able to get railroad passes to take him to Ocean Springs. See Connely, *Louis Sullivan*, 220, 233, 249.

3. Harold C. Bradley to [Jon Phillip] Buschke, September 30, 1965, in Menocal, *Architecture*, 180–84. Sullivan and Elmslie designed a home for Bradley in Madison, Wis., in 1907. Bradley said in his letter that Sullivan at that time "was obviously and often under the influence of liquor – not drunk, but somewhat tipsy, sometimes vague or sleepy." Sullivan to Bennett, June 9, 1909, Mrs. Freeman.

4. Sullivan to Bennett, August 1, 1909, Mrs. Freeman.

5. Connely, *Louis Sullivan*, 249; Elmslie to Purcell, November 12, 1909; Sullivan to Bennett, October 23, 1909, Mrs. Freeman.

6. Elmslie to Bennett, December 7, 1909, Mrs. Freeman.

7. Mrs. Bennett to Nickel, February 19, 1957, RNC; Sullivan to Bennett, January 4, 1910, Mrs. Freeman.

8. Sullivan to Bennett, January 4, 1910, Mrs. Freeman. For more information on Dr. Arndt, see Warn, "Bennett and Sullivan," 9, 10.

9. Elmslie to Purcell, November 12, 1909. Elmslie mentioned in this letter that the Cedar Rapids bankers had toured Bennett's bank. See also Lathrop, "Prairie School Bank," in *Prairie School Architecture,* 59. For descriptions of the Cedar Rapids bank as originally built, see Morrison, *Louis Sullivan,* 210–13, and Schuyler, "People's Savings Bank," 45–56.

10. Bennett to Purcell, April 14, November 14, 1910.

11. Bennett to Purcell, April 7, 1911.

12. Bennett to Sullivan, December 7, 1911, copy in author's possession; Bennett to Purcell, December 8, 1911. The December 7 letter was first published by Robert R. Warn, "Louis H. Sullivan, ' . . . an air of finality,' " *Prairie School Review* 10 (Fourth Quarter 1973): 6. St. Paul's Church in Cedar Rapids, which Sullivan had been commissioned to design, was eventually built. But Sullivan's original plans were altered by a third-rate architect who was called in after Sullivan left the job. See Morrison, *Louis Sullivan,* 213–16.

13. Bennett to Purcell, November 24, 1913. The lot is described in a letter written by Mrs. Bennett to Nickel, May 1, 1957, RNC.

14. Bennett to Purcell, November 15, 1911; Sullivan to Bennett, December 26, 1911, Mrs. Freeman; Bennett to Purcell, November 4, 1911.

15. Sullivan to Bennett, December 6, 1911, Mrs. Freeman.

16. Bennett to Elmslie, February 15, 1912; Bennett to Purcell, August 3, 1912.

17. There is a detailed discussion of the house, along with plans, in Warn, "Louis H. Sullivan," 8–10.

18. Warn, "Louis H. Sullivan," 8–10. Warn's article includes two perspective drawings of the home's interior done in 1973 by architect William Broderson on the basis of Sullivan's plans.

19. Purcell, "Parabiography for 1913," manuscript. For examples of the residential work of Wright and other Prairie School archi-

tects of this period, see Brooks, *Prairie School.*

20. Mrs. Bennett to Nickel, February 23, 1957, RNC.

21. Bennett to Purcell, September 12, 1912; Mrs. Freeman, interview; Warn, "Louis H. Sullivan," 10; Mrs. Bennett to Nickel, May 1, 1957, RNC.

22. Lathrop, "Prairie School Bank," in *Prairie School Architecture,* 59; Morrison, *Louis Sullivan,* 216–19.

23. Morrison, *Louis Sullivan,* 219–20; Warn, "Bennett and Sullivan," 13.

24. Connely, *Louis Sullivan,* 262; Wright, *Autobiography,* 289.

25. Warn, "Louis H. Sullivan," 16. The recollections of the school board member, Henry Miller, were in an interview with Nickel, December 2, 1961, RNC. Although Miller recalled the proposed high school building as having two stories, Mrs. Guy (Winifred) Bennett thought the school was to have been a one-story structure; Mrs. Bennett, interview with Nickel, May 25, 1958, RNC.

26. *Journal-Chronicle,* April 13, 1917, p. 1. The draftsman was A. O. Budina. His comment on the school fiasco is in a letter to Nickel, July 23, 1957, RNC.

27. Morrison, *Louis Sullivan,* 220–23.

28. Sullivan to Wright, December 25, 1919, April 1, 1918, *Frank Lloyd Wright: Letters to Architects,* ed. Bruce B. Pfeiffer (Fresno, Calif.: California State University Press, 1984), 16, 5.

29. Sullivan to Wright, May 18, May 23, June 1, 1918, *Frank Lloyd Wright,* 6–9; Elmslie to Purcell, October 12, 1949. Elmslie in his letter recalled how much Sullivan was irritated by the noise of the elevated trains.

30. Morrison, *Louis Sullivan,* 223–24. There is also a good deal of information about the Columbus bank in John Szarkowski, *The Idea of Louis Sullivan* (Minneapolis: University of Minnesota Press, 1956), 2–13.

31. Connely, *Louis Sullivan,* 275–79; Elmslie to Purcell, December 20, 1943.

32. Sullivan to Wright, January 20, 1919, *Frank Lloyd Wright,* 12; Elmslie to Purcell, August 26, 1951.

33. Sullivan to Wright, December 25, 1919, *Frank Lloyd Wright,* 16.

34. Sullivan to Wright, November 30, 1920, August 19, 23, 1921, *Frank Lloyd Wright,* 18–20.

35. Morrison, *Louis Sullivan*, 224; Connely, *Louis Sullivan*, 281.

36. Here and below, Connely, *Louis Sullivan*, 282–84.

37. Connely, *Louis Sullivan*, 284–88. The story of Sullivan's last commission is in Szarkowski, *Idea*, 17; Gross, interview with Nickel.

38. Wright to Sullivan, August 28, 1923, Sullivan to Wright, September 3, 1923, *Frank Lloyd Wright*, 34, 37.

39. Connely, *Louis Sullivan*, 298–302.

40. Sullivan, "Essay on Inspiration," in Menocal, *Architecture*, 161; Connely, *Louis Sullivan*, 302; Wright, *Genius*, 75. Although Wright received the drawings in 1924, he did not get around to publishing them until 1949 in *Genius and the Mobocracy*. Moreover, he marked up some of the drawings for inexplicable reasons. For more information on the fate of the drawings, see Paul E. Sprague, *The Drawings of Louis Henry Sullivan: A Catalogue of the Frank Lloyd Wright Collection at the Avery Architectural Library* (Princeton, N.J.: Princeton University Press, 1979).

41. Elmslie to Fred Strauel, April 15, 1924.

42. Sullivan, *Kindergarten Chats*, 62.

43. That Sullivan himself recognized this failing is evident from his letter to Bennett on January 4, 1910, Mrs. Freeman.

44. Adolf Loos, "Ornament and Crime," in Ludwig Munz, *Adolf Loos, Pioneer of Modern Architecture* (New York: Praeger, 1966), 226–31. Morrison wrote in 1935: "At present . . . the reaction against all kinds of ornament is so widespread that we judge quality in this aspect of architecture with difficulty"; *Louis Sullivan*, 201. It was not until the 1950s that scholars began studying Sullivan's ornament as an integral part of his architecture.

45. Beman's comment is quoted in a letter from David Gibson to Hugh Morrison, January 23, 1936, copy in the possession of David Bowers.

46. Even Sullivan's own later banks do not compare in richness of ornament to the Owatonna bank. One reason for this is that Owatonna was the largest and most costly of Sullivan's banks. Another reason is that Owatonna is the only one of Sullivan's banks that was detailed by Elmslie, who had a fondness for extravagant ornament.

47. Elmslie to Wright, June 12, 1936, copy in NAA. In this letter, Elmslie mentions Wright's derogatory comment about the bank.

48. For an interesting view of two of Sullivan's banks, see Robert Venturi, *Complexity and Contradiction in Architecture*, 2nd ed. (New York: Museum of Modern Art, 1977), 62–63, 88–89.

Chapter 6: *Elmslie and Bennett – Triumphs and Tragedies*

1. Elmslie to Purcell, August 13, 1916.

2. Bennett to Purcell, August 30, 1929.

3. Elmslie to Purcell, November 11, December 6, 1909.

4. Gebhard, "Purcell and Elmslie," 103; Brooks, *Prairie School*, 130, 146.

5. Brooks, *Prairie School*, 130–31; Gebhard, "Purcell and Elmslie," 90. See also William Gray Purcell, *St. Croix Trail Country: Recollections of Wisconsin* (Minneapolis: University of Minnesota Press, 1967). This book, published after Purcell's death, is an account of his boyhood in Wisconsin. Elmslie's tendency toward artistic excess was discussed by Purcell in an untitled, undated document. As an example of Elmslie's exuberance, Purcell cited a paneled ceiling cornice Elmslie designed for a house in 1910. According to Purcell, the cornice was to contain twenty-two moldings within its twenty-four-inch width, requiring "704 mitred and glued joints, all to be made on the job." Purcell said that even the master carpenter employed by the firm of Purcell and Elmslie agreed that this cornice was simply too complicated to execute. Elmslie himself later said: "It is a pity that I allowed my facility [for drawing ornament] to lead me into extravagance"; Elmslie to Purcell, December [?], 1949.

6. Gebhard, "Purcell and Elmslie," 90; Elmslie to Purcell, September 29, 1909.

7. Elmslie to Purcell, July 20, 1908. Information about Bonnie Elmslie was provided by Tim Samuelson, letter to author, August 15, 1983.

8. Elmslie to Purcell, August 30, September 29, 1909; Purcell, tape-recorded interview with Nickel, July 11, 1959, RNC. Elmslie related Sullivan's remark in a letter to Purcell, September 11, 1945. Elmslie and Hunter were married by the Reverend Charles H. Bixby of

St. Paul's Episcopal Church, Chicago. A copy of the marriage certificate was provided to the author by Tim Samuelson.

9. Brooks, *Prairie School,* 219.

10. Elmslie's claim is in a letter to Wright, June 12, 1936, copy in NAA. There is a good description of the Merchants Bank in Brooks, *Prairie School,* 202-5.

11. Purcell, interview with Nickel; Edith Elmslie, tape-recorded interview with Richard Nickel, June 9, 1957, RNC. A copy of Bonnie Elmslie's death certificate was provided to the author by Tim Samuelson.

12. Elmslie to Purcell, January 14, 1913.

13. Elmslie to Purcell, February 20, September 3, 10, 1913.

14. Elmslie to Purcell, August 13, 1916. Mark Hammons of Minneapolis, a student of the Purcell and Elmslie Archives at NAA, estimates that Purcell may have spent more than fifty thousand dollars of his father's money on the firm.

15. William L. Steele, [William G.] Purcell, and [George G.] Elmslie, "Woodbury County Court House," in Brooks, *Prairie School Architecture,* 130-61; Brooks, *Prairie School,* 298-300.

16. Gebhard, "Purcell and Elmslie," 274; Brooks, *Prairie School,* 305; Elmslie to Purcell, October 9, 1918.

17. Elmslie to Purcell, October 9, 1918.

18. Purcell to Elmslie, October 18, 1918; Purcell, note on letter from Elmslie, December 23, 1944. Hammons's research indicates that Elmslie was hospitalized at least three times for nervous disorders. Elmslie was still trying to keep the partnership alive as late as 1920. In a letter to Purcell, he wrote: "If the office goes I feel that we are proclaiming to the world . . . that we are down and out"; Elmslie to Purcell, October 20, 1920.

19. Bowers, "National Farmers' Bank."

20. Elmslie to Purcell, November 21, December 6, 1909. Bennett's letters from this period contain numerous references to his activities on behalf of Purcell and Elmslie. His comment on the "new architecture" is in a letter to Purcell and Elmslie, April 7, 1911.

21. Bennett to Purcell, May 2, 1911; Bennett to Purcell and Elmslie, January 5, 1912.

22. Purcell to Bennett, April 13, 1910; Bennett to Purcell and Elmslie, September 25, 1911, September 18, 1913. It is likely that all eight small bank commissions which Purcell and Elmslie received from 1910 to 1920 were obtained at least in part through Bennett's efforts. His letters from this period show he was aware of bank building plans around the Upper Midwest and would frequently alert Purcell and Elmslie to possible jobs. Moreover, there is known to be a direct link between Bennett and one of Purcell and Elmslie's bank commissions, for the First State Bank of Le Roy, Minnesota, dating from 1914. This bank's head cashier at the time was Harry Tompkins, who had formerly worked as an assistant cashier in Bennett's bank.

23. There are brief descriptions of these two houses in David Gebhard and Tom Martinson, *A Guide to the Architecture of Minnesota* (Minneapolis: University of Minnesota Press, 1977), 303.

24. Bennett to Purcell, November 24, 1913. Purcell's comment is in "Purcell and Elmslie Parabiography, 1910-1914." The original plans of the house are in NAA. In addition, see Robert R. Warn, "Two House Projects for the Carl K. Bennett Family by Louis Sullivan and Purcell and Elmslie," *Northwest Architect* 36 (March-April 1972): 64-72, and Warn, "Louis H. Sullivan," 6-15.

25. John T. Schlebecker, *Whereby We Thrive: A History of American Farming, 1607-1972* (Ames, Iowa: Iowa State University Press, 1975), 209-11; Curtis L. Mosher, *The Causes of Banking Failure in the Northwestern States* (Minneapolis: Federal Reserve Bank, 1930), 15-16.

26. Bennett described his visits to Chicago in several letters to Purcell and Elmslie, in NAA. Among the items Bennett commissioned through Purcell and Elmslie was a mural for his office in 1923. The mural was painted by John Norton, who had worked with the architects on several projects. Morrison called the mural "undoubtedly the best painting to be found anywhere in association with Sullivan's architecture"; Morrison, *Louis Sullivan,* 210. The mural remains in the president's office today. Bennett had also commissioned a painting of the bank itself in 1914. The small oil painting was done by Albert F. Fleury, a French-born artist who worked in Chicago and had known Sullivan for many years. Their relationship went back to at least 1889, when Fleury painted two large murals for the Auditorium Theater. Later, he produced color renderings of many of Sullivan's buildings and a popular postcard series showing

Chicago street scenes. Fleury's painting of the Owatonna bank remains in the possession of the bank. Information about Fleury was supplied to the author by Tim Samuelson.

27. For information on Dr. L. L. Bennett's death, see *Daily People's Press,* February 4, 1916, p. 1.

28. Mosher, *Causes of Banking Failure,* 10, 11; *Daily People's Press,* October 22, 1926, p. 8.

29. *Bankers Magazine* 113 (September 1926): 289; Minnesota Legislature, *Report of Special Joint Committee of the House and Senate Appointed to Make a Study and Survey of the Banking Situation in the State of Minnesota,* 1927.

30. Sullivan to Bennett, December 26, 1911, Mrs. Freeman; First National Bank of Owatonna v. Guy Bennett, File No. 5622, Steele County District Court, DAM-MHS.

31. N. P. Peterson v. Carl Bennett, File No. 5495, Steele County District Court, DAM-MHS.

32. *Journal-Chronicle,* April 5, 1929, p. 1, 2. Although Bennett must have been aware of the bank's serious problems by 1924, he downplayed the situation in a letter to Purcell that year: "While we are not in that section of the farming country which has been hit hard, still we are somewhat affected by the difficulties of agriculture and prefer to keep a large supply of cash on hand rather than to take on notes"; Bennett to Purcell, May 2, 1924, letter in the possession of David Gebhard, Santa Barbara, Calif.

33. *Journal-Chronicle,* January 15, 1926, p. 1, 10.

34. Bank statements in the *Journal-Chronicle,* April 23, 1926, p. 5, July 9, 1926, p. 9.

35. *Journal-Chronicle,* August 13, 1926, p. 1; Mrs. Bennett, interview with Nickel.

36. *Daily People's Press,* September 2, 1926, p. 3, September 26, 1926, p. 8; Mrs. Bennett, interview with Nickel.

37. *Journal-Chronicle,* September 10, 1926, p. 1; *Daily People's Press,* September 26, 1926, p. 8.

38. *Daily People's Press,* September 9, 1926, p. 1.

39. *Journal-Chronicle,* September 17, 1926, p. 1, November 5, 1926, p. 1. The official cause of the bank's failure, according to the U.S. Comptroller of the Currency, was "incompetent

management and local financial depression from unforeseeable agricultural disaster." This information was provided by Ellen Stocksdale of the comptroller's office in a telephone conversation with the author, September 28, 1982.

40. Robert Adair, interview with author, July 19, 1983. Mr. Adair is a long-time resident of Owatonna. His father, James Adair, was a friend of Carl Bennett's. See also *Daily People's Press,* September 26, 1926, p. 8.

41. Owatonna Public Library Board, Minutes, September 8, 1926, Owatonna Public Library. Bennett was absent from this meeting but did attend several later meetings before resigning from the board. See *Journal-Chronicle,* September 24, 1926, p. 1.

42. *Journal-Chronicle,* October 1, 1926, p. 1; *Daily People's Press,* September 26, 1926, p. 8, October 31, 1926, p. 1. One reason why reorganization efforts failed was that depositors could not agree on how to settle the numerous lawsuits that were filed after the bank closed.

43. Mrs. Winston, interview. Most of the details of Bennett's later life were provided by Mrs. Winston and her sister, Mrs. Freeman.

44. There is information about the Bennetts' bankruptcy proceedings in numerous Steele County District Court files at DAM-MHS.

45. Two dormitories for students at Pillsbury Baptist Bible College now stand where Bennett had hoped to build his house. The long strip of land that was to be his garden is now a parking lot. The author is indebted to Mrs. Leonard Bennett for pointing out the exact location of Carl Bennett's property on Main Street.

46. *Journal-Chronicle,* March 8, 1929, p. 1.

47. E. C. Moulton v. National Farmers' Bank, File No. 5621, Steele County District Court, DAM-MHS; Mrs. Bennett to Purcell, March 12, 1929, Gebhard.

48. Here and two paragraphs below, Mrs. Bennett to Purcell, March 12, 1929, Gebhard.

49. Purcell to Mrs. Bennett, March 24, 1929, Gebhard; Elmslie discussed his "loan" to Bennett in a letter to Purcell, February 17, 1939; E. C. Moulton v. National Farmers' Bank.

50. Herbert E. Skinner v. Carl and Lydia Bennett, File No. 6328, Steele County District Court, DAM-MHS; Mrs. Freeman, interview; Bennett to Purcell, August 30, 1929.

51. Here and below, Mrs. Freeman, interview.

52. Here and below, Mrs. Freeman and Mrs. Winston, interviews.

53. *Daily People's Press,* August 30, 1941, p. 8; Gross, interview with Nickel; Elmslie to Mrs. Bennett, September 24, 1941, Mrs. Freeman.

54. Purcell, note on letter from Elmslie, September 10, 1944; Brooks, *Prairie School,* 306–7.

55. For more on this building, see Donald L. Hoffman, "Elmslie's Topeka Legacy," *Prairie School Review* 1 (Fourth Quarter 1964): 22–23.

56. Brooks, *Prairie School,* 306–9.

57. Elmslie to Wright, October 30, 1932, copy in NAA; Elmslie to Purcell, August 3, 1942.

58. Purcell, note on document dated December 8, 1952; Elmslie to Purcell, September [?], 1944. For more information about Sullivan's tombstone, see Lenore Pressman, "Graceland Cemetery: Memorial to Chicago Architects," *Prairie School Review* 12 (Fourth Quarter 1975): 13–18.

59. Elmslie to Mumford, May 29, 1931; Elmslie to Talbot Hamlin, June 25, 1941, copy in NAA.

60. Elmslie to Wright, June 12, 1936. Wright's review appeared in the *Saturday Review of Literature,* December 14, 1935, p. 6. For an unvarnished account of Wright's life, see Robert Twombly, *Frank Lloyd Wright: His Life and Architecture,* rev. ed. (New York: John Wiley and Sons, 1979).

61. Elmslie to Fred Strauel, December 7, 1934; Purcell to Strauel, April 20, 1938; Elmslie to Purcell, October 24, 1939.

62. Elmslie to Purcell, April 14, 1939, September 4, 1943, April 15, 1946.

63. Elmslie, "Autobiographical Sketch."

64. Elmslie's written remarks can be found in "To Louis Sullivan: The Gold Medal of the American Institute of Architects," *Journal of the American Institute of Architects* 6 (July 1946): 3–5; Elmslie to Purcell, July 9, 1947.

65. Elmslie to Purcell, April 14, 1939.

Chapter 7: *A True and Lasting Work of Art*

1. Bennett to Sullivan, December 7, 1911, copy in author's possession.

2. Bowers, "National Farmers' Bank."

3. Information on the Evans family comes from Curtiss-Wedge, *History of Rice and Steele Counties,* 1115–17; Henry A. Castle, *Minnesota: Its Story and Biography* (Chicago: Lewis Publishing Co., 1915), 1284–85; [Joseph A. A. Burnquist], *Minnesota and Its People* (Chicago: S. J. Clark Publishing Co., 1924), 4: 199.

4. Even though he did little to preserve the bank building, Evans apparently was aware of its architectural signficance, as demonstrated by an article that appeared in *Commercial West,* a Chicago business paper, in 1929. The article, very probably submitted by Evans, described the bank building as being "nationally known as a masterpiece." However, the bulk of the article was lifted, without attribution, from Bennett's 1908 article for *The Craftsman;* see *Commercial West,* June 8, 1929, p. 23, 59.

5. Bowers, "National Farmers' Bank." Bowers had access to a number of letters and memoranda written by Evans in 1926 as he was searching for a new home for his bank. Bowers generously made these letters, as well as his research notes, available to the author.

6. Here and two paragraphs below, Bowers, "National Farmers' Bank."

7. *Journal-Chronicle,* September 6, 1929, p. 1, 2.

8. *Daily People's Press,* March 22, 1940, p. 8. The bank's name was changed to the Security Bank and Trust Company in February 1930 when the bank was granted trust powers. Another change had occurred in May 1929 when the bank became affiliated with Northwest Bancorporation of Minneapolis.

9. Bowers, as part of his history of the bank, attempted to track down the seven wickets removed from the bank. He learned that three of them were purchased in 1940 by Stephen C. Stuntz, Jr., then a University of Wisconsin student. Stuntz was interested in Sullivan's work and during the summer of 1940 came to Owatonna to look at the bank. Stuntz learned that the wickets had been sold to a scrap dealer and quickly acquired three of them. He later gave one of the wickets to Hugh Morrison, a Dartmouth College professor who a few years before had published the first full-length study of Sullivan's work. Stuntz entered the U.S. Army in 1941 and served as an intelligence officer. He was killed in 1945 when the aircraft he

was aboard was lost at sea over the Pacific Ocean. As a memorial, his family in Virginia donated one of the wickets to a church in a community not far from Washington, D.C. The wicket is still there today. The third wicket has been kept by members of Stuntz's family. The author obtained information about Stuntz in an interview with his brother, Mayo Stuntz, December 21, 1983. A fourth wicket was acquired in 1982 by the Toledo Museum of Art. The museum's records indicate that the wicket had been in the hands of collectors in Chicago, Seattle, London, and New York before ending up in Toledo. The fate of the other three wickets removed from the bank in 1940 is unknown, although they presumably are in the possession of collectors. In 1968 three copies of the wicket at the Art Institute of Chicago were cast in brass. One is in the Norwest Bank of St. Paul, one was donated to Southern Illinois University, and the third is owned by a collector in Stillwater, Minnesota.

10. Here and two paragraphs below, Bowers, "National Farmers' Bank."

11. Clifford C. Sommer, interview with author, November 26, 1983.

12. Sommer, interview; Bowers, "National Farmers' Bank."

13. Bowers, "National Farmers' Bank."

14. Sommer, interview.

15. Here and two paragraphs below, Bowers, "National Farmers' Bank."

16. Miriam Alburn, "Owatonna Bank Causes Architecture Storm," *Minneapolis Tribune*, November 2, 1956, p. 6. Catlin's comments are in Alburn's article.

17. Here and below, Sommer, interview. Members of the committee were Catlin; Donald Torbert, associate professor of art at the University of Minnesota; Ralph Rapson, head of the university's school of architecture; H. Fred Koeper and Robert Bliss, both assistant professors at the school of architecture; and Victor Gilbertson and John Lindstrom, both members of the Minneapolis chapter of the American Institute of Architects.

18. For more information on Harris, see *Harwell Hamilton Harris: A Collection of His Writings and His Buildings* (Raleigh, N.C.: North Carolina State University Press, 1965). See also *Current Biography Yearbook, 1962,* s.v. "Harris, Harwell H."

19. Sommer, interview.

20. Bowers, "National Farmers' Bank."

21. Sommer, interview; Bowers, "National Farmers' Bank."

22. Marlow Ihling to Harwell Harris, February 6, 1957, Norwest Bank of Owatonna; Sommer, interview.

23. Here and below, Sommer, interview.

24. Here and below, "Interview with Louis Mario DeNardo, April 29, 1958." This three-page document, at the Norwest Bank of Owatonna, apparently was part of a press packet that was prepared for rededication ceremonies at the bank in June 1958.

25. Sommer, interview.

26. Sommer, interview; "Mrs. Ivy Baker Priest Speaks at Owatonna Bank Celebration," *Northwestern Banker,* July 1958, p. 51; *Daily People's Press,* June 11, 1958, p. 3. The story of the quarry owner and the man who helped unload the flatcars is in Harris, "Design Dimensions," 8.

27. "Sullivan's Owatonna Bank," *Northwest Architect* 22 (July-August 1958): 28–39. This is a printed version of Fitch's speech.

28. Mrs. Bennett to Richard Nickel, [1959?], RNC. The plaque installed in 1981 also contains the names of Sullivan and others associated with the building of the bank.

29. Stories about the remodeling included "Making a Monument Work," *Architectural Forum* 109 (July 1958): 99–104; "Save the Heritage," *Time,* June 23, 1958, p. 62, 65; *New York Times,* June 15, 1958, sec. 8, p. 1, 12.

30. Harris's comment is in "Sullivan's Owatonna Bank," 29. It should be noted that most architectural critics and scholars have expressed high praise for Harris's work in the bank. Typical are the comments of Gebhard and Martinson, *A Guide,* 301: "It was fortunate in every way that when the building had to be modified and expanded in the late 1950s Harwell H. Harris was engaged to do the design. . . . He modified the interior but retained its basic Sullivan quality. The fitness of Harris's detailing is evident in the interior, but its presence has in no way compromised the original."

31. Here and below, Bowers, "National Farmers' Bank."

32. In 1983 the bank became the Norwest Bank of Owatonna in accord with a name change by the parent bank corporation.

33. Information on the proposed addition was provided by Bowers.

34. Kenneth E. Wilcox, interview with author, August 20, 1982.

35. Here and below, for additional information on the 1982 remodeling, see a story by the author in the *St. Paul Pioneer Press,* September 5, 1982, p. 1B, 4B. See also "The Vicissitudes of a Famous Landmark," *Architecture Minnesota* 10 (January-February 1984): 44–47.

36. Wilcox, interview.

37. Sullivan, "What Is Architecture," in *Kindergarten Chats,* 227.

38. Sullivan, "What Is the Just Subordination, in Architectural Design, of Details to Mass?" in *Kindergarten Chats,* 186.

39. Harris, "Design Dimensions," 16.

40. Mrs. Freeman, interview.

BIBLIOGRAPHY

American Terra Cotta Index, ed. Statler Gilfillen. Palos Park, Ill.: Prairie School Press, 1974.

Andrews, Wayne. *Architecture, Ambition and Americans.* New York: Harper and Brothers, 1947.

Appelbaum, Stanley. *The Chicago World's Fair of 1893: A Photographic Record.* New York: Dover, 1980.

Bach, Ira. *Chicago's Famous Buildings.* 3rd ed. Chicago: University of Chicago Press, 1980.

Bennett, Carl K. "A Bank Built for Farmers." *The Craftsman* 15 (November 1908): 176–85.

Blake, Peter. *Frank Lloyd Wright: Architecture and Space.* Baltimore: Penguin, 1964.

Bonta, Juan Pablo. *Architecture and Its Interpretation: A Study of Expressive Systems in Architecture.* New York: Rizzoli, 1979.

Bowers, David P. "The National Farmers' Bank of Owatonna: A Documentation Project for the Northwestern Bank of Owatonna, Minnesota." Unpublished report, Norwest Bank of Owatonna, 1976.

Bragdon, Claude. *Architecture and Democracy.* New York: Knopf, 1918.

———. "Letters from Louis Sullivan." *Architecture* 64 (July 1931): 7–10.

Brooks, H. Allen. *Frank Lloyd Wright and the Prairie School.* New York: George Braziller, 1984.

———. *The Prairie School: Frank Lloyd Wright and His Midwestern Contemporaries.* Toronto: University of Toronto Press, 1972. Reprint. New York: Norton, 1976.

———, ed. *Prairie School Architecture: Studies from "The Western Architect."* Toronto: University of Toronto Press, 1975. Reprint. New York: Van Nostrand, 1983.

Burchard, John and Albert Bush-Brown. *The Architecture of America: A Social and Cultural History.* Boston: Little, Brown and Co., 1961.

[Burnquist, Joseph A. A.] *Minnesota and Its People.* Chicago: S. J. Clarke Publishing Co., 1924.

Bush-Brown, Albert. *Louis Sullivan.* New York: George Braziller, 1960.

Castle, Henry. *Minnesota: Its Story and Biography,* 4 vols. Chicago: Lewis Publishing Co., 1915.

Chafee, Richard. "The Teaching of Architecture at the Ecole des Beaux-Arts." In *The Architecture of the Ecole des Beaux-Arts.* Edited by Arthur Drexler. New York: Museum of Modern Art, 1977.

Chucker, Harold. *Banco at Fifty: A History of Northwest Bancorporation, 1929–1979.* Minneapolis: Northwest Bancorporation, 1980.

Coles, William A. and Henry H. Reed, Jr., eds. *Architecture in America: A Battle of Styles.* New York: Appleton-Century-Crofts, 1961.

Condit, Carl. *American Building: Materials and Techniques from the First Colonial Settlements to the Present*. Chicago: University of Chicago Press, 1968.

——. *The Chicago School of Architecture: A History of Commercial and Public Building in the Chicago Area, 1875–1925*. Chicago: University of Chicago Press, 1964.

Connely, Willard. "The Last Years of Louis Sullivan." *Journal of the American Institute of Architects* 23 (January 1955): 32–38.

——. "The Later Years of Louis Sullivan." *Journal of the American Institute of Architects* 21 (May 1954): 223–28.

——. *Louis Sullivan: The Shaping of American Architecture*. New York: Horizon, 1960.

Crook, David H. "Louis Sullivan and the Golden Doorway." *Journal of the Society of Architectural Historians* 26 (December 1967): 250–58.

Curtiss-Wedge, Franklyn. *History of Rice and Steele Counties, Minnesota*, 2 vols. Chicago: H. C. Cooper, Jr., and Co., 1910.

Daniels, Jonathan. *The Time Between the Wars*. Garden City, N.Y.: Doubleday, 1966.

Darling, Sharon S. *Chicago Ceramics and Glass: An Illustrated History from 1871 to 1933*. Chicago: Chicago Historical Society, 1979.

——. *Chicago Metalsmiths*. Chicago: Chicago Historical Society, 1977.

Duncan, Hugh D. *Culture and Democracy: The Struggle for Form in Society and Architecture in Chicago and the Middle West during the Life and Times of Louis H. Sullivan*. Totowa, N.J.: Bedminster Press, 1965.

Eaton, Leonard K. *American Architecture Comes of Age: European Reaction to H. H. Richardson and Louis Sullivan*. Cambridge, Mass.: MIT Press, 1972.

——. *Two Chicago Architects and Their Clients: Frank Lloyd Wright and Howard Van Doren Shaw*. Cambridge, Mass.: MIT Press, 1969.

Egbert, Donald D. *The Beaux-Arts Tradition in French Architecture, Illustrated by the Grands Prix de Rome*. Edited by David Van Zanten. Princeton, N.J.: Princeton University Press, 1980.

Elmslie, George G. "The Chicago School: Its Inheritance and Bequest." *Journal of the American Institute of Architects* 37 (July 1952): 32–38.

——. "Functionalism and the International Style." *Architecture and Engineering* 120 (February 1935): 69–70.

——. "Sullivan Ornamentation." *Journal of the American Institute of Architects* 6 (October 1946): 155–58.

Fitch, James. *American Building: The Forces that Shaped It*. Boston: Houghton Mifflin, 1948. Rev. ed. *American Building: The Historical Forces that Shaped It*. Boston: Houghton Mifflin, 1966.

Frampton, Peter and Yukio Futagawa. *Modern Architecture: 1851–1919*. New York: Rizzoli, 1983.

Furnas, J[oseph] C. *The Americans: A Social History*. New York: Putnam, 1969.

Futagawa, Yukio and Albert Bush-Brown. *The National Farmers' Bank, Owatonna, Minn., 1907–08; Merchants' National Bank, Grinnell, Iowa, 1914; Farmers' and Merchants' Union Bank, Columbus, Wis., 1919*. Tokyo: A.D.A. Edita, 1979.

Gebhard, David. *A Guide to the Architecture of Purcell and Elmslie: 1910–1920*. Roswell, N.M.: Roswell Museum and Art Center, 1960.

——. "Letter to the Editor." *Prairie School Review* 4 (Third Quarter 1967): 33–36.

——. "Louis Sullivan and George Grant Elmslie." *Journal of the Society of Architectural Historians* 19 (May 1960): 62–68.

——. "William Gray Purcell and George Grant Elmslie and the Early Progressive Movement in American Architecture from 1900 to 1920." Ph.D. diss., University of Minnesota, 1957.

—— and Tom Martinson. *A Guide to the Architecture of Minnesota*. Minneapolis: University of Minnesota Press, 1977.

Giedion, Sigfried. *Space, Time and Architecture*. 1941. 5th ed. Cambridge, Mass.: Harvard University Press, 1967.

Greenough, Horatio. *Form and Function: Remarks on Art, Design and Architecture*. Edited by Harold A. Small. Berkeley: University of California Press, 1957.

Hamlin, Talbot. "George Grant Elmslie and the Chicago Scene." *Pencil Points* 22 (September 1941): 575–86.

Hanks, David. "Louis J. Millet and The Art Institute of Chicago." *Bulletin of The Art Institute of Chicago* 67 (March-April 1973): 13–19.

Harris, Harwell H. "Design Dimensions."

North Carolina Architect (September 1966): 8–17.

——. *Harwell Hamilton Harris: A Collection of His Writings and His Buildings.* Raleigh, N.C.: North Carolina State University, 1965.

Hitchcock, Henry-Russell. *Architecture: Nineteenth and Twentieth Centuries.* Baltimore: Penguin, 1963.

——. *The Architecture of H. H. Richardson and His Times.* Rev. ed. Hamden, Conn.: Archon Books, 1961.

Hoffman, Donald. "The Brief Career of a Sullivan Apprentice: Parker N. Berry." *Prairie School Review* 4 (First Quarter 1967): 7–15.

——. "Elmslie's Topeka Legacy." *Prairie School Review* 1 (Fourth Quarter 1964): 4–22.

Johnson, Diane C. *American Art Nouveau.* New York: Harry N. Abrams, 1979.

Jordy, William H. *American Buildings and Their Architects.* Vol. 3. *Progressive and Academic Ideals at the Turn of the Century.* Garden City, N.Y.: Doubleday, 1972.

Kaufman, Mervyn D. *Father of Skyscrapers: A Biography of Louis Sullivan.* Boston: Little, Brown and Co., 1969.

Kaufmann, Edgar, ed. *Louis Sullivan and the Architecture of Free Enterprise.* Chicago: Art Institute of Chicago, 1956.

Kennedy, Roger G. "The Long Shadow of Harvey Ellis." *Minnesota History* 40 (Fall 1966): 97–108.

——. *Minnesota Houses: An Architectural and Historical View.* Minneapolis: Dillon Press, 1967.

Landau, Sarah Bradford. "Arcaded Buildings of the New York School, c. 1870–1890." In *In Search of Modern Architecture: A Tribute to Henry-Russell Hitchcock.* Edited by Helen Searing. Cambridge, Mass.: MIT Press, 1982.

Larson, Paul. "The Prairie School in its Midwestern Setting." In *Prairie School Architecture in Minnesota, Iowa, Wisconsin.* St. Paul: Minnesota Museum of Art, 1982.

Larson, Philip. "Ornament as Symbol." In *Prairie School Architecture in Minnesota, Iowa, Wisconsin.* St. Paul: Minnesota Museum of Art, 1982.

Lathrop, Alan K. "The Prairie School Bank: Patron and Architect." In *Prairie School Architecture in Minnesota, Iowa, Wisconsin.* St. Paul: Minnesota Museum of Art, 1982.

Leuchtenburg, William. *The Perils of Prosperity: 1914–32.* Chicago: University of Chicago Press, 1958.

Lowe, David. *Lost Chicago.* Boston: Houghton Mifflin, 1978.

Manson, Grant. "Sullivan and Wright: An Uneasy Union of Celts." *Architectural Review* 118 (November 1955): 297–300.

Menocal, Narciso G. *Architecture as Nature: The Transcendentalist Idea of Louis Sullivan.* Madison: University of Wisconsin Press, 1981.

Millet, Louis J. "The National Farmers' Bank of Owatonna, Minn." *Architectural Record* 24 (October 1908): 249–54.

Morrison, Hugh. *Louis Sullivan: Prophet of Modern Architecture.* 1935. Reprint. New York: Norton Library, 1962.

Mosher, Curtis L. *The Causes of Banking Failure in the Northwestern States.* Minneapolis: Federal Reserve Bank, 1930.

Mumford, Lewis. *The Brown Decades: A Study of the Arts in America.* 1931. Reprint. New York: Dover, 1955.

——. *Sticks and Stones: A Study of American Architecture and Civilization.* 1924. 2nd rev. ed. New York: Dover, 1955.

Murray, Robert K. *The Harding Era: Warren G. Harding and His Administration.* Minneapolis: University of Minnesota Press, 1969.

O'Gorman, James F. *The Architecture of Frank Furness.* Philadelphia: Philadelphia Museum of Art, 1973.

Paul, Sherman. *Louis Sullivan: An Architect in American Thought.* Englewood Cliffs, N.J.: Prentice-Hall, 1962.

Pearlman, Daniel H. *The Auditorium Building: Its History and Architectural Significance.* Chicago: Roosevelt University, 1976.

Peisch, Mark L. *The Chicago School of Architecture: Early Followers of Sullivan and Wright.* New York: Random House, 1964.

Pevsner, Nikolaus. *Pioneers of Modern Design.* 1960. Rev. ed. London: Penguin, 1974.

Pierson, William H., Jr. *American Buildings and Their Architects.* Vol. 2. *Technology and the Picturesque, the Corporate and the Early Gothic Styles.* Garden City, N.Y.: Doubleday, 1978.

Pressman, Lenore. "Graceland Cemetery: Memorial to Chicago Architects." *Prairie School Review* 12 (Fourth Quarter 1975): 13–18.

Purcell, William G. *St. Croix Trail Country:*

Recollections of Wisconsin. Minneapolis: University of Minnesota Press, 1967.

——. "Sullivan at Work." *Northwest Architect* 8 (January–February 1944): 11.

Saloutos, Theodore. *The American Farmer and the New Deal.* Ames, Iowa: Iowa State University Press, 1982.

Schlebecker, John T. *Whereby We Thrive: A History of American Farming, 1607–1972.* Ames, Iowa: Iowa State University Press, 1975.

Schuyler, Montgomery. *American Architecture and Other Writings.* Edited by William Jordy and Ralph Coe. 1961. Reprint. New York: Atheneum, 1964.

Scully, Vincent J. *American Architecture and Urbanism.* New York: Praeger, 1969.

——. *Frank Lloyd Wright.* New York: George Braziller, 1960.

——. "Louis Sullivan's Architectural Ornament: A Brief Note concerning Humanist Design in the Age of Force." *Perspecta* 5 (1959): 73–80.

Severens, Kenneth W. "The Reunion of Louis Sullivan and Frank Lloyd Wright." *Prairie School Review* 12 (Third Quarter 1975): 5–21.

Shannon, David. *Twentieth Century America: The United States since the 1890s.* Chicago: Rand McNally, 1963.

Southworth, Susan and Michael Southworth. *Ornamental Ironwork: An Illustrated Guide to Its Design, History, and Use in American Architecture.* Boston: David R. Godine, 1978.

Sprague, Paul E. "The Architectural Ornament of Louis Sullivan and His Chief Draftsmen." Ph.D. diss., Princeton University, 1969.

——. *The Drawings of Louis Henry Sullivan: A Catalogue of the Frank Lloyd Wright Collection at the Avery Architectural Library.* Princeton: Princeton University Press, 1979.

——. "The National Farmer's Bank, Owatonna, Minn." *Prairie School Review* 4 (Second Quarter 1967): 5–21.

Sparks, Earl S. *History and Theory of Agricultural Credit in the United States.* New York: Thomas Y. Crowell, 1932.

Stevenson, Russell, ed. *A Type Study of American Banking: Non-Metropolitan Banks in Minnesota.* Minneapolis: University of Minnesota Press, 1934.

Sullivan, Louis H. *The Autobiography of an Idea.* 1924. Reprint. New York: Dover, 1956.

——. *Democracy: A Man Search.* Edited by Elaine Hedges. Detroit: Wayne State University Press, 1961.

——. *Kindergarten Chats and Other Writings.* Edited by Isabella Athey. New York: George Wittenborn, 1947. Reprint. New York: Dover, 1979.

——. *A System of Architectural Ornament According with a Philosophy of Man's Powers.* New York: American Institute of Architects, 1924. Reprint. New York: Eakins Press, 1967.

——. *The Testament of Stone: Themes of Idealism and Indignation from the Writings of Louis Sullivan.* Edited by Maurice English. Evanston: Northwestern University Press, 1963.

"Sullivan's Owatonna Bank." *Northwest Architect* 22 (July–August 1958): 28–39.

Szarkowski, John. *The Idea of Louis Sullivan.* Minneapolis: University of Minnesota Press, 1956.

Tselos, Dimitri. "The Chicago Fair and the Myth of the 'Lost Cause.'" *Journal of the Society of Architectural Historians* 26 (December 1967): 259–68.

Turak, Theodore. "French and English Sources of Sullivan's Ornament and Doctrines." *Prairie School Review* 11 (Fourth Quarter 1974): 5–30.

Twombly, Robert. *Frank Lloyd Wright: An Interpretive Biography.* New York: Harper and Row, 1973. Rev. ed. *Frank Lloyd Wright: His Life and Architecture.* New York: John Wiley and Sons, 1979.

Upham, Cyril B. and Edwin Lamke. *Closed and Distressed Banks: A Study in Public Administration.* Washington, D.C.: The Brookings Institution, 1934.

Vaughn, Edward J. "Sullivan and Elmslie at Michigan." *Prairie School Review* 6 (Second Quarter 1969): 20–23.

"The Vicissitudes of a Famous Landmark." *Architecture Minnesota* 10 (January–February 1984): 44–47.

Venturi, Robert. *Complexity and Contradiction in Architecture.* 1966. 2nd ed. New York: Museum of Modern Art, 1977.

Vinci, John. *The Art Institute of Chicago: The Stock Exchange Trading Room.* Chicago: Art Institute of Chicago, 1977.

Warn, Robert R. "Bennett and Sullivan: Client and Creator." *Prairie School Review* 10 (Third Quarter 1973): 5–15.

——. "Louis H. Sullivan, ' . . . an air of finality.' " *Prairie School Review* 10 (Fourth Quarter 1973): 5–19.

——. "Two House Projects for the Carl K. Bennett Family by Louis Sullivan and Purcell and Elmslie." *Northwest Architect* 36 (March–April 1972): 64–72.

Weisman, Winston. "A New View of Skyscraper History." In *The Rise of an American Architecture.* Edited by Edgar Kaufmann, Jr. New York: Praeger, 1970.

——. "Philadelphia Functionalism and Sullivan." *Journal of the Society of Architectural Historians* 20 (March 1961): 3–19.

Wesley, Edgar B. *Owatonna: The Social Development of a Minnesota Community.* Minneapolis: University of Minnesota Press, 1938.

Wilson, Richard G. and Sidney K. Robinson. *The Prairie School in Iowa.* Ames: Iowa State University Press, 1977.

Wright, Frank Lloyd. *An Autobiography.* 1932. Reprint. New York: Duell, Sloan and Pearce, 1943. Rev. ed. New York: Horizon, 1977.

——. *Genius and the Mobocracy.* New York: Duell, Sloan and Pearce, 1949.

——. *Letters to Architects.* Edited by Bruce B. Pfeiffer. Fresno, Calif.: California State University Press, 1984.

——. *Writings and Buildings.* Edited by Edgar Kaufmann and Ben Raeburn. New York: Horizon, 1960.

INDEX

PICTURE CREDITS

The photographs and other images used in this book appear through the courtesy of the institutions listed below. The names of the photographers, when known, are given in parentheses.

Pages 7, 10 (courtesy Arabella Bennett Winston), 14 (courtesy Arabella Bennett Winston), 19, 163 (Clark Dean), 165 (Duane of Owatonna), 170 (Clark Dean)—Minnesota Historical Society

Pages 11, 66, 91, 157, 169 (David Bowers); 70, 71, 74 left and right, 75, 79, 81, 83, 84 (all Henry Fuermann); cover (oil painting by Albert F. Fleury, 1914)—Norwest Bank of Owatonna

Pages 23, 60, 68, 90, 98, 106, 109, 125, 128, 129, 130, 131, 133, 136, 137, 149—Northwest Architectural Archives, University of Minnesota, Minneapolis

Pages 33, 117—Commission on Chicago Historical and Architectural Landmarks

Pages 40, 55, 113 (all Richard Nickel)—Richard Nickel Committee, Chicago

Page 45 (W. H. Jackson)—*The White City* (Chicago: White City Art Co., 1894)

Pages 49 (Louis Sullivan?, courtesy Ryerson and Burnham Libraries), 119 (courtesy Department of Architecture)—The Art Institute of Chicago

Page 57—Avery Architectural and Fine Arts Library, Columbia University (Collection of Drawings by Louis Sullivan LHS/FLLW nos. 77 and 119)

Pages 77, 172, 173—Val Michelson and Associates, Inc., Architects

Page 93—*Prairie School Review*, Third Quarter 1964

Page 95—Virginia Millet Hawes, Winnetka, Illinois

Page 158—Minneapolis Star and Tribune

Page 171—St. Paul Pioneer Press and Dispatch

Page 175—Alan Ominsky

Color Section
Pages [1-4, 6-8]—Alan Ominsky

Page [5]—Jerry Mathiason

COLOPHON

The text and captions of this book are set in
Plantin by Compugraphic. The main and chapter
titles are Letraset Galadriel and Friz Quadrata
Bold, respectively.

The paper used throughout the book is
seventy pound Sterling Litho Matte.

Composition is by Stanton Publication Services,
and color separations by Color House, both of
Minneapolis; printing and binding are by Edwards
Brothers, Ann Arbor. Both the cover and text of
this volume were designed by Judi Rettich.